A FEARFUL
FREEDOM

A FEARFUL FREEDOM

Women's Flight from Equality

Wendy Kaminer

ADDISON-WESLEY PUBLISHING COMPANY, INC.

Reading, Massachusetts   Menlo Park, California   New York
Don Mills, Ontario   Wokingham, England   Amsterdam   Bonn
Sydney   Singapore   Tokyo   Madrid   San Juan

Library of Congress Cataloging-in-Publication Data

Kaminer, Wendy.
  A fearful freedom : women's flight from equality / Wendy
    Kaminer.
    p. cm.
  ISBN 0-201-09234-4
  1. Sex   discrimination   against   women—Law   and
legislation—United States.
  2. Sex discrimination against women—United States.
I. Title.
KF4758.K35 1990
342.73'0878—dc20
[347.302878]   89-28509

Jacket design by Linda Koegel
Text design by Anna Post George
Set in 10-point Palatino by C&C Associates

ABCDEFGHIJ–MW–9543210
First printing, March 1990

087893

To Alyssa, Julia, and Charles Frederick

Contents

Acknowledgments *xi*

Introduction *xiii*

1. Feminism, Equality, and Sexual Difference: How We View Nature *1*
2. Theories of Rights: How We View Law *11*
3. Constitutional Standards of Equality and Women's Rights *21*
4. Λ History of Egalitarianism and Protectionism and the Ideology of Sexual Difference *35*
5. A History of Protective Labor Laws and the Equal Rights Amendment *61*
6. Equality and the Sexual Revolution *79*
7. Equality in the Workplace: Title VII of the 1964 Civil Rights Act *91*
8. Equality in Education: Title IX of the 1964 Civil Rights Act *113*
9. Federal Resistance to Expanding Civil Rights *123*
10. Pregnancy, Child Care, and the Workplace *133*
11. Equality in the Home: Divorce, Child Custody, and Surrogacy *145*
12. Equality and Reproductive Choice *163*

13. Equality in Criminal Justice, Sexual Violence, and
Pornography   *183*
Conclusion   *205*
Notes   *217*
Index   *239*

Acknowledgments

Radcliffe College provided me with the space and support I needed to write this book. May its research institutes prosper. Thanks to Elizabeth McKinsey, Ann Bookman, Ann Colby, Patricia King, Barbara Haber, and staff people at the Bunting Institute, the Murray Center, and the Schlesinger Library. Thanks to Mead Data Central for free research assistance.

My editor, Jane Isay, encouraged me to write a good book and helped turn it into a better one. I'm equally indebted to my agent, Edite Kroll, for her intelligence, integrity, and perseverance. Thanks to Nancy Rosenblum, Muriel Morisey Spence, and Martha Davis for good conversation and reviews of my manuscript. Thanks to Betsy Moore, Sam Frederick, Michelle Scott, Fritz Gold, Phyllis Landau, Michael Laiken, and Harrison Moore, for everything. And to Mark Coovelis, Fae Myenne Ng, and the good luck typewriter.

Introduction

Sixty years ago, suffragist and author Helen Hamilton Gardener bequeathed her brain to researchers at Cornell University. Having "spent" her life using "such brain as [she] possessed in trying to better the condition of humanity, and especially of women," as she wrote in her will, this tenacious woman found an appropriate way to spend her death. Scientists needed to examine the brains of "women who think," she asserted, in order to dispel notions of natural female inferiority.[1] Prevailing skepticism about women's capacity to think was made clear by the excitement Gardener's bequest generated at the *New York Times*. On 9 October 1927 the Sunday *Times* ran a full-page feature on the "controversy over mental equality" and this straightfaced report on Gardener's brain: "It reveals a wealth of cortical substance, or gray matter, that is only equaled, but not exceeded, by the best brains in the Cornell collection, which includes those of a number of doctors, professors, lawyers, and naturalists."[2]

Gardener would have been gratified but hardly surprised by these findings. She had initiated her own study of the human brain some fifty years earlier, in response to "pseudo-scientific" theories about feminine stupidity and the dangers thinking posed to women's reproductive functions. In 1880 Dr. William Hammond, a former United States Surgeon General, proclaimed that "the brain of a woman was inferior in at least nineteen different ways to the brain of a man," providing at least nineteen different excuses for inequality. Gardener couldn't quite disprove this assertion, but she could reveal the ignorance on which it was based. Neurologists knew very little about men and even less about women, she wrote in an essay, "Sex in Brain." They had yet to examine the brain of any "remarkable woman," and she urged Susan B. Anthony and Elizabeth Cady Stanton to donate their brains to science when they were "done" with them.[3] Meanwhile, the scientific community was busy compiling statistics about the brain weights of famous men. Byron was said to have had a huge brain, weighing 2,238 grams, Turgenev's weighed in at 2,012, and Daniel Webster's at 1,518. But no man's brain was a match for the brain of a large whale, Gardener noted; it weighed nearly 7,000 grams. Even a very young whale boasted 2,312 grams of what scientists called "intellectual producing substance," which made it seventy grams smarter than Byron. If absolute brain weight determined intelligence, Gardener concluded, "Almost any elephant is . . . perhaps an entire medical faculty."[4]

Legions of elephants have lumbered away in the years since Gardener's death. Smart, educated women are no longer anomalies. Feminism, birth control, and the steady march of women into the labor market are slowly transforming the workplace, the family, education, and even the practice of religion, as women infiltrate the clergy. Laws and language are changing (we no longer say *man* when we mean *humankind*), along with a few ideas about nature itself: We no longer agree that women are naturally unsuited to practice white-collar professions or engage in competitive sports. But the time for an Equal Rights Amendment has not yet come; and if few among us would assert that women are naturally dumber than men, many still believe in natural differences between the sexes that ought to be recognized by custom and law. We don't draft women or send them into combat. We don't expect men to stay home with their children, and wage-earning women are still clustered in low-paying, women's jobs. The equality Helen Gardener sought has proved elusive, emancipation has been a painful, halting process for women, and feminism is regarded with a mixture of anxiety, anger, and scorn.

Whether it started with the pill or passage of the 1964 Civil Rights Act, prohibiting sex discrimination in employment, or formation of the National Organization for Women in 1966, the contemporary feminist movement is now over twenty years old, and equality is out of fashion.

The private concerns of women—children and family—and the costs of careerism are defeating the drive and desire of many to participate equally in public life. Egalitarian feminists of the 1970s are accused of ignoring, even exacerbating, the problems of wage-earning mothers, displaced homemakers, and pink-collar women in order to advance the interests of aspiring professionals. Equal education and employment opportunities are said to have benefited only middle- and upper-class women who were able to take advantage of them and willing to pursue careers singlemindedly, just like men. The day-care crisis is attributed to feminist disregard for children and the demands of family life.[5] Feminist-inspired reforms, no-fault divorce, and the substitution of temporary maintenance awards for alimony are shown to have hurt traditional homemakers and their children.[6] In the shadows of feminism, one-third of all families headed by women are poor.[7] The intractable problems of combining wage earning and motherhood and achieving economic independence have made biology look like destiny after all.

The practical problems of women have created a theoretical crisis for feminists. If woman is not mistress of her fate, if nature limits her earning power and enhances her devotion to domesticity, then, for most women, equal rights and opportunities are irrelevant and inappropriate; positing equality as an ideal for women reproaches them for what they cannot and would not change. If nature is retarding the assimilation of women into the full-time professions and men into full-time family life, then the hope that men and women will one day trade roles as easily as they trade clothes must give way to some acceptance of traditional divisions of labor and the stereotypes on which they are based. If wage earning is necessary but not natural for women, then instead of a chance to equal men, they need renewed respect for their womanly roles. Feminism, once a movement for equal rights, has become a movement for special protections, or special rights, too, a movement divided over the most basic feminist question about human sexuality and law: Should the sexes be governed by one law as equals or by two respecting their differences?

To me, the answer—equality—has always been clear and the question about sexual difference confused by a legacy of discrimination. In Helen Gardener's day, discrimination masquerading as respect for difference excluded women from higher education and the professions; today it maintains a dual labor market and denies them "masculine" jobs requiring stamina, strength, and the capacity to command. To me, opposition to drafting women or hiring them as construction workers or electing one President is as quaint as the belief that intelligence can be measured in grams. The assertion that all women are one type and all men another is as suspect as an assertion about racial or ethnic homogeneity. If women are uniformly different from men, they must uniformly resemble each other, but we don't; we don't all look alike. To me, feminism has always been a civil rights movement that opposes reducing people to type, defying double standards of law based on assumptions of feminine frailty and the notion that men and women were destined to star on different stages. The challenge for feminists today is maintaining that defiance and a vision of justice as respect for individual choice and variation, not resignation to "natural," collective conformity. The challenge is remembering that biology is not destiny and restoring belief in the possibility of change.

·1·

Feminism, Equality, and Sexual Difference: How We View Nature

Imagine all the men in the country taking as much responsibility for child care as all the women and all the women making as much money as all the men. Feminists have always been dreamers. One hundred fifty years ago votes for women, access to higher education and the professions, and the freedom to divorce an abusive husband were the vagaries of a fractious few. Fighting for women's rights in the 1800s, when women were considered stupider, weaker, and lower on the evolutionary scale than men, demanded great leaps of faith.

Much has been ceded to women since then—intelligence, an independent will, athletic ability, and some constitutional rights—but much is still denied—economic equality, assistance with child care, and political power. We've managed to enter a postfeminist world without ever knowing a feminist one. Motherhood and the ideas about femininity that go with it are still handicaps for women in the workplace and the political arena: Occupational choice, opportunities, and salaries are still determined by sex and reproduction. Feminism requires resilience. The familiar litany of statistics about the wage gap between men and women, occupational segregation, the dearth of female legislators and judges, and the feminization of poverty cripple the imagination. Keep-

1

ing faith with feminism you feel starry eyed and self-indulgent. Try imagining a world in which it is not remarkable or incredibly hard for women to have careers and be parents too—a world of female doctors and male nurses and househusbands, equal numbers of male and female senators, and day-care centers staffed by men and women who make as much money as investment bankers. Imagine women not being penalized for having children and not being pitied when they don't. It's hard—hard to imagine being free to invent your own life, according to your own ideas about sex and gender. It's hard to imagine equality.

But imagining is how we begin. Feminists must always be dreamers, as well as politicians. We may linger long or end in compromise, but we begin with an ideal. In my ideal world, sex, like race, is not used to measure or predict intelligence, character, talent, ambition, or desire. Women are not presumed to be more nurturing, compassionate, and intuitive than men, better at child care, and worse at executive decision making—anymore than blacks are presumed to be more rhythmic, better at basketball, and worse at math. Presumptions about women's nature will be as suspect as presumptions about the nature of any racial or ethnic group. Sex-based divisions of labor based on these presumptions may not be eradicated, but they will be considered unjust. In my ideal world, justice for women will include freedom for every woman to shape her own nature and choose her own role.

This is not a terribly popular ideal. The notion that natural differences between men and women dictate different roles for them, at home and in the workplace, still prevails. Widespread opposition to legal equality emerged with a vengeance in the battle over the Equal Rights Amendment and is clearly reflected in our male-only draft registration laws, upheld by the United States Supreme Court,[1] and the exclusion of women from combat. "The principle that women should not intentionally and routinely engage in combat is fundamental and enjoys wide support among our people," the Senate Armed Services Committee reported in 1980, rejecting proposals to draft women and place them in combat.[2] Drafting women would weaken the "national resolve" during wartime, the Committee decided. It would also raise the unsettling possibility of drafting mothers as well as fathers. Who would take care of the children?

Whether you consider double standards of male and female citizenship discrimination or simply common sense depends on your view of sex and gender and your vision of family life. Is the average woman, whoever she may be, naturally unsuited to combat? Or with appropriate

2

training and socialization would she be as good or bad a soldier as any man? Would he be as good or bad a parent as any woman? If she went to war, would he keep the home fires burning?

Fifteen years ago, the feminist answer was clear: Male and female roles were cultural, not biological, constructs, so feminists talked about gender, instead of sex, when they talked about differences between men and women.* Feminist research into early child development illuminated the link between education, socialization, and gender roles; children were taught to be masculine or feminine, by the way they were dressed or the games they were given to play and, in later years, by the academic subjects in which they were encouraged to excel. The masculinization of math and science was no more natural, feminists asserted, than the feminization of ironing.[3] In this view, presumptions about male and female natures, or the military prowess of men and women, were self-fulfilling prophecies. Of course military service should be equally open and equally onerous. Women could, and should, if they chose, be soldiers, cops, or firefighters, just as men could, and probably should, vacuum and teach kindergarten.

But the prospect of a female draft helped defeat the Equal Rights Amendment and shape the view of feminism as a movement to masculinize women and emasculate men, as if women in uniforms would grow hair on their chests and men donning aprons would not. This postfeminist world of ours has been marked by considerable hostility toward feminism. "What is a feminist?" I sometimes ask women who scowl at my mention of the word. A feminist is a "bra burner," they tell me—an angry, man-hating, strident, childless woman. A feminist is a "self-hating" female who denies her true maternal nature and wants women to be just like men. What is equality? Equality is "unnatural," like a woman in a pinstriped suit.

Not just traditional family women but wage earners and careerists, who harbor some feminist beliefs, share this disdain for feminism. It's evident too among young, aspiring professionals who grew up with the women's movement and are reaping its benefits. "I'm for equal pay and equal work and all that," college students tell me. "But I'm not a feminist." Young women don't like to call themselves feminists, one Harvard woman says: "People will think that they're gay." A discussion we attend about the future of feminism draws only a handful of students. "'Why are you going to that?' my friends asked," one student

*I generally use the term *sexual difference*, simply because it's more common.

reports. "'People will think you're a feminist.'" What is a feminist? The answer is familiar. Feminists are "angry and aggressive"; they're "bra burners" who believe that women are "the same as men."

This image of a feminist as a woman who's hostile toward children or hateful toward men (or just like them) or obsessed with burning her bra is pervasive, yet it doesn't remind me of any feminist I know. It's a twenty-year-old caricature I thought we'd leave behind, along with caricatures of dumb blondes, spinsterish career women, and happy housewives that prevailed in the 1950s. Its persistence reflects the rigidity of sex/gender stereotypes and their dominion over identity. Labeling a feminist a man-hating virago is a defense of femininity that demonstrates its power as a refuge and a role for women. If we're not "feminine"—softer, better at relationships and child care and ironing than men—what are we?

Equality doesn't presume sameness, but it does promise choice and the unsettling search for identity that goes with it. The feminism of the 1960s and 1970s was frightening because its model of womanhood was inclusive—of whatever women freely chose to do. Along with independence, this offered women new responsibilities, not just to support themselves but to define themselves as well. By their actions, women, once liberated, would define femininity instead of being defined by it.

Inequality was unnatural, equal rights advocates asserted; discrimination, not reproduction, was its cause. Women were not naturally unfit for the practice of law or medicine anymore than men were naturally incapable of changing diapers. Gender was mere social artifice, feminists declared, echoing John Stuart Mill and Simone de Beauvoir. (Woman was a "product elaborated by civilization," not a "creation of nature," de Beauvoir wrote in *The Second Sex*.)[4] In the early 1970s, the message was clear: Women were socialized to be feminine and fulfill the subordinate roles that culture, not nature, assigned to them. Culture, or science, might even reallocate the job of childbearing. Some suggested that artificial reproduction would free women.[5]

But culture has changed only slightly since then, nature has changed not at all, and technology is complicating rather than solving the problem of reproduction. Limited gains and unexpected losses of the past ten years—the trauma of childbearing women and mothers of preschool children entering the workforce—have shaken feminist faith in equality and the possibility of sexual assimilation. Disappointment has put them on the defensive. Middle-class women entered the 1970s with great expectations. Graduate schools and the male professions were opening up, however grudgingly. Sexual freedom was becoming feminized; the double standard didn't quite disappear, but it did command less respect. The notion that women could "have it all"—a career and a family or an endless succession of wonderful dates—was popularized by the women's magazines before being exposed as a myth. Encountering discrimination in the workforce and trouble in combining careers and family life might have strengthened women's resolve, but it didn't. Instead, tired and disillusioned, the new postfeminist woman turned on feminism, as if it had broken a promise that equality would come easy.

Feminism responded to the setbacks and conservatism of the 1980s with a retreat from egalitarianism, which challenged the ideology of sexual difference, and a revival of protectionism, which invoked it, as a matter of public policy. Some feminists lost their resolve too or simply changed their minds about what was good for women. Perhaps the drive for equality overlooked women's special needs as mothers and their commitment to family life, they conceded. Born-again advocates of preferential treatment for women accused equal rights advocates of betraying their sex, and their children, in a selfish effort to emulate men. Women needed "more than equal treatment," they asserted;[6] women needed compensatory measures such as special maternity benefits, custody rules favoring mothers, and fault-based alimony laws.[7] The movement that began with an appeal to women's strengths and capacity to vie with men as equals began raising the spectre of the handicaps imposed on them by nature. On their way to equality, feminists stumbled over the feminization of poverty and the awesome fact that only women get pregnant.

They also discovered pornography and an epidemic of sexual violence; almost only women get raped. Like the equal rights movement, the sexual revolution was characterized by dissident feminists as a fearful hoax. Equality was assailed for depriving women of the protection they needed as wives and mothers. Sexual freedom was blamed for exposing them to the brutality of unbridled males. Some antipornography activists began demanding less than equal First Amendment rights for men, as if sexism were a matter of men having too much freedom instead of women too little.

Underlying all these demands to protect women as mothers, wage earners, and victims of sexual violence are sexual stereotypes of which some men and women would like to be free. There's always been a strain of female chauvinism in the women's movement; recently, there's been an outburst of it. The view of women as naturally peace-loving, compassionate, more moral and better at parenting than men has shaped the women's peace movement, antipornography protests, and battles over child custody and surrogate motherhood. While men are maligned as militaristic creatures who read pornography and are ruled by "urges" rather than ethics, women are romanticized as mothers and guardians of an ethic of caring.

In the early 1980s the old notion that women are morally different than men and, in some ways, superior, was given new credibility by psychologist Carol Gilligan in her frequently cited book, *In a Different Voice*. Women resolve moral conflicts differently, Gilligan suggested; they tend to be more concerned with preserving relationships and satisfying emotional needs than they are with parceling out rights. They tend to cultivate a "morality of responsibility" instead of a "morality of rights."[8]

This is an immensely popular theory, although for feminists, who speak in several different voices, it's a rather controversial one.[9] It deftly articulates and justifies what many women feel about themselves, and coming from a Harvard-based feminist psychologist, this assurance that women do indeed care more than men gives women's feelings the weight of scientific fact.

The debate about values that erupted in the 1970s heralded a feminist debate about assimilation. If feminists were attacked for undermining traditional family values, they had their own doubts about the "masculine" values equality seemed to require embracing. In the last decade, as Carol Gilligan's theories trickled down from academia to the popular press, nostrums about dressing for success, fast-tracking, and competing for rungs on the corporate ladder gave way to some feminist breast beating about female machismo.

Enough has been written about women's disdain for competition and the discomfort it causes them: Competition isn't "sisterly," and it isn't as selfless as women are supposed to be. Competition requires and sanctifies self-interest, and women are supposed to be primarily interested in the welfare of others. "Women don't compete; they cooperate," we're often told.

The ideal of feminine selflessness is shared by some feminists and antifeminists alike, although they differ about the value of competitiveness in men. According to conventional antifeminist wisdom, men vie with each other for honor, wealth, and good-looking wives. The women they win are supposed to nurture their mates and facilitate their battles, standing watch on the sidelines, like cheerleaders. Women are supposed to vie with each other only for men (or in beauty pageants).

Feminist champions of femininity denigrate economic competition among men, advocating a cooperative model for them too. They see sexual competition among women as a survival skill, forced on them by a sexist system: Women are forced to go after men the way men go after jobs.

Feminists who put their faith in sisterhood have difficulty reconciling their demand for jobs and economic equality with the fact that jobs are awarded competitively. For baby boomers, some of whom have grown up into feminists, the competition has been fierce. Prestigious degrees, honors, high-paying, high-status jobs are scarce, and for many women, success has taken precedence over sisterhood. In an ideal world, competition would, no doubt, give way to cooperation. People would simply agree on the allocation of resources, caring as much about their neighbors as they do about themselves. In the meantime, women who want power will have to join the fray and fight for it.

The trouble is that without some sense of solidarity none or few of the spoils traditionally monopolized by men would be available to any women at all. For women, and minority males, cooperation is not simply a utopian ideal; it's a practical necessity: Many must fight for access to places few may attain. In a world of economic disparities and sexual discrimination, sisterhood is as much a matter of self-interest for women as competition, and women must always balance their needs with the needs of their community.

Concern for community and an understanding of the ways in which the interests of each woman converge with those of her community is basic to feminism; it is, after all, a movement based on the perception that in this culture women are a separate class with a separate history of discrimination and domesticity. This is not nostalgia for femininity and a belief that what women share is character—the capacity to "care" and compromise and make peace. It is a recognition that despite economic, racial, and ethnic divisions among women, they share a past—of economic and political powerlessness, dependence and vulnerability to sexual abuse, of child rearing, homemaking, and community service.

The irony for feminists is that the separate women's world created by discrimination and traditional divisions of labor have always been a source of strength for women as well as a fount of frustration, a realm of freedom from male domination as well as a cage. In the nineteenth century, women's separateness fostered women's solidarity, which fostered feminism, and feminists have always been divided in their allegiance to idealized femininity. Egalitarianism was briefly ascendent in the 1970s, but the feminist movement never has been a monolithic quest for equality. It's always been a movement divided by two views of the sexes and two goals.

The first women's rights advocates of the mid-1800s drew from John Mill and Mary Wollstonecraft a belief in the natural equality of all human beings and sought to extend the natural rights of men to women. They stressed what the sexes shared—the capacity to reason and the right to determine their own destinies, instead of how they differed biologically. But in the years after the Civil War, women reformers ("social feminists") dominated the drive for suffrage, stressing women's moral superiority and blaming society's ills on the animal passions of men that virtuous women, enfranchised, would curb. They based their demand for the vote on an assertion of sexual difference and the view of women as more pacific, moral, and compassionate, and better at delivering social services. Taken to its logical if frenzied extreme, femininity was somewhat subversive. Women used the virtues ceded to them in the private sphere to claim the vote and a role in public life. Femininity became a pedestal from which women could preach.

It was, however, a dangerous basis for legal reform. Woman's virtues—moral and emotional sensitivity—were inextricably linked to her most crippling vulnerabilities—physical and intellectual weakness. These were the qualities associated with motherhood and domesticity, which may have won women the vote and lost them the battle for full equality. As mothers, women were protected instead of empowered. Throughout much of this century, protective labor laws barred women from "unfeminine" occupations and limited their hours of work, perpetuating the dual labor market. Protective family laws deprived women of equal guardianship and property rights, preserving the patriarchal family. Protective criminal laws subjected women prostitutes to imprisonment for sexual misconduct in which men indulged with impunity and distorted the prosecution of rape cases, protecting only "good" women from sexual assaults. Protectionism institutionalized white, middle-class standards of femininity, dividing women not just from men but from each other along class and racial lines.[10] By glorifying double standards of male and female behavior, it rationalized double standards of justice. It objectified women, depriving them of the right to be treated and judged as individuals, not fungible members of the female sex. Discrimination has always been justified by presumptions about difference.

"Yes, but . . ." advocates of preferential treatment might respond. "The discrimination facing wage-earning women today reflects a cruel disregard for their differences: Only women get pregnant. We need special disability benefits so that women with high-risk pregnancies don't have to choose among their health, their baby's health, and their jobs. We need special child-care leaves and more flexible work schedules. Women have special, prior commitments to family life; they will suffer discrimination in the workplace as long as they are expected to perform in it just like men."

Yes, but . . . Not only women can care for children. Not all women have children. Not only women workers are temporarily disabled and deserve a humane workplace and job security. Not only women should not be asked to sacrifice their health or their families on the altar of their jobs. Culture, not nature, has forced women, and not men, to choose between work and love. Culture, not nature, made women better at washing dishes and socks and created a crisis in day care.

Men and women may not be the same, but what we call masculine and feminine characteristics may be distributed unpredictably, in varying degrees among them. My own vision of a feminist world does not deny the possibility of sexual differences. It does question their relevance as well as the effort to quantify them. If there are natural sex and gender differences, they exist and develop in the context of culture. Perhaps they are, in the end, what we make of them.

Nature doesn't simply dictate human limits; it outlines human potential. It provides us with malleable raw material, which we remain responsible for shaping. Even to answer the question of nature—to say that women are naturally more nurturing, more emotional, and less analytic than men or that men are more warlike than women—doesn't answer the question of culture or justice. It doesn't tell us what roles men and women should be encouraged or allowed to play and what rights they ought to enjoy. If nature gave men and women different characters, should culture minimize or maximize their differences? Women were once presumed to be naturally dumber than men. Was their dumbness good reason for denying them an equal education? Or should they have been educated energetically? Men were presumed to be more lustful and violent than women. Did their "animal passions" justify the historic failure to prosecute rape cases?

The question of nature ought not to be confused with the question of justice. Justice doesn't simply accommodate nature by codifying natural inequities. Justice tames nature with a cultural ideal of what's fair.

Choice is fair, because human nature is variable. Despite their reproductive differences, men and women are not simply male and female prototypes. Perhaps women differ as much from one another as

9

they do from men. Perhaps the fact of reproduction need not consign them to a secondary place in the workforce. That it has so far is a tribute to discrimination, men's disdain for housework, and the dearth of day care, none of which are biological imperatives.

This does not mean a feminist world will take shape soon. Institutional barriers to equality are nearly as formidable as biological ones, and to many women the differences may seem academic. A woman stuck in an inhospitable workplace without adequate benefits or day care may not be interested in distinguishing between the cultural and natural causes of her problems. Most women are more concerned with daily economic and domestic struggles than ideology. Most have some personal or familial needs that preempt feminist principles. No woman would, or should, turn down a child-care leave because comparable leaves are not extended to men. How many women ask to be drafted?

But for feminists in the midst of an arduous journey to equality, the choice between special protections and equal rights is a painful one between the needs of the present and goals of the future, between treating the symptoms of sexism or curing the disease. Preferential treatment for women is a short-term solution that perpetuates the problem, trapping women in a cycle of legal privileges and institutionalized discrimination. Preferential custody rules suggest children belong first with their mothers. Do women then belong at home? Preferential maternity policies—special pregnancy disability benefits and women-only child-care leaves—suggest that they do.

Feminists have to find a way to compensate women for discrimination without compromising their fight for equality. We have to find a way to maintain at least some feminine values while we integrate the masculine world. Like immigrants who want to preserve their culture and be Americans too, women are caught between a woman's culture—the private world of children and shopping and female friendships—and the drive for independence and an equal share of public life. We may pay for assimilation, but not dearly; the private women's world has never been edenic. By sacrificing a part of their cultural heritage, women will ease their cultural burdens. We can't copyright a feminine value system without endorsing the sexual stereotypes it reflects or the oppression it perpetuates.

In the long run, ideology matters; dreams turn into political agendas. Principles have practical consequences. Political acts have ideological ones. Out of the tension between ideals and practical exigencies, on a tightrope balancing principles and needs, feminists—and other advocates of social justice—are made.

·2·

Theories of
Rights:
How We View Law

The first hard lesson for feminists is recognizing the difference between a movement to end injustice and a movement that caters to women. Being a feminist does not mean taking every woman's side in every conflict or putting the interests of women above those of men. If sexual justice means that rights, opportunities, and power will be distributed without regard to sex, then in a feminist world some men may be better off than some women—not because they're men but because they're smarter, stronger, saner, or simply luckier.

This is not, however, what everyone means by justice. Protectionist feminists will argue that not taking account of sex in a competition between men and women is inherently unfair because women are naturally handicapped by pregnancy. Separatist feminists will dismiss a competitive economy and rights-based legal system as male-identified, declaring that women are naturally cooperative and more concerned with feelings than with rights. Socialist feminists will condemn "rights talk" as liberalism, arguing that there is no justice, sexual or otherwise, when resources are distributed unequally in a competitive marketplace. Communitarians will add that liberalism and an ethic of rights foster callous, radical individualism, alienation, and anomie, asserting

11

that rights should be supplanted by some mystical commitment to community.

So it is not enough for a feminist to declare her interest in justice. There are several competing models of it from which she must choose. We have no shared ideal of justice, no consensus. Instead we have shared anxieties—about nature, cultural values, sexual assimilation, liberty, equality, and public welfare.

One central concern uniting feminists on all sides of the debate over sexual justice today is the gap for women between guarantees of legal equality and facts of social inequality. How should the law treat women who are still only potentially equal? The controversy over divorce asks this question, pointing out the inequities of treating homemakers as the economic equals of their husbands, as some judges have been inclined to do. Feminists have stressed that equality sometimes requires treating differently situated people differently: A woman who has been out of the workforce for ten years raising children may have a right to receive alimony or maintenance payments from her husband, while he has no equivalent claim to receive them from her. A woman who suffered discrimination in the early years of her career may have a right to be evaluated by different standards than men when decisions about promotions are made.

Does this infringe on the rights of men who are held to higher promotion standards? Not if they enjoyed an advantage over women early on in their careers. And not if we focus on what Ronald Dworkin has called the "right to treatment as an equal" instead of the "right to equal treatment." In defense of affirmative action, Dworkin argues that a white male law school candidate has the right to be treated as the equal of a minority candidate, meaning his application must be weighed with equal fairness, interest, and concern. He may not have the right to equal treatment in the allocation of places in the law school class. Given the need to increase minority participation in the legal profession, instead of an equal claim to a place in the law school a white candidate has the right to have the merits of his claim given equal consideration.[1]

Dworkin's distinction between equal treatment and treatment as an equal neatly illustrates the conflict between social equality and some individual rights. It presumes that integrating the legal profession and improving the status of minorities is a public priority that takes precedence over the right to equal treatment of white males. But it also makes clear that affirmative action doesn't give minorities special or extra rights: It gives both minority and white candidates rights to what might be called equal consideration instead of equal treatment in order to equalize their positions in society.

Whether the principle of color-blind or gender-blind equal treatment is more or less important than achieving racial or sexual equality is an ideological, not an empirical question. We have to make some moral choices between rights. We have to choose sides, because extending equal opportunities—equal treatment instead of equal consideration—to women and minority males hasn't equalized their status. The experiment that began twenty-five years ago with the 1964 Civil Rights Act has proved that in a world in which some are born rich or middle class and some are born poor, handicapped by a history of discrimination, equal opportunities do not ensure equal access, much less equal results.

Some feminists have responded by questioning the principle of equality and the benefits of equal rights for women, suggesting that biology, not culture, has disabled women in the effort to exercise their rights. Others who blame culture argue that rights should be determined in the context of gender roles and relations. This demands affirmative action. Some contend it also demands such measures as special pregnancy disability benefits, because of divisions of labor within families and a history of discrimination against wage-earning mothers.

So the suggestion that legal rights should be shaped by social realities doesn't end the debate for feminists about special rights and equal rights for women. Feminists who agree that men and women are not essentially different in character may also agree that gender roles—the circumstances of women's lives—sometimes require their different treatment; but they may disagree about precisely what circumstantial differences are relevant when we allocate rights.

When is the fact that only women get pregnant relevant in the workplace? Does it require different maximum-hour laws for men and women that existed over sixty years ago or different disability benefits? Does it matter whether a wage earner is disabled by pregnancy or a bad back? Should disability policies concerning paid or unpaid leaves and job reinstatement be determined by the cause of disabilities or their effect on workers?

Feminists disagree decisively in answering these questions about the relevance of pregnancy to workers' rights, but they tend to agree that pregnancy is central to the determination of reproductive rights, giving women and not men the right to make decisions about abortion. And they tend to agree that divisions of labor within a family are relevant to determining the rights of husbands and wives on divorce. There is an emerging feminist consensus that differently situated people should be treated differently—when the differences in their circumstances are relevant. (There is little consensus about the question of relevance.) This is allied to a "contextual" approach to the allocation of rights; it stresses the personal and social circumstances in which rights are exercised.

During the past ten years feminists and other civil rights activists have had to confront the irony of extending rights to people who are in no position to exercise them. Affirmative action is one response to this; so is increased concern about the underclass and people who are disenfranchised by the conditions of their lives. In the minority community, poverty and social justice are displacing equal legal rights as focal issues. Drug abuse, AIDS, teenage pregnancy, illiteracy, the decline in public education, and inadequate health care make the existence of rights academic for many. Feminists too have shifted their focus to social problems, such as the child-care crisis, the plight of displaced homemakers and single mothers, and the feminization of poverty. These are, of course, pressing problems, but they are not the fault of the equal rights movement, as some feminist advocates of protectionism have charged. Before there were feminists, there were women with problems—pervasive social problems that laws may alleviate but cannot easily solve.

The recent revival of anti-egalitarianism among feminists and demands for protections instead of equal rights partly reflects a confusion of social and legal issues, which misapprehends the place and power of law and simplifies its relationship to social change. Law changes attitudes slowly. We can and should legislate parental leaves, but we can't force men to take them; fathers will not become caregivers soon. We can award larger and more equitable divorce settlements to women homemakers, but we can't prohibit the perception of middle-aged women as less valuable professionally and less desirable sexually than middle-aged men. We can criminalize acts of sexual abuse but not images of it. A compelling sociological argument against pornography is not a compelling legal one. We can raise consciousness about pornography; but men may long persist in reading it with impunity, and we shouldn't blame the First Amendment when they do. If law is supposed to lead us to justice, we can hardly blame it when social mores lag behind.

Confusion about law and social work was emblematic of feminism at the turn of the century. It was manifested quite clearly in the juvenile court system. The juvenile courts were conceived by reformers as benign, discretionary, social, or pseudosocial familial institutions, not justice-ridden courts of law. Judges and other court personnel—social workers, psychologists, and doctors—were supposed to play parental roles in the lives of delinquents, whose own parents were generally presumed to have failed them. This was supposed to be good for children; it spared them "criminal treatment." The delinquent was "not a criminal but a ward with special needs which the state has the power of supplying," penologist Miriam Van Waters explained in 1922, when she was referee of the Los Angeles County Juvenile Court. Juvenile courts were "social agencies," she said, for which a juvenile offense was only a symptom of "ill health," like "the cough of a patient in a clinic."[2]

This well-intended socialization, or feminization, of the juvenile courts gave delinquents a moral claim to the care and attention of the state but no legal rights. They were institutionalized for indeterminate periods without the benefit of counsel, the right to confront or cross-examine witnesses, and other constitutional rights afforded adult suspects. Analogizing punishment to parental discipline and calling it rehabilitation deprived juveniles of the fairness guaranteed by due process until a 1967 United States Supreme Court decision applied the Constitution to juvenile court proceedings.[3]

There is something stereotypically feminine about this misguided focus on the needs of juveniles instead of their rights. It echoes the different moral voice that psychologist Carol Gilligan has attributed to women—the sensitivity to behavior and tendency to nurture instead of judge. Miriam Van Waters's description of the juvenile court system reflects a mistrust of rights and a view of justice as something cold, judgmental, and mechanized—a view shared by protectionist feminists today. "The old common law dealt only with individual rights, which were supposed to be always in conflict," Van Waters observed. "The new social justice deals with human welfare and human interests, which in truth are always identical. The old law had two remedies, punishment and redress. The newer justice tries to prevent delinquency, just as the traffic signals of our highways mark out dangers."[4] "The juvenile court is not a mere piece of judicial machinery. It has touched so many vital sources of public welfare that it is best described as a social institution. Its work is constructive and preventative. Its keynote is service for childhood."[5]

To condemn this "new" service-based approach to justice because it turned out to be more oppressive to juveniles than the old one is not to suggest laws may not be tempered by mercy or an understanding of human behavior and the social causes of crime. In fact, criminal liability

15

has always been limited by concepts of insanity and various forms of diminished capacity; the increasing reliance on traumatic stress disorders in criminal cases today demonstrates that sensitivity to the emotional, psychological, and social nuances of a case is not incompatible with respect for rights. But rights come first; they protect people (especially when they're accused of crimes) more than Miriam Van Waters's vague ideas about "human welfare and human interests." Rights are more trustworthy than judges or social workers, and the displacement of rights by a commitment to "caring" is a prescription for discretionary injustice.

Feminist dissatisfaction with rights does however, point out the failure of traditional theories of constitutional law to account fairly for social needs. *Harris v. McRae*,[6] the Supreme Court decision that upheld the cut off of Medicaid funds for abortions exemplifies a cruel disregard for poverty and its relation to the exercise of rights. In holding that the right of privacy guaranteed by *Roe v. Wade*[7] did not oblige the government to pay for abortions, as it paid for childbirth and sterilization, the Court essentially held that rights need only be respected in theory, not in fact. It made the right to have an abortion irrelevant to women who couldn't pay for one and refused to admit this was tantamount to saying poor women had no abortion rights at all.

This decision was not, however, the inevitable result of rights-based theories of justice (or even privacy theories in particular). It resulted from the refusal to translate economic needs into constitutional rights that has shaped the Court's approach to welfare. The Court has not recognized a fundamental constitutional right to subsistence or the receipt of welfare benefits. In *Dandridge v. Williams*, a 1970 case that derailed the welfare rights movement of the late 1960s, the Court held that a Maryland law limiting the amount of Aid to Families with Dependent Children funds available to any family unit, regardless of the number of children it contained, did not discriminate against large families or violate any constitutional rights.[8]

The Court in *Dandridge* acknowledged that welfare laws involve "the most basic economic needs of impoverished human beings," but it declined to consider these needs fundamental rights. It declined, therefore, to review the Maryland law as strictly as it reviews laws effecting fundamental rights, such as rights of speech or religion or fair trial. It likened the regulation of welfare benefits for poor families to economic regulations of commercial enterprises and upheld it as a reasonable economic policy.

In cases following *Dandridge* the Court continued rejecting claims of economic rights, in deference to legislative decision making: "The legislature's efforts to tackle the problems of the poor and needy are not subject to a constitutional straitjacket," Justice Rehnquist declared in *Jefferson v. Hackney*,[9] another AFDC case. In a subsequent case involving an Oregon eviction law, *Lindsey v. Normet*, [10] the Court rejected a claim by tenants that the " 'need for decent shelter' and the 'right to retain peaceful possession of one's home' are fundamental interests which are particularly important to the poor."

Whether these cases reflect the class biases of individual justices or insensitivity to the problems of the poor, they clearly confirm the Court's view of public welfare as a legislative and not a judicial problem. "The intractable economic, social, and even philosophical problems presented by public welfare assistance programs are not the business of this Court," Justice Stewart declared in *Dandridge*. Or as Justice White explained in *Lindsey v. Normet*, "The Constitution does not provide judicial remedies for every social and economic ill."

This was a general truth that didn't exactly apply to the case. The Court was not being asked to provide remedies for every social or economic ill. It was asked to provide the framework for legislative remedies, which is precisely what the Constitution intended it to do. Besides, the extension of political rights to free speech or trial by jury is not predicated on the belief that they will remedy all political ills. Why should economic rights be expected to solve all economic problems? Economic rights are also not as alien to the Court as the welfare cases suggest: It has always recognized some, such as the rights of property owners to be compensated for property appropriated by government. Neither is the Court always this deferential to legislative functions: The recognition of political rights has sometimes imposed quasi-legislative or executive roles on courts by requiring them to oversee school desegregation or the improvement of state prison systems. Courts may not be well equipped to run school systems, but they have a clear constitutional role to play in protecting the rights of students to racial equality.

Poverty, like school segregation, effectively denies its victims their constitutional rights. Poor women don't have abortion rights. Homeless people lose the right to vote if having an address is a requirement for registration. Indigent defendants don't generally enjoy the same fair trial rights as wealthy ones. Poverty creates a class of people with limited rights of citizenship—people for whom rights simply don't matter.

It is the obligation of courts to make rights matter. We might consider recognizing economic needs—for food, shelter, and medical care—as enabling rights. They enable people to participate as citizens and exercise the full panoply of political rights to which they're now only theoretically entitled.

The Supreme Court's refusal to incorporate basic economic needs into its vision of justice is not therefore a consequence of its commitment to individual rights. It results instead from a restricted construction of rights, a failure to examine the context in which rights exist. It also reflects the Court's choice of values—its preference for the rights of property owners over the rights of tenants. Rights are expressions of values: We value the right to practice religion freely for its own sake, not simply as a remedy for some social or political ill.

Courts and legislatures, not the feminist movement for equal rights, are to blame for not making rights matter to poor women. Not just abortion rights but welfare rights are of special concern to women, since the majority of poor families are headed by women. The tendency of protectionist feminists and other critics of egalitarianism, notably advocates of the new communitarianism, to blame feminists for the problems of women reflects a rejection of sexual equality that has more to do with traditional notions of femininity than concern for social ills.

Communitarianism, an instructive and often overlooked example of antifeminism, is difficult to define because its precepts are so vague. It posits a concern for community, a sense of connectedness with fellow citizens as an alternative to individual rights in the search for "values" and social justice. A commitment to rights is associated with an insular self-centeredness, a "cancerous" individualism at the heart of our "atomistic" society; it's blamed for alienation and anomie.[11] The communitarian antidote is a "vision of self-government that goes beyond voting rights, important though they are . . . a vision of community that embraces the rich array of civic resources intermediate between the individual and the nation."[12]

Precisely what this community looks like—how it's structured, how it allocates resources and ensures that people will be treated fairly—is not specified. This is a labile sort of nation. An airy vision of self-government and fellowship may have any number of meanings to any number of citizens in some warm and fuzzy community.[13]

But if the substance of communitarianism is murky, its association of equal rights feminism with feminist selfishness is clear. Feminism is implicitly linked with the narcissism of the 1970s—the obsession with "self-actualization" that presumably fostered ambition and an unsisterly spirit of competitiveness in women. It challenged the traditional family, which is presented both as a basis and a paradigm of community: The family was once "an integral part of a larger moral ecology tying the individual to community, church, and nation," the authors of *Habits of the Heart*, a popular communitarian critique of individualism, mournfully report.[14] It's not fair to call this family, which emerged in the early nineteenth century, patriarchal, they insist, despite the fact that wives couldn't hold property, exercise guardianship of their children, or refuse to sleep with their husbands. "To a certain degree, [women] were 'separate but equal' in their own sphere."[15] Political philosopher Michael Sandel has observed that "there is nothing intrinsically conservative about family,"[16] a statement that is true only when it is generalized to the point of meaninglessness. In the context of our culture, an assertion that the family is not essentially conservative reflects remarkable ignorance or willful misunderstanding of sexual injustice.

From a communitarian perspective, feminism's greatest failing, apart from its reliance on rights, is its presumed preference for the atomistic economic and political marketplace over the family. Communitarians reproach feminists for undermining feminine values, for choosing an ethic of rights over an ethic of caring. "The equality of women could result in complete loss of the human qualities long associated with 'women's sphere,' " the authors of *Habits of the Heart*, suggest, endorsing popular antifeminist biases.[17] While there is general, public recognition that many women have been propelled out of the family and into the workplace by economic need, there is not much general, public support for women working by choice and not necessity. Economic necessity is a "good" reason to "abandon" the domestic sphere. Self-fulfillment is a "bad" one. Women should work not because they want to but because they must.

It's obvious that current concern for community (and communitarian antipathy to egalitarian feminism) reflects anxiety about new roles for women. Our "vision" of community has always been based on a vision of women volunteers. Maternal, self-sacrificing women have always been the repository of our community values. The first question people ask of women who work for money is "Who will take care of the children?" The second is "Who will take care of the community?"

To believers in traditional masculine and feminine roles, there is something oxymoronic about a feminist community, yet without a sense of community women would never have banded together as feminists. A commitment to individual rights is not incompatible with concern for community, as the movement for minority rights has shown. Indeed, the minority civil rights movement is extolled by communitarians as an "affirmation of responsibility for uniting all of the diverse members of society into a just social order,"[18] or a "moment of self-government . . . an example of the kind of civic engagement that can flow from local attachments and communal ties."[19] It was also a movement to acquire individual rights. The suggestion that a minority civil rights movement is communal while a feminist civil rights movement is selfish is more a statement of gender bias then a theory of rights or justice.

·3·

Constitutional Standards of Equality and Women's Rights

Does equality mean justice for women? What does nature require of law? Whether you focus on the integrity of individuals or the interests of their communities, in fashioning laws for men and women you begin with an ideological assessment of male and female nature: Either you believe biology is destiny or you don't. You shape policies that encourage women's dependence on men or allow for their equality.

Until the 1970s our laws chose dependence for women in the belief that nature did too. Of course, laws are shaped by politics and the simple desire for power, as well as by ideologies; discriminatory, gender-based laws that prevailed in this country only twenty years ago protected the interests of men, as racial discrimination protected the interests of whites. But ideology is not simply propaganda or an afterthought—a rationalization of power—and law is not simply political. Protectionism, a discriminatory double standard of law for men and women, was also a practical consequence of protectionist ideals about sexual difference, implemented by legislatures and endorsed by the United States Supreme Court. Ideology also determines the allocation of rights, as the abortion debate demonstrates: Either you believe a fetus is a human being or only a potential one. You prohibit or permit abortions accordingly and shape the fate of countless women. The abortion debate, with its profound political consequences, is almost entirely ideological, like the debate about the Equal Rights Amendment.

"When He created them, God made physiological and functional differences between men and women," Senator Sam Ervin declared in 1970, explaining his opposition to equality and the ERA: "These differences confer upon men a greater capacity to perform arduous and hazardous physical tasks. Some wise people even profess the belief that there may be psychological differences between men and women. . . . They assert that women possess an intuitive power to distinguish between wisdom and folly, good and evil."[1]

Today, this might pass for one form of feminism; today feminists are among the "wise people" who believe in moral and psychological differences between men and women. But had he lived to hear them, Ervin would have been surprised by the number of fin de siècle feminists echoing his views. When Congress approved the ERA in 1970, at the height of the equal rights movement, the line between male chauvinists and feminists was clear, and so was feminist mistrust of biological determinism. Ervin's deterministic, protectionist philosophy precluded the reform of gender roles sought by egalitarians: In his view, natural differences mandated traditional divisions of labor, which made women responsible not just for bearing children but for nurturing and training them. Man provides a "habitation" for his family, Ervin intoned; women "make the habitations homes."[2] Laws imposing support obligations on men and domestic ones on women only reflected the natural order, not a cultural one that law can and perhaps ought to change. In this way, by insisting that the status quo is natural, the protectionist ideology of sexual difference has always minimized the power of law to effect sociosexual change.

The traditional ideology of racial difference questions law's power as well. The Constitution does not guarantee "social, as distinguished from political equality," the Supreme Court held in *Plessy v. Ferguson* in 1896, upholding a Louisiana law establishing separate railway cars for blacks and whites: "Legislation is powerless to eradicate racial instincts or to abolish distinctions based upon physical differences," the Court explained, dismissing the possibility of "social prejudice [being] overcome by legislation."[3] That blacks may have been more concerned with how they were treated than whether they were liked, that segregation may have exacerbated the social inequality it enforced, only occurred to the Court some sixty years later. In 1954, in *Brown v. Board of Education*, it overruled *Plessy v. Ferguson* and found segregated schools unconstitutional.[4] Rejecting the fiction that separate facilities for blacks were also equal ones, the Court began the slow process of dismantling the Jim Crow laws it once condoned.

Segregation "generates a feeling of inferiority" among black school-children, the Court in *Brown* observed, but, of course, segregation reflected presumptions of black inferiority, presumptions the Court in *Plessy v. Ferguson* tacitly confirmed. Each case is grounded on a different racial ideology: One reinforces white supremacy; the other recognizes natural racial equality. Both cases turn ideas about racial difference into principles of constitutional law that regulate behavior. Whether it codifies prejudice or uses its power to shape ideals, law is our primary link between ideology and behavior.

What ideals will it shape for women? What behavior will it encourage? One woman's ideal—the notion that women are gentler than men—is another woman's prejudice. What's natural behavior to one—full-time homemaking—is an enforced social role to another. Shaping ideals and determining behavior involves choosing sides ideologically. When judges and legislators make rules about divorce proceedings or the treatment of women in the workplace, they enter a feminist debate about equality, assimilation, and motherhood.[5]

The debate erupts periodically over practical problems posed by pregnancy for women with lives outside the home. Is pregnancy a natural handicap for women, a difference for which law must account? The Supreme Court faced these questions in a 1987 case involving special pregnancy disability benefits. In a controversial decision, the Court upheld a California law providing pregnant women with up to four months' disability leave and a guarantee of reinstatement in their former jobs; California law does not require that men who are disabled have their jobs reserved for them. This case, *California Federal Savings and Loan Association v. Guerra*,[6] illuminated the debate about protectionism and equality and the divisions it's causing among feminists.

It began in 1982, when Lillian Garland took a pregnancy leave from her job as a receptionist at a California bank. When she was ready to return to work, three months later, neither her former job nor a similar one was available. Garland complained to the state's fair employment office and soon got back her job. The bank went to federal court to challenge the state law that gave it to her. It was joined at the Supreme Court by the Reagan Administration, which urged the Court to invalidate the California law. Also filing briefs opposing special treatment of women were the National Organization for Women and the American Civil Liberties Union, to the chagrin of quite a few feminists. Challenges to the law were brought under the federal Pregnancy Discrimination Act, which prohibits discriminating against pregnant women in the extension of disability benefits. It was argued that the Act required employers to treat women the same as men, not better or worse than them. The California bank and the Reagan administration wanted special benefits for women eliminated; NOW and the ACLU wanted comparable benefits extended to men. Lillian Garland wanted to keep her job, and the state of California wanted to keep its pregnancy disability law intact. The state argued that special pregnancy benefits compensated women for their special "biological burden."

The Supreme Court upheld the law, not so much because of biology but because of discriminatory custom: As Justice Marshall noted, the Pregnancy Discrimination Act was intended to remedy prior discrimination against pregnant wage earners. Proponents of preferential treatment were partially vindicated, briefly: One week later, in *Wimberly v. Labor and Industrial Relations Commission of Missouri*,[7] the Court upheld a Missouri law denying unemployment benefits to women who leave their jobs on account of pregnancy. Justice O'Connor explained that women were being treated no worse than men who left their jobs for reasons unrelated to their work or employers. Together, these two cases mean that states may choose to extend special benefits to pregnant women wage earners, but they are not compelled to do so. Pregnant women in the workforce must be treated as well, or better, and may be treated as badly as men.

To some feminists, this is precisely what's wrong with equality: It doesn't recognize pregnancy as a unique condition requiring unique treatment and so cannot relieve the hardships of wage-earning women. But the effects of pregnancy on the worker—temporary inability to work and increased medical costs—are common and can readily be addressed in a general worker disability plan. (The problem of pregnancy-related disabilities must be separated from the need for child-care leave, which can and should be extended to both sexes.) Of course, pregnancy is unique, but should its uniqueness matter in the workplace? Shouldn't disabled male workers have their jobs reserved for them as well? The notion that women are affected by pregnancy, or the mere possibility of it, in a way that no man is ever affected by a slipped disc or prostate surgery has always been used to justify their marginal status in the workforce.

It also inspired, perversely, two key decisions by the Supreme Court in the mid-1970s that denied pregnant women the right to any disability coverage at all, either under the Fourteenth Amendment or Title VII of the 1964 Civil Rights Act (prohibiting sex discrimination in employment). In the first case, *Gedulgig v. Aiello*,[8] upholding the exclusion of pregnancy from an employee disability plan under the Fourteenth Amendment, Justice Stewart noted that "there is no risk from which men are protected and women are not." Or as Justice Rehnquist concluded in the second case, *General Electric Company v. Gilbert*,[9] decided under Title VII, pregnancy is "significantly different from the typical covered disease or disability."

These cases show how the "only women get pregnant" argument can readily be turned against women in setting legal standards of equality. Under the Fourteenth Amendment, traditional equal protection analysis rests on notions of comparability, requiring the "similar treatment" of groups of people that are "similarly situated." If, in the pregnancy disability cases, the Court had looked to the effects of disabilities on workers, rather than their causes, it might have found all disabled male and female workers similarly situated, pregnant or not. But it didn't, taking instead an arbitrary, narrow view of comparability that reflected an arbitrary, traditional view of pregnant women as a sort of separate species: Only women get pregnant.

If, however, the Court exaggerated the relevance of pregnancy as a cause of worker disabilities, it minimized its importance in determining how different workers were affected by the same disability exclusions. A rule that hurts only pregnant people hurts only women and ought to be called discriminatory. But in both race and sex cases decided under the Fourteenth Amendment, the Court does not generally ask who's hurt; it asks whether any hurt was intended. The Supreme Court has so far refused to look beyond the face or intent of a law to its effect, refusing to adopt a result-oriented approach to constitutional equality.*

Thus, the *Gilbert* and *Gedulgig* pregnancy disability cases are favorite targets of feminists on both sides of the debate. To advocates of preferential treatment for women, they illustrate the limitations of traditional antidiscrimination law in cases involving physical characteristics unique to one sex (when men and women are not "similarly

---

*Cases involving the discriminatory enforcement of laws present one exception to this rule. Note too that statutory standards of equality, set by Congress, differ from constitutional standards set by the Court. When the Court reviews an allegedly discriminatory employment practice, under Title VII, it examines the effects of the practice, its "disparate impact" on women and minorities. *General Electric Company v. Gilbert* was a Title VII case, and the Court held that the pregnancy disability exclusion had not been shown to have had a discriminatory effect on women. For a discussion of disparate impact analysis under Title VII, see Chapter 7.

situated"). To egalitarians, who believe that pregnancy can or should be compared to other physical conditions affecting workers or that the Court should consider the discriminatory effects of legislation, these cases are simply bad law: The trouble with antidiscrimination law is the Court's crabbed construction of it.

Sex discrimination is, however, a relatively new concept for the Supreme Court, inspired by egalitarian feminism. Throughout most of our history, the ideology defining women's legal rights and disabilities, and determining their fate, was a traditional, protectionist one that assigned men and women different characters and consigned them to separate spheres: Men were given the world and women the home (or at least the homes of their husbands and fathers). Laws governing domestic relations, employment practices, social programs (like Social Security, and civic obligations (jury and military service) extended greater rights, responsibilities, and benefits to men, because men were presumed to be wage earners and women homemakers.

Like racial segregation laws, these laws dividing men and women reinforced the group differences they assumed: Protective labor laws that barred women from men's jobs and family laws that gave men the obligation to support and power to control their families made assumptions about women, domesticity, and dependence come true. The Supreme Court routinely confirmed the constitutionality of these assumptions until the early 1970s, long after it had begun to question legislative assumptions about race. It also continued blaming women for the disruptive, sexist behavior of men after it stopped blaming minorities for the racist behavior of whites. The Court that, in 1948, denied women the right to work as bartenders because of "social problems" they might cause did not deny black families the right to live in white neighborhoods because of racial tensions their presence might allegedly create.[*]

The Supreme Court has generally been more sensitive to racism than sexism under law, because since its passage in 1868 the Fourteenth Amendment has been recognized as a prohibition of racial discrimination. What constitutes discrimination—segregation laws or standardized job tests that disqualify disproportionate numbers of blacks—is often a difficult, devisive question for the Court, but the underlying constitutional claim of minorities to equal protection of law, or nondiscrimination, is acknowledged in principle if not always effected in fact. In 1880,

---

[*]Compare *Goesaert v. Cleary*, 335 U.S. 464 (1948), the case upholding a prohibition on women bartenders, to *Shelley v. Kraemer*, 334 U.S. 1 (1948), invalidating private agreements prohibiting the sale of property to blacks.

in *Strauder v. West Virginia*,[10] the Supreme Court affirmed that the Equal Protection clause meant that laws "shall be the same for the black as for the white." Declaring the exclusion of blacks from jury service discriminatory, a "brand upon them" (in 1961 the Court would consider women's exemption from jury service a privilege),[11] the Court recognized that blacks enjoyed constitutional "immunity" from "legal discriminations, implying inferiority in society." Six years later, in 1886, when it upheld racial segregation laws in *Plessy v. Ferguson*, the Court managed to subvert its own principle of nondiscrimination, but not without feigning respect for it. The separate but equal doctrine announced in *Plessy* gave segregation an appearance of constitutionality.[12]

But while the Constitution's prohibition of racial discrimination has been recognized for over a century, its prohibition of sexual discrimination has been recognized for less than twenty years. It was not until 1971, in response to the equal rights movement, that the Supreme Court began to question the law's differential treatment of the sexes. In the heady, early days of the movement, when Congress approved the ERA, egalitarian feminists successfully challenged sexual stereotyping under law and the wage-earner/homemaker classification of men and women. A range of state and federal laws based on this classification, giving men greater familial authority and concomitant obligations, were finally found unconstitutional. The potentials of egalitarianism and the pitfalls of protectionism for women are delineated by recent legal history.

In 1971 the Supreme Court brought women under the aegis of the Fourteenth Amendment for the first time. In *Reed v. Reed*[13] it invalidated an Idaho law favoring men as estate administrators in cases involving competing male and female applicants. (*Reed* involved conflicting claims by adoptive parents of a minor who died intestate.) Two years later, in *Frontiero v. Richardson*,[14] the Court invalidated a federal statutory scheme that denied women in the military equal benefits for their dependents. (A serviceman was automatically allowed to claim his wife as a dependent, without proof she was dependent in fact; a servicewoman was not allowed to claim her husband as a dependent unless he was in fact dependent on her for more than half of his support.) This case, *Frontiero*, was followed by *Weinberger v. Weisenfeld*,[15] invalidating a federal law barring widowed fathers from receiving the same survivor benefits as widowed mothers. A third case, *Califano v. Goldfarb*,[16] invalidated a Social Security provision that provided unequal benefits for the surviving spouses of female wage earners.

A cynical feminist viewing these cases—*Frontiero, Goldfarb, Weisenfeld*—might point out that they all involve extensions of benefits to men—husbands and widowers of wage-earning women. But it is surely a benefit to all workers to be able to care for their families, as the trial court in *Goldfarb* noted: "Mrs. Goldfarb was entitled to the dignity of knowing that her social security tax would contribute to their joint welfare when the couple or one of them retired and to her husband's welfare should she predecease him. She paid taxes at the same rate as men and there is not the slightest scintilla of support for the proposition that working women are less concerned about their spouses' welfare in old age than are men."[17] But the support for this proposition was, of course, conventional wisdom about woman's nature and role that the judicial system took so long to question. To suggest that wives don't worry about providing financially for their husbands reflects the traditional view of women as childlike dependents, which followed from traditional ideas about motherhood. To assume that women don't in fact contribute to their families' support is to suggest that they shouldn't.

This suggestion shaped a range of laws defining women's place, like those permitting women to marry without parental consent at an earlier age than men: Women were generally allowed to marry at eighteen and men at twenty-one because women were expected only to marry and men were expected to establish themselves professionally. Today, age-of-consent laws are the same for both sexes, and in 1975 the Supreme Court declared unconstitutional a Utah law setting a differential age of majority for males and females that established differential parental obligations of support for sons and daughters:[18] The obligation to support a daughter ended when she turned eighteen and would presumably be supported by her husband. Sons were supported until they reached twenty-one and were presumed to be able to support their families. In upholding this law (before it was struck down by the Supreme Court), Utah's highest court explained that "it is the man's primary responsibility to provide a home and its essentials for the family." The Utah court also noted that "girls tend generally to mature physically, emotionally and mentally before boys, and . . . to marry earlier."[19] Rejecting these "old notions," the Supreme Court observed that "women's activities and responsibilities are increasing and expanding. . . . If a specified age of minority is required for the boy in order to assure him parental support while he attains his education and training, so, too, it is for the girl."[20]

The Court's rejection of the wage-earner/homemaker distinction in these cases was clear and generally supported by feminists. But in recognizing expanding roles for women and extending their rights, the Court extended their responsibilities as well and rescinded one of their dearest privileges—alimony. In 1979 in *Orr v. Orr*[21] the Court struck down an Alabama law making only men liable for alimony. Although the state had a legitimate interest in protecting needy, dependent spouses on divorce or in compensating women for past discrimination during marriage, the Court observed, these interests were not served by making alimony an exclusively female entitlement. Alimony payments were set at individualized hearings during which judges could inquire into the circumstances of both spouses and determine whether the wife, in fact, was in need or the victim of discrimination.

Assumptions about male and female roles would no longer justify treating men and women differently, because the assumptions were flawed and also self-fulfilling: "No longer is the female destined solely for the home and rearing of the family, and only the male for the marketplace and the world of ideas," the Court noted. This was not to deny needy divorced homemakers a right to alimony. It was to affirm that alimony could fairly be provided, on a case-by-case basis, through gender-neutral laws that did not "carry the inherent risk of reinforcing stereotypes about the 'proper place' of women and their need for special protection." No longer was sex a legitimate "proxy for need."[22]

These landmark cases of the 1970s do not deny the possibility of sexual difference. They do suggest that whether or not there are differences between them, men and women ought to be treated as individuals and not emblems of sex and gender. Legislative generalizations about women, even when based on statistical averages or demographic trends, are always overinclusive: Not all women share what may be general characteristics of their sex. Those who do can fairly be served by gender-neutral laws that focus on the characteristics at issue instead of on sex. Perhaps most spouses in need of alimony are women; their right to alimony ought to derive from their need and not from the fact that they're women.

This does not ignore the effects of sex discrimination. The Court in *Orr v. Orr* relied on the fact that alimony payments could be tailored to the needs and equities of every case; making alimony legally available only to women was unnecessary as well as unfair to the minority of men dependent on their wives. The Court also distinguished between protective legislation (like alimony laws), reflecting assumptions about women's proper place, and compensatory legislation, responding to a history of discrimination. It acknowledged that culture, or law, should sometimes give back to women what it once took away.

In another line of sex-discrimination cases decided during the 1970s, the Supreme Court upheld "benign" sex-based classifications aimed at redressing inequality. In *Kahn v. Shevin*[23] the Court upheld an annual

$500 property tax exemption available to widows and not widowers. The law was intended to reduce economic disparities between men and women, the Court observed, disparities that resulted from "overt discrimination or from the socialization process of a male dominated culture." Culture had made the job market "inhospitable to the woman seeking any but the lowest paid jobs." One year later, in *Schlesinger v. Ballard*,[24] the Court upheld a federal law providing more lenient treatment for women naval officers who were passed over for promotion. (Male officers twice passed over were automatically discharged; women who were not promoted could be discharged only after thirteen years of service.) The law did not reflect "archaic and overbroad generalizations about women," the Court observed; rather it was an attempt to remedy previous discrimination against women in the military. Finally, in *Califano v. Webster*[25] the Court upheld a Social Security law that established different formulas for computing retirement benefits for male and female wage earners. (Benefits were based on average monthly wages; women could exclude three additional low-earning years in determining their average wages.) The Court stressed that this provision "operated directly to compensate women for past economic discrimination," discrimination that had created a considerable wage gap between men and women. The differential formula for computing their average wages was "not 'the accidental by-product of a traditional way of thinking about females,' " the Court held (quoting itself), "but rather was deliberately enacted to compensate for particular economic disabilities suffered by women."

In upholding remedial, sex-specific legislation based on economic fact rather than cultural prejudice, the Court has recognized that women are still only potentially equal. Not nature but cultural roles long thrust upon them have made it difficult for women to compete in the marketplace. In this view, ignoring the effects of discrimination is a way of continuing it. The same opportunities for promotion for male and female officers, for example, are not necessarily equal ones. Should women always be treated as equals in principle when they are not yet equal in fact? The principle of gender neutrality enunciated by the Court in the 1970s, and supported by egalitarian feminists, does not require that laws presume equality that has yet to be achieved.

It requires, instead, affirmative action based on the notion that law ought to account for the effects of discrimination; positing equality as a goal sometimes requires the differential treatment of unequals, as a strategy, in the meantime.

But recognizing the need for affirmative action requires acknowledging systemic inequities that make it impossible for minorities and women to take advantage of the "equal" opportunities presented to them. It requires a willingness to admit that not all Americans are raised equally or given equal chances to succeed. Affirmative action doesn't just threaten the economic advantages of white men; it questions the romanticized image of America as a country in which life is fair.

That's an image to which an increasingly conservative Supreme Court apparently clings. In 1989 the Court retreated from its qualified endorsement of affirmative action, under the sway of a new conservative majority, consisting of Chief Justice Rehnquist, Justice White, and Reagan appointees Justices O'Connor, Scalia, and Kennedy. In *Martin v. Wilkes*[26] the Court held that affirmative action plans adopted by employers with a long history of discriminating against minorities might be subject to subsequent legal challenges by whites. (This means that affirmative action plans intended to compensate women for prior discrimination will be subject to subsequent challenges by men.) In *City of Richmond v. Croson*[27] the Court invalidated a plan to increase the share of minority firms in public contracts, holding that remedial quotas for minorities are as suspect as any other racial classification.*

The Court has always been most vigilant in guarding against racial discrimination. One irony of the *Croson* decision is that the stringent constitutional protection traditionally afforded minorities may now be used against them to protect the majority complaining of "reverse discrimination." Another is that the less stringent constitutional protection traditionally afforded women should mean less stringent constitutional protection for men complaining of reverse sexual discrimination. Despite its new distaste for affirmative action, the Court that has been more tolerant of laws differentiating between the sexes that hurt women should be equally tolerant of differential laws that help them.**

---

*The affirmative action debate, *Martin v. Wilkes*, and *City of Richmond v. Croson* are discussed further in Chapter 9.

**In a 1987 case, *Johnson v. Transportation Agency, Santa Clara County*, 480 U.S. 616 (1987), the Court upheld a plan aimed at providing women with traditionally masculine jobs, holding that a county highway department could consider the sex of qualified applicants, among other factors, in making promotional decisions: In choosing between more or less equally qualified men and women, an employer may choose a woman, on account of her sex, in order to integrate its workforce. *Johnson* has not been overruled, but the composition of the Court has changed since it was decided; it would probably be decided differently today.

Is affirmative action a kind of protectionism? Perhaps. But it differs from traditional protective laws in the way a "benign" sex-based classification, like one aimed at equalizing male and female opportunities for promotion, differs from a "privilege," like alimony, based on asssumptions about appropriate gender roles. Affirmative action isn't protectionism but compensation, a way of enabling women and minority males to compete and a recognition that for victims of discrimination, life has never been a meritocracy. Unlike traditional protective laws, affirmative action rests not on assumptions about natural differences between the sexes but on the unnatural ways in which women have been handicapped by a history of discrimination.

In its endorsement of benign sex-based classifications and the principle of remediation and in its rejection of the wage-earner/homemaker distinction, the Supreme Court addressed some important cultural inequities for women. (Affirmative action is a response to cultural inequities, not a reflection of biases about human nature; it's about gender roles, not sexual difference.) But while the Court challenged traditional gender roles and the laws that enforced them, it left standing the essential ideology of sexual difference.

The Supreme Court has not extended to women the same constitutional protection extended to racial minorities. Because it has not concluded that men and women are naturally equal, as racial groups are equal, the Court employs a different standard of review in race and sex cases under the Fourteenth Amendment. Different standards for women and minorities were invoked early on in 1971 in *Reed v. Reed*, the first decision to strike down a law for discriminating against women, under the Fourteenth Amendment.

Reed was a landmark case for women, but as a matter of constitutional law it was fairly tame. The Court in *Reed* simply found that a preference for men as estate administrators was unreasonable. The principle of this decision—that legislation must bear a reasonable relation to a legitimate state objective—is a very traditional one. It is an expression of judicial deference to legislative decision making that requires courts to determine only if a piece of legislation is rational, not if it's right. This "rational relation" test used to review the constitutionality of legislation is a permissive one that most laws can pass. That the law at issue in *Reed* did not is a measure of how irrational traditional assumptions about gender roles were beginning to appear.

Deference to legislation—the principle that courts are supposed to review the reasonableness of a law, not its wisdom—does not, however, apply in cases involving fundamental rights (such as rights of speech) or racial discrimination. In these cases, the Court employs a "strict standard" of review. A racial classification must not simply be a reasonable way of achieving a legitimate state objective; it must be a necessary way of achieving a compelling one, which it virtually never is.[28]

The Court has not applied this higher standard to laws discriminating against women (or men). If it had, it might have invalidated the widows' property tax exemption at issue in *Kahn v. Shevin*.[29] The state's purpose in granting an exemption to widows and not widowers—compensating women for economic discrimination—could have been served by a gender-neutral law that applied to all surviving spouses whose incomes fell below a certain level. In race cases, when it applies a strict standard of review, the Court essentially requires the state to find the least discriminatory alternative way of achieving its purpose. In sex cases, however, the Court has fashioned an "intermediate" standard. "Classifications by gender must serve important governmental objectives," not compelling ones, the Court has held; and the classifications "must be substantially related to achievement of those objectives," not essential to them.[30]

What these lawyerlike semantic distinctions signify is the Court's attachment to a few "old notions" about sexual difference. The intermediate standard allows the Court to uphold some sexually discriminatory laws as natural and necessary, when they involve reproduction.

The Court often has trouble locating discrimination in laws differentiating between the sexes on the basis of their reproductive roles—laws that are often "protective" of women. In 1981, in *Michael M. v. Superior Court*,[31] it upheld a California statutory rape law applying only to men because only women get pregnant. The law prohibited sexual intercourse with underage females, not underage males, and provided that intercourse between a male and an underage female was a crime for the male only. This was justified by the Court as an attack on the problem of teenage pregnancy. Since only girls are exposed to the risk of pregnancy, Justice Rehnquist reasoned, it serves as a "natural sanction" for sexually active females. Criminal sanctions for males simply "'equalize' the deterrents." The familiar "only women get pregnant" refrain has also been effective in limiting the rights of unwed fathers. In 1979, in *Parham v. Hughes*,[32] the Supreme Court upheld a Georgia law denying an unwed father the right to sue for wrongful death of a child he had failed to "legitimate." Rejecting a sex discrimination claim in this case, the Court noted that "mothers and fathers of illegitimate children are not similarly situated," because of problems in establishing paternity.[33]

Reproductive differences and the differences in sexual behavior they're presumed to create have also been used to deny women equal employment opportunities. In 1977, in *Dothard v. Rawlinson*,[34] the Court upheld an Alabama law prohibiting women from working as guards in male prisons because prisoners would be "moved" to assault them. The fact that Alabama's prison system had been declared unconstitutionally violent and inhumane—"particularly inhospitable for human beings of whatever sex"—was used to justify the state's exclusion of women prison guards, not to define its obligation to enact penal reforms. The fact that male prison guards were also subject to assaults was conveniently ignored.

What's striking about these cases is the irrelevance of the biological differences on which they are based. Difficulties in establishing paternity are not simply biologically compelled: They reflect cultural patterns of neglect and desertion by fathers, which limiting fathers' rights may confirm and encourage. Nor is male sexual aggressiveness (or female passivity) a simple fact of life, as statutory rape laws and discrimination against women prison guards assume. The Court doesn't recognize discrimination in these cases, or in preferential pregnancy disability plans, because it doesn't recognize that the biological differences involved in them don't matter. The Court can't see discrimination when it can't see the difference between biology and culture.[35]

Of course, defining that difference and its relevance to law has always been the challenge for feminists. Feminists themselves, and other reasonable people, always will disagree about what's natural to men and women and what results from socialization, which is why a "sameness/difference" debate is polarizing the feminist community today. But it's clear that whatever the fixed, natural order may be, popular images of it change: Slavery was once considered as natural as childbirth. If there are absolutes, we have only shifting, relativistic views of them, which sometimes translate into laws. Basic to feminist theory is the perception that law has always been implicated in the transformation of economic interests and cultural prejudice into immutable biological truth.

·4·

A History of Egalitarianism and Protectionism and the Ideology of Sexual Difference

"The natural and proper timidity and delicacy of the female sex evidently unfits it for many of the occupations of civil life," United States Supreme Court Justice Bradley declared in 1873 in a case denying women the right to practice law. Women's familial obligations, dictated by "the Creator," compelled their exclusion from public life: "The family institution is repugnant to the idea of a woman adopting a distinct and independent career from that of her husband." Justice Bradley admitted that some women were unmarried and free to pursue careers, but they were exceptions: "The paramount destiny and mission of women are to fulfill the noble and benign offices of wife and mother. . . . The rules of a civil society must be adapted to the general constitution of things and cannot be based upon exceptional causes."[1]

That the "rules of a civil society" should maintain what were considered natural, separate spheres of activity for men and women was the dominant ideology of Victorian America. It reflected sexual stereotypes that persist today with less power but considerable tenacity: Men were aggressive, competitive, smart, and strong; they were ceded the qualities necessary for success in the industrial marketplace. Women were nurturing, emotional, moral, and weak; they were given the qualities needed to ensure domestic harmony. This view of individual men and women as sexual archetypes justified the protectionist wage-earner/homemaker laws that prevailed until the 1970s; in the nineteenth century it barred all but a very few unmarried women from professional life and wedded others to poverty or dependence. The stereotypes that denied women their equal power to reason justified denying them their rights.

Egalitarian feminism had to begin with a challenge to protectionist stereotyping and the neat, dualistic "natural" order it implied. Equality offered instead a messier, more complex vision of human sexuality and of men and women as variable, potentially reasonable human beings.

In 1791, with the daring assertion that women were "rational creatures," just like men, Mary Wollstonecraft extended eighteenth-century ideals about the natural rights of men to women and set forth the basic theory of egalitarian feminism. However different they may be, whatever different duties they fulfill, she wrote, men and women are endowed with the same capacity to reason and the same right to determine their own destinies. Wollstonecraft laid claim to reason; women were not mere vessels of emotion, she declared. They could think as well as feel if they were educated and encouraged to do so. It was their social conditioning that degraded women by "cramping their understandings and sharpening their senses."[2]

Wollstonecraft stressed the power of culture to shape character. She blamed the frivolity, "fondness of dress," obsession with love and domestic trivialities, and the sheer silliness of leisure-class women on a "false system of education" and the tendency of men to view women "rather as women than human creatures." But women who were bred to be "creatures of sensation," idle and inane, could just as easily be bred to exercise their reason. Wollstonecraft stressed the need for an education that encouraged independent thought, to remake women and unmake femininity. Her mandate for women was revolutionary: "to obtain a character as a human being, regardless of the distinction of sex."[3]

Egalitarianism always tests distinctions—sexual, racial, ethnic, economic, and intellectual. How seriously should we take IQ tests? Are the differences between people real or imagined? If they're real, are they relevant? Is the social order we make of them fair? The real distinction between men and women is a great mystery, John Stuart Mill suggested in 1840: Presumptions about women were mere prejudices, reflections of "custom and general feeling," because women never had been allowed naturally to develop. Like Galatea, they were made, not born;

brute strength had given men the power to dictate what women should be. "What is now called the nature of women is an eminently artificial thing," Mill remarked.[4] Or as suffragist Helen Hamilton Gardener remarked eighty years later, "After a woman's waist and brain are put into tight laces and shaped to fit the fashion, it is rather a poor time to judge of her natural figure, either physical or mental." [5] Moreover, whatever restraints nature might have imposed on women did not justify the unnatural ones imposed on them by men. Early women's rights advocates stressed the clear and simple moral claim to equal rights: "The legal subordination of one sex to the other," Mill wrote, "is wrong in itself."[6]

The nineteenth-century American women's movement began with this moral appeal for legal equality, informed by a belief in universal reason and natural rights and the conviction that women were weak, not by nature, but by law and social conditioning, dependent on men because they were denied the means to be independent. Their privileges were few, and they paid for them dearly: If a few women found respectful male partners and some found benign male protectors, others suffered under petty despots in marriages they could not dissolve (divorces were scandalous and, for many, impossible to obtain). At midcentury married women were under the legal patronage of their husbands, with no general right to hold property or wages in their own names; single women were deprived of their dignity and opportunities to support themselves. Elizabeth Cady Stanton characterized the care and protection extended by men to women as "care and protection such as the wolf gives the lamb—such as the eagle the hare he carries into his eyrie!!"[7]

So the first women's movement, which began officially in 1848, did not begin with a plea for expanded privileges and protections for women, in respect of their reproductive roles. It began with an assertion of rights, a "Declaration of Sentiments," issued at Seneca Falls, New York, and modeled after the United States Declaration of Independence. Equality of the sexes is "self-evident," it proclaimed, and along with suffrage—the most controversial of their demands—early women's rights advocates called for equal economic rights, educational and employment opportunities, divorce and child-custody rights, and a single standard of sexual morality. Underlying these demands was a belief that men and women were "invested by the Creator with the same capabilities, and the same consciousness of responsibility for their exercise," which meant that both men and women had both a right and duty to participate in public life.[8] The framers of the Seneca Falls declaration did not promise that women, once emancipated, would save the world, or simply make better mothers in service to the public good. They didn't argue that emancipation was expedient. They presented it as a moral imperative.*

Egalitarianism demanded not only pervasive political and economic changes but profound ideological ones as well. In 1850 declaring that men were not smarter, more sensible, and tougher than women was like declaring in 1512 that the earth was not the center of the universe. Science and religion, as well as law, defined women as naturally inferior, which made sexual subjugation, not sexual equality, naturally just.

The convergence of authority on the "woman question" made women's rights to hold property, attend college, and enter the male professions, even their capacity to function outside the home, less than self-evident. It was evident instead that women who reasoned, argued, and spoke out on public issues were unnatural, irreligious, and a threat to traditional family values. Science dismissed assertive, achievement-oriented women as sexual anomalies—evolutionary blips. Religion condemned them as unholy. Law barely acknowledged their existence, confirming that "exceptional" women, like those who sought admission to the bar, need not be considered by men when they handed out rights. On the subject of women, law was reactive, reflective, like a ventriloquist's dummy. Instead of defining sexual justice, it dumbly codified social, scientific, and religious prejudices about women. Instead of rights, women were left with the moral claim of their dependence.

"The power of woman is her dependence," a group of Massachusetts clergymen reminded abolitionists and feminists Angelina and Sarah Grimke during their notorious speaking tour of New England in the 1830s. "When [woman] assumes the place and tone of man as public reformer, our care and protection of her seems unnecessary . . . and her character becomes unnatural. If the vine . . . thinks to assume the independence and the overshadowing nature of the elm, it will not only cease to bear fruit, but fall in shame and dishonour into the dust."[9]

Whether they incurred the wrath of God or simply men, women who acted less differently than women were supposed to act put themselves at risk. The vilification of women like the Grimke sisters who voiced

---

*Many of the first women's rights advocates, including Lucy Mott, Susan B. Anthony, Sarah and Angelina Grimke, and Sojourner Truth, were active abolitionists. Inspired and trained by the fight for abolition, they began the women's movement with newly acquired public speaking and political skills and a sense of moral outrage.

unfeminine opinions was a measure of popular resistance to expanding women's roles and also a warning to feminists.

If women were supposed to be actively Christian, their Christian activities were narrowly proscribed. The church welcomed women charity workers and relied on their religiosity, at home and in the community: Women were active followers of the nineteenth-century evangelical movements; the Second Great Awakening of the 1830s was largely a movement of women and clergymen. Religious belief even led some women into public life, as moral reformers and temperance workers. But their crusades against alcohol and commercial vice were, in part, attempts to implement church teachings.[10] Secular political activism was denied them, and public issues in which the church was less interested or less unified or less reliant on women's "moral influence"—issues such as abolition—were reserved for men.

Abolition, involving questions of natural rights and a wrenching challenge to the social order, was an especially dangerous subject for women. "There were no bounds to the efforts made to crush the actions of women who . . . used their powers in the anti-slavery movement," British journalist Harriet Martineau remarked.[11] Martineau, who toured the United States in the 1830s and made more trenchant observations about women than de Tocqueville ever imagined, considered the failure of many women to act on their professed antislavery beliefs evidence of the moral bankruptcy of femininity. It was certainly evidence of masculine intimidation and feminine fear. Women abolitionists, women's rights activists, and others who preferred being "independent," "overshadowing elms" instead of clinging vines, could expect to end up alone, impoverished, infertile, and damned. No wonder so many preferred to stay home.

During the first half of the nineteenth century, the onset of industrialization and a system of wage labor for men turned domesticity into a calling for women. During the 1840s a plethora of popular treatises on femininity and submissiveness—how-to books for middle-class women—helped shape an emerging cult of True Womanhood. True Women were frail, tender, loyally supportive (like the family dog), and not terribly rational or pragmatic. Their virtues were "not of this world," one lady's book intoned. Home was their only "appropriate sphere of action," according to the laws of God and nature. "The religion and politics of men have their widest sphere in the world without; but the religious zeal and the patriotism of women are most beneficially and powerfully exerted upon the members of her household. . . . When our husbands and our sons go forth into the busy and turbulent world . . .

their hearts will be at home where their treasure is; and they will rejoice to return to its sanctuary of rest, there to refresh their wearied spirits, and renew their strengths for the toils and conflicts of life."[12]

The True Woman was thus an unemployed wife, or a spinster with a benevolent father or brother who tended her nieces, nephews, and neighbors. Poor, unprotected women who had to face the "toils and conflicts" of life themselves were ignored, pitied, or condemned to prostitution. The diminution of women's employment opportunities occasioned by the characterization of wage work as unwomanly went largely unnoticed. What was noticed, by middle-class women, were the hardships of life without a male protector: When it is virtually impossible for women to support themselves, when "feminine occupations of a profitable nature are few," Harriet Martineau wrote, "there is the strongest temptation to prefer luxury with infamy to hardship with unrecognized honour."[13] Instead of fighting to create a place outside the home, middle-class women agreed to sanctify their place within it.

To the champions of True Womanhood, which probably included, in varying degrees, most white middle-class women, egalitarianism was not only an offense against God and nature, it was bad for women. Equal rights would deprive them of the protections they enjoyed as wives and mothers, leaving them stranded in the brutal world of business and politics, to which they were innately unsuited. Catherine Beecher, an early advocate of "educated motherhood," declared that the "domestic subordination" of women was in their own best interests: Men could be trusted to vote for them and manage their affairs and, "as if in compensation," for their deference, women are "always treated as superiors . . . preference is given to woman, in all the comforts, conveniences, and courtesies of life."* In her view, the subordinancy of women in real or surrogate maternity was determined by "the Creator." True Womanhood was a form of Christian womanhood, which was a bulwark of democracy. The "principles of democracy" were identical with the "principles of Christianity."[14]

A rejection of domesticity was made to look like a rejection of God and nation, and it was, in fact, a rejection of popular Christian ideals about women. Elizabeth Cady Stanton was one of the few feminist

---

*Beecher, who never married, recognized that not all women could be wives. But her view of femininity was not inconsistent with spinsterhood. Spinsters could lead useful, womanly lives dedicating themselves to the care of others—as nurses, domestic servants, or teachers. Beecher, a pioneer of modern teacher training, wanted to educate women to make them better mothers if they did marry and better teachers if they didn't.

leaders with the courage or foolhardiness to acknowledge this. When women protested "their civil and political degradation" or their "unequal position in the Church," Stanton observed, "they were referred to the Bible for an answer." Condemning the religious idealization of women as silent, suffering, and submissive—daughters of Eve, doing penance—she attacked the "Bible position" on women as if the Bible itself were another political tract: "I do not believe that any man ever saw or talked with God," she wrote.[15]

Toward the end of her life, Stanton developed her own sacred vision of sexual equality and an androgynous God in *The Woman's Bible*, a much maligned book that was denounced by the National American Women's Suffrage Association. Some say that "it is not *politic* to rouse religious opposition," Stanton complained (and it surely was not). But convinced that sexual injustice and the underlying belief in female inferiority was systemic, she remained convinced that emancipation required "an entire revolution in all existing institutions. . . . All reforms are interdependent. . . . Whatever is done to establish one principle on a solid basis, strengthens all."[16] Susan B. Anthony viewed the NAWSA disavowal of Stanton's bible as a form of religious persecution or, at least, intolerance, urging suffrage leaders to "inspire in women a broad and catholic spirit." Religious bigotry was no basis for "better government," she vainly suggested to women whose view of government and social change was shaped partly by religion.[17] (Temperance and moral reform movements were overtly evangelical, and the volunteer tradition, which fueled the suffrage movement, carried on a tradition of "good works.") Of the countless women who were willing to demand votes or criticize social services or denounce the liquor industry, few were willing to take on the Bible. Feminism was no match for religion.

Science was more formidable, and science might have saved women from religious misogyny. With authority equal to that of the Bible and the power to establish new truths about the origin of species, it surely could have established new truths about women. Instead, science confirmed misogynist views of male and female nature spread by the religion it threatened to displace.

Darwin turned religious and social prejudices about female and racial inferiority into scientific facts. Citing a developmental link between women and the "lower races," he provided a biological justification for sexual and racial oppression: "Man is more courageous, pugnacious, and energetic than woman and has a more inventive genius," he wrote in *The Descent of Man*. "With women the powers of intuition, of rapid perception, and perhaps of imitation, are more strongly marked than in man; but some, at least, of these faculties are characteristics of the lower races, and therefore of a past and lower state of civilization."[18] In what became the popular scientific view, women and blacks simply occupied a lower rung on evolution's ladder; they were "living representatives of an ancestral stage in the evolution of white males."[19] French scientist Paul Broca, a leader in the new "science" of craniometry, or skull measurement, "proved" that women were dumber than men because their brains were smaller. Gustave Le Bon, a disciple of Broca, said that women's brains were like the brains of gorillas; their intellectual inferiority to men was so obvious that "only its degree [was] worth discussion." Le Bon characterized women as "the most inferior forms of human evolution. . . . They are closer to children and savages than to an adult, civilized male."[20]

Smart, successful, or strong women were considered monstrous, masculinized freaks of nature, unworthy of scientific consideration. Le Bon declared that "distinguished women, very superior to the average man," were "as exceptional as the birth of any monstrosity, as, for example, of a gorilla with two heads; consequently, we may neglect them entirely."[21] According to Otto Weininger, author of *Sex and Character*, an immensely popular misogynist tract that appeared around the turn of the century, "A woman's demand for emancipation and her qualification for it are in direct proportion to the amount of maleness in her. . . . All women who are truly famous and are of conspicuous mental ability . . . reveal some of the anatomical characters of the male, some external bodily resemblance to a man." (George Eliot, for example, had a "broad, massive forehead.") "Those so-called women who have been held up to admiration in the past and present, by the advocates of women's rights, as examples of what women can do, have almost invariably been what I have described as sexually intermediate forms."[22]

As an archetype, woman was "mindless," Weininger wrote. Femininity—meaning submissiveness, emotionalism, stupidity, and sensuality—came naturally to natural women, who were ruled by reproduction. "Man possesses sexual organs; her sexual organs possess women." Lacking control, self-consciousness, and spirit, "Women have no existence and no essence; they are not, they are nothing."[23]

Weininger, a proto-fascist who killed himself in his early twenties shortly after publication of his book, can fairly be called crazy, but *Sex and Character* was influential and widely read, and its bitter, frightened attack on both femininity and feminism is one logical extreme of Darwin's theories about human sexuality. According to Darwin, men were the primary actors in the human evolutionary drama, because of nature's reproductive scheme. Men choose women, vying with each other for the choicest; men support women and their young, vying for meat and worldly success. The processes of sexual selection, "the contest with rival males," and natural selection, "the general struggle for life," developed man's "imagination" and "reason" as well as his "courage, perseverance, and determined energy. . . . Man has ultimately become superior to woman." Having fallen behind in development, women—destined for passivity, natural selectees instead of selectors—never would catch up. What evolution had produced in the past—sexual differences that determined character and intelligence—it would exaggerate in the future. Men must "struggle in order to maintain themselves and their families," Darwin observed—never imagining women struggling too. "This will tend to keep up or even increase their mental powers, and, as a consequence, the present inequality between the sexes."[24]

Scientific "evidence" like this was hard to dispute. In describing the inferiority of women, science had one great advantage over religion—an air of objectivity. Science "proved" what religion could only declare; it offered fact instead of belief. Darwin wasn't supposed to be expressing a personal preference or even a tenet of faith; he was supposed to be revealing a fact.

Facts about sexual difference abounded during the late nineteenth century. Popular, pseudoscientific notions of sexual differentiation stressed man's ascent from some primeval, hermaphrodic sludge; sex differentiation was a form of development, and greater differentiation meant a higher degree of civilization. As the human race matured, the sexes would continue separating, as Darwin predicted. Men would grow smarter, while women, it seems, would keep having babies. Men were in the process of becoming and women were standing still. Grounded by reproduction, weighed down by her uterus, woman was earthbound, sensate, stupid. Man was ascending into the realm of spirit and intellect, as if becoming disembodied, like some highly evolved alien on *Star Trek*.[25]

In Darwinian terms, progress was a movement toward inequality, a process of male development, but progress was not assured. Man, after all, still resembled the animals from which he had descended. Carrying his past within him, he was liable to "reversion," Darwin hinted. His superiority was as "tentative" as natural selection itself.[26] Evolutionary science began raising the frightening prospect of natural degeneration, and atavism became a popular explanation of criminality. It was as if the mere existence of women, criminals, and black males proved the hold white man's past had on him.

The image of women dragging down men began to be taken quite literally. Sirens and mermaids, in fact, were popular subjects for painters.[27] Female sexuality, always suspect, now threatened men with atavistic devolution, as it had once threatened them with damnation. "Bad" women were animals, sensual and cruel, like Zola's Therese Raquin, a feline temptress (with "African blood that burned in her veins"),[28] who leads her lover into murdering her husband, or Nana, the mindless, amoral prostitute who preys on men and is likened to the racehorse that bears her name. Thackery's Becky Sharp was a "Syren" with a monster's tail.[29] Women were a natural force of corruption. Nana turned "society sour," Zola explained, "just as women having a period turn milk sour."[30] Sexual abstinence became an ideal for men, a way to distance themselves from the "lower animals" and preserve the energy believed contained in bodily fluids. Sex sapped man's thinking power just as education sapped woman's power to reproduce. (Higher education made women sterile, according to medical authorities.)

Reproduction consumed women, claiming whatever intellectual energy nature had mistakenly bestowed on them, making them not just maternal but childish. Suspicions about what women shared with children had been confirmed by Darwin. Although "male and female children resemble each other closely, like the young of so many animals in which the adult sexes differ widely," he observed, "they likewise resemble the mature female much more closely than the mature male." Women did eventually assume some "distinctive characters" of her own, he added, which made her the "intermediate between the child and the man," at least in terms of the formation of her skull.[31]

Skull formation provided further evidence of sexual and racial inferiority and a biological explanation for criminal behavior that might otherwise have been blamed on social injustice. Craniology became another obsession of nineteenth-century science, thanks largely to the efforts of Cesare Lombroso. Lombroso identified criminals by their "anomalous skull shapes," brain weights, and facial features, along with other physical "abnormalities." The habitual criminal was on a different or at least a slower evolutionary track; he represented "one branch of a decadent stem that also included lunatics, epileptics, alcoholics, prostitutes, and paupers."[32] The female criminal, Lombroso discovered, had a decidedly masculine skull. She was also shorter and fatter than the normal woman, although prostitutes had "longer hands and bigger calves." The cranial capacities of female offenders were below normal, and they were usually ugly, although in less "refined" nations, such as Russia, they were not so much uglier than normal.[33]

Today, Lombroso's theories may seem quaint or too stupid to be taken seriously, but at the turn of the century, he was a respected scientific authority who helped shape Progressive notions of criminal justice. If biology, not social or economic conditions, caused crime, it was argued, the penal system should focus on the biology or the character of the criminal, not the crime. This justified, indeed demanded, differential indeterminate sentencing: Two people convicted of the same crime would serve different sentences because of their different characters and capacities for rehabilitation. Assessments of character would be made by craniologists and the new social scientists—penologists and other experts in criminology.

This reflected, of course, a highly deterministic view of human behavior; "normal" men and women were no more free of their genetic inheritances and had no more control over their characters and destinies than "abnormal" ones. In this view, the notion that fairness required similar treatment of people convicted of similar offenses was as anachronistic as the belief that deprivation, poverty, and abuse might be causes of crime, as unreasonable as the assertion that social conditioning and discrimination might explain femininity.

Biological determinism relieved society of any obligation to remedy inequality and engendered resignation in the victims of it—women, minority males, the poor and working classes. The belief that all men, if not women, were created equal (and in a democratic society would be equal) gave way to the Social Darwinist notion that some were created more equal or fitter than others, the belief that success and failure reflected the natural selection of the marketplace, that economic disparities reflected prior biological ones. Equality itself was tacitly redefined to mean equal opportunities, not equal results, imposing no affirmative obligation on society to ensure that people were equally able to take advantage of whatever opportunities were presented to them. In this way, biology provided a rationalization for inequality in a putatively egalitarian society that idealized economic and social mobility and witnessed the rise of the middle class. Science "proved" that the problem was in the players, not the playing field, that inequality was a natural phenomenon that society never could or should control: According to Cesare Lombroso, "We are governed by silent laws which never cease to operate and which rule society with more authority than the laws inscribed on our statute books."[34]

Concern about these laws, along with fear of racial degeneracy, erupted, perhaps inevitably, into the passion for eugenics that dominated discussion of social issues at the turn of the century. Darwin himself had bemoaned man's rather irresponsible breeding habits: "Man scans with scrupulous care the character and pedigree of his horses, cattle and dogs before he matches them; but when he comes to his own marriage he rarely, or never, takes any such care. . . . Both sexes ought to refrain from marriage if they are in any marked degree inferior in body or mind."[35]

Darwin was concerned partly with consanguineous marriages and what he considered the congenitally weak—people who would not survive if sympathy and a compulsion to aid the helpless did not constitute a "social instinct" in the strong. But by the turn of the century, eugenics was a racist response to the emancipation of blacks, increasing immigration, and the fear that native-born whites would eventually be outnumbered. "From the rate at which immigrants are increasing, it is obvious that our very life-blood is at stake," one eugenics textbook warned in 1916: "For our own protection, we must face the question of what types or races should be ruled out."[36] Eugenicists supported restricting immigration to whites and justified segregation and miscegenation laws that persisted in the South well into this century.[37]

This overtly racist movement was covertly sexist: Eugenics threatened the reproductive freedom of all women. While blacks were encouraged not to "breed," native-born whites were expected to do so patriotically and as a sort of public service to "the race." Taken to its extreme, as it was, eugenics justified involuntary sterilization of blacks and convicted felons and compulsory pregnancy for whites. Birth control, for white women, was labeled "race suicide."[38] Feminism itself, by advocating not just family planning but equal education and employment for women, was race suicide too: Educated professionals tended to marry later, if at all, and have fewer if any children.

Eugenicists therefore had little use for feminists and less for advocates of birth control for middle- and upper-class whites. But early twentieth-century birth control advocates were not above using eugenics, exploiting fears about the breeding capacities of blacks and immigrants, and presenting birth control as a means of ensuring the continued dominance of native-born whites. Margaret Sanger became unabashedly racist, turning from a concern for reproductive freedom to advocacy of population control.[39] Feminist reformers not directly involved in the birth control movement also found some use for eugenics: It lent support to pronatalist, feminist reforms, such as mothers' pensions and protective labor laws.*

Feminism mounted no greater challenge to science than it had to religion. Popular feminism reflected the popular scientific view that biology was destiny and women could only complement and never equal men. The feminist movement for equal rights became a movement for womanly reforms and protections—prohibition and censorship as well as special labor laws for women.

What began at Seneca Falls by celebrating the common human heritage of both sexes ended seventy years later, with passage of the suffrage amendment, in a celebration of femininity. After the Civil War an amalgam of temperance and antivice crusaders, social service volunteers, and Progressives fought for votes and the entry of women into public life in the name of their superior moral virtue, blaming society's ills on the absence of their "gentle influence" outside the home. Women's rights advocates—egalitarian feminists like Elizabeth Cady Stanton—were supplanted by protectionist women reformers, or "social feminists"—like Frances Willard, charismatic leader of the Women's Christian Temperance Union, and Julia Ward Howe. In the late 1860s the split in the feminist movement and a bitter battle over constitutional amendments extending voting rights to blacks and not women split the suffrage movement into two rival camps that remained apart for twenty years. Susan B. Anthony and Elizabeth Cady Stanton, blindly enraged by the support of their abolitionist allies for the Fifteenth Amendment (extending the vote only to blacks), formed the relatively radical, if racist in origin, National Woman Suffrage Association. Lucy Stone, Julia Ward Howe, Henry Beecher, and others formed the American Woman Suffrage Association, a more reformist organization that helped make feminism palatable to mainstream American women.**

The frenzy of femininity in which middle-class white women had been exhorted to indulge turned out to be somewhat subversive. What were considered women's special virtues and values gave them a special role to play in the public as well as the private sphere. The home would no longer be the world for women; instead, they would make the world a home. According to Frances Willard, women were "the less tainted

*Protective labor laws are discussed in Chapter 5.
**The suffrage movement, in general, became increasingly tainted with racism. Both radical and reformist suffragists invoked the spectre of black and immigrant men voting in arguing for the enfranchisement of native-born white women.

half of the race"; their moral superiority gave them an obligation to "go forth into the world" and make it "homelike."[40]

So while egalitarian feminists demanded the vote partly for its own sake because disenfranchisement was morally wrong, social feminists saw it as a means of achieving reforms to protect women, children, and the growing working class from the abuses of industrialization. Armed with ballots, women promised to eliminate alcohol, commercial vice, and political corruption, to improve education, health, and welfare systems. It was as if by seeking the vote, suffragists were doing their communities a favor. To protectionist social feminists, voting was less a right than a public service women were willing to render.

Egalitarians who stressed individual rights for women and individual fulfillment instead of communal needs were readily accused of being "selfish" and therefore unwomanly. To declare, as Mary Wollstonecraft did, that a woman's first duty was to herself was to attack the sex/gender stereotypes on which most people based their identities as well as their familial roles. Selfishness is considered a cardinal sin in women; it's inconsistent with cultural ideals of motherhood, which is why egalitarians have always been branded as unnatural, self-hating betrayers of children. This rather hysterical reaction to demands for equal rights does have the political virtue of appealing to feelings about women and children rather than ideas, but it has always been simplistic and grossly unfair.

Egalitarian feminism has never been a clear and simple rejection of femininity, much less of motherhood. Elizabeth Cady Stanton, who had seven children, was not above invoking or believing in women's virtues, especially when demanding maternal custody rights, nor was she insensitive to the hardships and pleasures of motherhood. In 1848, when she organized the convention at Seneca Falls, she was a thirty-three-year-old housewife with three children, beset with "nursing and housekeeping cares." She retreated periodically from public life to care for her children: "I swear by all saints that whilst I am nursing this baby I will not be tormented with suffering humanity," she wrote to Susan B. Anthony in 1853.[41] Years later, Stanton described her own domestic experiences and the general lack of support for housework and child care as inspiration for her feminism.[42]

Mary Wollstonecraft's experience with motherhood and femininity was not just hard but tragic. Afflicted with the very feminine weakness of falling helplessly and hopelessly in love, she attempted suicide after one unhappy affair and died at thirty-eight in childbirth—knowing too well that nature treated men and women differently. She used motherhood to support her demands for education, pointing out that educated women would make better mothers, who would, in turn, raise better citizens. But she characterized the feminine virtues of "patience, docility, good humor, and flexibility" as negative virtues "incompatible with any vigorous exertion of intellect."[43] Positive virtues were intelligence and will, virtues fostered only by equality and respect for individual autonomy. Underlying women's claim to equal rights was a claim to autonomy and a right of self-interest.

Women's right to equality was based on their natural claim to "self-sovereignty," Elizabeth Cady Stanton wrote at the end of her life. In a speech entitled "The Solitude of Self," this mother of seven and political organizer, who spent most of her life in a crowd, stressed the "individuality of each human soul." Every man and woman is autonomous and unique: "We come into the world alone, unlike all who have gone before us, we leave it alone, under circumstances peculiar to ourselves." Women needed to assume responsibility for their own lives, as men did, because "each soul must depend wholly on itself . . . as an individual [woman] must rely on herself." It wasn't selfish for women to look after themselves; it was self-deceptive for them not to: "No matter how much women prefer to lean, to be protected and supported, nor how much men desire to have them do so, they must make the voyage of life alone." For Stanton, it wasn't benevolence that denied women rights of self-interest and the capacity to care for themselves, but a way of playing God: "Who, I ask you, can take, dare take himself, the rights, the duties, the responsibilities of another human soul?"[44]

This assertion of autonomy distinguished egalitarians from protectionists, who persisted in portraying women solely in relation to their communities. Egalitarians posed fearful existential as well as economic challenges to feminists and antifeminists alike. In a society that defined women by their service to family and community, a society in which women existed only in relationship to others, acknowledging their separateness was heresy and treason. To Stanton it was a matter of self-preservation. Demanding your rights was no more selfish than breathing.

The "whole question of women's rights turns the point of the marriage relation," Stanton stressed in 1853.[45] Or as contemporary feminists have said, the personal is political. Personal relations are inextricably bound to political rights, largely through laws about family life.

In the nineteenth century marriage provided women with their most coveted privileges and crippling disabilities. Traditional domestic rela-

49

tions laws, which have always been the province of the states, reflected the common law fiction that wives did not exist as separate individuals but merged into the persons of their husbands. (This was the civil death of women defined by the English jurist Blackstone.) In the early 1800s wives were generally denied the right to control their own property or wages, make wills, or enter contracts and conduct their own businesses; daughters often had limited inheritance rights. These laws gradually changed during the latter half of the nineteenth century, with the enactment by the states of married women's property laws, championed by radical and reformist feminists alike. They were championed as well by the fathers and brothers of women who wanted to protect their fortunes from men who married into the family. New York's Married Women's Property Act, the first in the nation (passed in 1848), shielded a wife's property from her husband's creditors.

Still, the traditional view of men as natural heads and masters of their families was not readily displaced and commands some support today. By 1900, after widespread reform, a married woman could not control her own property in one-quarter of the states; in one-third of them she did not possess her own earnings. A range of similar inequalities persisted well into this century.* In the 1920s women's services "belonged" to their husbands in all but eight states; several states limited their right to contract and enter into businesses, and in about one-third of the states, women did not have equal rights to dispose of real estate. Fathers enjoyed greater guardianship rights in many states; in New York, for example, fathers owned the services and earnings of their minor children and had the exclusive right to sue for injuries to them. Mothers, however, had sole custody and control of children born out of wedlock, who were not allowed to inherit from their fathers.[46]

In the nineteenth century, custody rights were primary concerns uniting most feminists. At common law fathers enjoyed virtually absolute rights to custody of minor children, rights that were generally respected in this country until the 1830s, when they began gradually being eroded. In the mid-1800s courts began following a "tender-years presumption" favoring a mother's claim to custody of infants, children under seven, and daughters. This was not a challenge to the father's

---

*Only eight years ago husbands in eight states had the right to manage property owned jointly with their wives. In many states, women still must take their husband's legal domicile as their own.

legal guardianship but to his "natural" capacity to care for young and female children. As a Maryland court explained in 1830,

> The father is the rightful and legal guardian of all his infant children, . . . In general, no court can take from him the custody and control of them, thrown upon him by law, not for his gratification, but on account of his duties, and place them against his will even in the hands of his wife. . . . Yet even a court of common law will not go so far as to hold nature in contempt, and snatch helpless, pulling infancy from the bosom of an affectionate mother, and place it in the coarse hands of the father. The mother is the softest and safest nurse of infancy, and with her it will be left in opposition to this general right of the father.[47]

The Cult of True Womanhood and romanticization of motherhood thus gave women a moral claim to custody that came to be recognized by courts. It coincided with a changing attitude toward children, as sociologist Viviana Zelizer has shown: The utilitarian view of children as productive, economically useful additions to the family unit that prevailed in agrarian America was gradually replaced by a sentimentalized view of them as emotionally precious and economically useless.[48] For fathers, custody of a child had traditionally meant custody of the child's earnings and services. Fathers didn't need and had no moral claim to children with immeasurable sentimental value and no commercial worth; they belonged, "naturally," with their mothers, and as children were made sacred, mothers were too.

But in their fight for greater custodial and guardianship rights of minor children, women enjoyed only partial success. True Womanhood and the sacrilization of children was a basis for claiming a right to care, not control, of younger children. Throughout the nineteenth century, in most states fathers retained greater guardianship rights.

Women did not gain custodial rights as much as custodial privileges, doled out at the discretion of the courts, and the extension of these new privileges hardly signified the expansion of gender roles required for an expansion of women's rights. It reflected instead a very traditional, narrow view of femininity that imposed strict standards of "good motherhood" on women. Sexually active women or those otherwise unfit in the eyes of traditional male judges were not likely to be granted custody. Women didn't directly gain whatever custodial rights were lost by their husbands. Instead, they were placed at the mercy of the courts, which took on themselves what had once been the father's power to decide the fates of minor children. The tender-years presumption was more an expansion of judicial authority than a grant of women's rights.[49]

Throughout the century, husbands exercised dominion over wives as well as minor children. Changing property laws and new judicial ideas about custody did not change the view of the family as a hierarchy with father at the top. New York's Married Women's Property Act was not intended to undermine man's role as "head and master of his household," a New York court declared in 1883: A woman was still obliged to render "due obedience and submission to her husband."[50]

Wifely submission was likely to be physical. Marital rape was legal (and only recently has been recognized as a crime in some states), and battering was ignored, rationalized, or considered a problem for social workers, not legislatures and courts. This traditional view of family violence as a social problem, not a legal one, reflected the view of it as a lower-class phenomenon (social workers served poor and immigrant families), a disinclination of courts to interfere in middle-class family life, and a refusal to grant women legal rights, instead of discretionary protections.[51]

It also reflected the protectionist double standard of sexual behavior that shaped ideals of criminal justice, discriminating against women as victims—of rape and battering—and as offenders as well. Rape, long considered a natural expression of male sexuality, tended, like battering, to be ignored, rationalized, or blamed on women victims charged with provoking their attackers. (Reform of the corroboration requirements of rape laws and of the use of a victim's sexual history to discredit her testimony has been an important achievement of contemporary feminism.) But while serious sexual offenses committed against women were likely to be trivialized, minor ones committed by women were prosecuted vigorously. Wayward women, who strayed from the narrow path of femininity, were punished much more severely than men for sexual misconduct and other public morals offenses.

The nineteenth century view of women as morally different from men justified differential standards of male and female criminality and the differential treatment of male and female criminals. Sexual behavior considered normal for men was criminalized for women, primarily through prostitution laws, and female felons, because they deviated so drastically from what was considered normal for their sex, were considered more evil than their male counterparts. In 1833 one penologist opined that because women were intended to be society's moral guardians, "the injury done to society by a criminal woman, is in most cases much greater than that suffered from a male criminal. . . . A woman, when she commits a crime, acts more in contradiction to her whole moral organization, i.e., must be more depraved, must have sunk already deeper than a man."[52] The "female born criminal" has a superior "diabolical cruelty," Cesare Lombroso stated sixty years later, at the turn of the century: "To kill her enemy does not satisfy her; she needs to see him suffer and know the full taste of death." Still, the "born criminal" was anomalous, Lombroso conceded; if women's "evil tendencies" were "more numerous and varied than men's [they] generally remain latent." Women usually fell out of virtue, not into violence, he suggested, "the natural form of retrogression in women being prostitution and not crime."[53]

Penal institutions of the nineteenth and early twentieth centuries reflected this view. While state prison populations, housing convicted felons, were predominantly male, reformatories were established to rehabilitate women convicted of minor sexual and public-order offenses. Individualized, indeterminate sentences were first applied to women believed amenable to rehabilitation. As a result, women were sent to reformatories for periods of years when convicted of acts like prostitution, for which men weren't even arrested, or for offenses like public drinking and disorderliness, for which a man might spend a month or two in a local jail.[54]

A reformatory sentence, however, was not considered punishment but rehabilitation. The reformatory movement, which flourished in the late nineteenth and early twentieth centuries, was supposed to be benevolent. It was led by reformers and protectionist social feminists who believed in gender differences and traditional middle-class ideals of femininity and hoped to do their fallen sisters a favor. Reformatories were designed to protect women, primarily lower-class women, from their unnatural, unfeminine selves. Reformers attempted to rehabilitate wayward women by domesticating them. Inmates were schooled in domestic arts and prepared for careers as servants to the middle class. Rehabilitation was a matter of spreading the middle-class gospel of True Womanhood to errant, lower-class white women and incidentally providing middle-class women with maids.[55]

Black women, believed inherently immoral (ranked lower on an evolutionary scale and excluded from the temple of True Womanhood), were considered unlikely candidates for rehabilitation and spared the services of reformatories. But they were spared only the law's benevolence. Black women, underrepresented in reformatories, were overrepresented in state prisons and more likely to be incarcerated for serious felony offenses. The number of black women inmates at one Tennessee penitentiary, for example, ranged from 70 percent of the female inmate population between 1860 and 1887 to 90 percent in 1900 to 65 percent between 1926 and 1934; during these years, the state's population of blacks declined. In New York State's prison for women, the percentage of black inmates rose from 12.5 percent to 40 percent during the same period, while the state's black population rose only a little more than 2 percent.[56]

Black women also suffered discrimination as victims of rape and sexual harassment. The cult of True Womanhood, which required that all rape victims be pure, was profoundly racist. Black women, condemned as naturally impure, were dismissed as no more worthy of protection than they were considered capable of being rehabilitated. The sexual servitude of black women in slavery (slave women were routinely raped and abused by their owners) and racist images of blacks as naturally promiscuous, unintelligent, and oversexed made black women fair game for sexual assaults. It was as if only white women could be "good" enough to be raped; black women were presumed to have consented or not to have cared: "A colored woman's virtue . . . has no protection," remarked one domestic worker who lost her job when she "refused to let the madam's husband kiss me."[57]

True Womanhood exacted a price from black men as well. In the years after the Civil War, allegations of rape became excuses for lynchings. Journalist Ida B. Wells estimated, conservatively, that some 10,000 black men were lynched between 1865 and 1895. Wells was a leader in an antilynching movement organized by black women, who recognized that myths about black sexuality excused and encouraged pervasive racial oppression. "The myth of the black rapist of white women is the twin of the myth of the bad black woman," historian Gerda Lerner has pointed out. Both were "designed to apologize for and facilitate the continued exploitation of black men and women. Black women perceived this connection very clearly."[58] For black men and women, rape, real and imagined, was a weapon of white supremacy.

Rape was an issue for white women too, but lynching was not. White social feminists and egalitarians tended to ignore lynching or endorsed prevailing views of black men as natural rapists. Frances Willard of the WCTU linked the "menace" posed by black men to a propensity for drunkeness: "The grogshop is the Negro's center of power," she stated. "Better whiskey and more of it is the rallying cry of the great, dark-faced mobs."[59]

Lynching delineated the connection between racism and sexism and traditional ideas of femininity championed by Willard and other leading social feminists. The white southern women who willingly collaborated with lynch mobs, or were too powerless and frightened not to, collaborated as well in the crippling stereotyping of women as passive, pure, and needful of protection. As black men were damned, white women were exalted, and both were dehumanized, imbued with great symbolic value and denied their individual worth. True Womanhood didn't cause the murders of black men, but it did excuse them. It didn't incite violence against women, but it denied justice to all except the purest victims of it.

The failure of protectionists to recognize the harm done to women by idealizing them was particularly grievous in cases of rape and abuse, but it was hardly intentional. The cult of female chastity was supposed to protect women, partly by making them morally superior to men.[60] The view of women as moral guardians of society was based on the wishful assertion that sexual passion in women was not natural or, at least, not difficult to repress. Chaste women were then presumed to be nature's check on lustful men. Chastity became both an argument for women to participate in public life (to raise the tone of it), and a way for them to exert control over men, particularly in marriage. It was, in part, a defense against marital rape and unwanted pregnancies.

The myth about feminine purity on which protectionism was based was not quite antisexual (mutual sexual pleasure in marriage was valued), but it did reflect some uneasiness about sex and social change. Chastity became an instrument of social control. By the end of the nineteenth century, protectionist feminists and others involved in movements for moral reform and "social purity" succeeded in making chastity an ideal for men as well as women. Long before contemporary antipornography protests, the sexual subordination of women generated a current of antilibertarianism in the women's movement. From the beginning, protectionists have been at odds with sexual freedom and concomitant first amendment rights.

Middle-class American women first went to war against commercial vice and pornography in the early 1830s with the formation of the New York Female Moral Reform Society and the growth of a network of voluntary, antivice associations in cities and towns of the Northeast. They began with an attack on prostitution and the demand for a single standard of sexual morality. Moral reformers held a surprisingly radical view of prostitution: They blamed it on men, the double standard, and the dearth of decent employment opportunities for single women. But they adopted a reactionary, repressive agenda for reform that included the criminal prosecution of men who patronized prostitutes and public condemnation of those who read pornography. With virtually no civil rights or social freedoms of their own, they had no apparent respect for the rights and freedoms of their oppressors. Their mission was to protect women by making men behave.[61]

The antivice movement peaked in the 1830s and 1840s but reemerged with renewed strength after the Civil War, when men picked up the banner of social purity that had previously been carried by women. The new social purity movement was partly a reaction to urbanization and the migration of young, single men and women to cities, away from the care and protection of their families: Exposed to "lewd and lascivious" literature, they would surely end up in brothels, gambling casinos, and dance halls. "Books are feeders for brothels," Anthony Comstock declared.[62] Comstock, executive secretary of the New York Society for the Suppression of Vice, and probably the most famous and influential antivice crusader of his day, was credited with passage of a landmark federal obscenity law in 1873, which bears his name, and charged with enforcing it, as a "special agent" of the United States Post Office. The Comstock law made it a crime to mail obscene or indecent literature, like "French postcards," or articles about contraception, as well as contraceptive devices. It marked the beginning of a new era in federal review of the morality of materials sent through the U.S. mails.[63]

Perhaps Darwinism fueled censorship and moral reform movements, as evolution gave new meaning to fears about "animal passions" of men. If human progress meant distancing man from his ancestors, it required unstinting control of the "baser" urges they shared. Perhaps Darwin was responsible for the spectre of "animal-level sex," which still haunts right-wing moral reformers today. But industrialization, immigration, and the growth of the modern city, complete with the modern slum, also exacerbated fears about change, disorder, and moral decay. And sexual repressiveness was an inevitable defense for women without the economic power or legal rights to fight the abuse visited on them by unrepressed men. The social purity movement was not simply an outgrowth of protectionist feminism, but it had a strong protectionist appeal.[64]

In his campaign to purify society, Anthony Comstock enjoyed the support of prominent social feminists. Frances Willard, Julia Ward Howe, and Elizabeth Blackwell all spoke out against the dangers of "impure" and "vicious" literature and made the stringent enforcement of obscenity laws a social priority. The role of censor was a natural one for Victorian women who believed in their own moral superiority: As "guardians of society, women should have their part in the guardianship of the press," Julia Ward Howe asserted. They would be "more strict and scrupulous than the average of the other sex."[65] Frances Willard exhorted women to "cleanse and purify" the world, by remaking it in their own virtuous image. To accomplish this mission, Willard involved the WCTU in progressive social reforms—improving education and penal institutions—and in a crusade to rid society of alcohol, prostitution, and pornography. She advocated the establishment of censorship boards in towns throughout the country to preview local theater productions and presided over the establishment of the WCTU's Department for the Suppression of Impure Literature.[66]

Contraception, as well as pornography, was considered dangerous by both protectionists and egalitarians. Associated not just with prostitution and venereal disease but with marital rape too, contraception deprived women of their best excuse for warding off unwelcome husbands. The first step for the nineteenth-century woman fighting for the right to control her own body was asserting her right to say no. She advocated "voluntary motherhood" through abstinence, not contraception. In prohibiting the mailing of contraceptives and information about contraception and abortion, federal obscenity laws reflected, in part, a resistance to birth control that prevailed among feminists into the early 1900s.[67]

Demands for censorship and sexual abstinence were not simply forms of puritanism; the impulse to purify society sprang partly from the need to make it safe for women. Sexual violence coupled with enforced feminine dependence made sexual repression look like the only defense against the abuses of masculine sexual freedom. In its fight for temperance, prohibitions of pornography, prostitution, and contraception, the WCTU sought to protect married women from drunken, abusive husbands and single women from sin, seduction, and abandonment. Social purity feminists also sought to protect the family, which was supposed to protect women. If marriage was a cage for women, the world outside was a jungle.

As long as women were denied educational and employment opportunities, they would identify their interests with the interests of their husbands in preserving the traditional family. The positive virtues Mary Wollstonecraft extolled—vigorous exertions of intellect—would not pay the rent for most women. Middle-class women clung to their feminine virtue, as they clung to the marriages virtue promised and ensured. Marriage required femininity, subordination, and self-abnegation in women, and marriage was all that women had; egalitarianism was too great a risk. Its demands for equal rights and individual autonomy were indeed an attack on traditional marriages and traditional divisions of labor, which protectionist social feminists anxiously respected. The ideal of male breadwinners wedded to female homemakers remained a feminist ideal throughout the nineteenth century. Social feminists never challenged the patriarchal family; they fought, instead, to curb its most flagrant abuses—wife beating, abandonment, marital rape, and male control of children. They never confronted the unsettling fact that changing the status of women meant changing the family along with the workplace, reallocating child care along with rights, responsibilities, and opportunities, and revisioning marriage.[68]

The view of marriage as a voluntary, egalitarian partnership was "at the foundation of all reforms," Elizabeth Cady Stanton stressed, but she doubted "the world [was] quite willing or ready to discuss [it]."[69] She discussed it in small groups of women, challenging the notion that wives belonged to their husbands, declaring women's right to sexual self-sovereignty, and arguing that marriage should be a dissoluable relationship between equals, not an indissoluable, holy hierarchical bond. She wanted divorces to be granted not just in cases of abuse but on grounds of incompatability, without allegations of fault.

This modern, secular view of marriage as a private arrangement based on mutual consent is still controversial today; 100 years ago it was revolutionary. Stanton did find some support among unhappy wives: "Women respond to my divorce speech as they never did to suffrage," she told Susan B. Anthony. "Oh, how they flock to me with their sorrows." But public sentiment was against her, and so were feminists who feared divorce as a license for men to abandon their wives. What was needed in marriage, according to Lucy Stone, a leader of the American Woman Suffrage Association, was not "equal license" to divorce but "equal restraints."[70] (Marriage depends more on duty than on love, Phyllis Schlafly wrote years later, in an attack on the ERA.)[71]

Stanton was either less hostile toward men or more hopeful for women. She viewed divorce reform in the context of expanding rights and opportunities and looked ahead to a time when, as the equals of men outside the home, women would not be forced to seek refuge within it:

"It is said that the 10,000 libertines, lechers and egotists would take a new wife every Christmas if they could legally and reputably rid themselves in season of the old one," she observed in her speech on "Home Life." "[This] objection is based on the idea that woman will always remain the penniless, helpless, resistless victim of every man she meets, that she is to-day. But in the new regime, when she holds her place in the world of work, educated to self-support, with land under her feet and a shelter over her head, the results of her own toil, the social, civil and political equal of the man by her side, she will not clutch at every offer of marriage, like the drowning man at the floating straw."[72]

But Stanton, lucky enough to have money of her own and a reasonably sympathetic husband, was a visionary. Equality was a distant goal. Protectionism was a practical compromise for women whose daily needs loomed larger than their dreams of the future.

Marriage was a kind of protective custody for middle-class women, and so was femininity. Those who were unable to wed could play surrogate domestic roles in public, as teachers, nurses, missionaries, or social service volunteers. Social feminism made femininity consistent with at least limited participation in public life. By the turn of the century, an exceptional, educated woman could even embark on a professional career, as long as she wasn't married. The notion that every woman should be able to marry, have children and a reasonably satisfying job, or simply pursue her own interests, did not take tenuous hold until the 1970s, following the expansion of civil rights for women and a slight shift in economic power.

Today, equality is only less distant, and protectionist demands for limits on no-fault divorce, a resumption of long term alimony, a presumptive maternal right to custody, and the prohibition of pornography are strong among feminists who are questioning the dreams of the 1970s and resigning themselves to tradition. Protectionism always has reflected resignation and an essentially tragic view of relations between the sexes, as Elizabeth Cady Stanton noted; it was founded on a view of women as perennial victims.

Protectionism, and the determinism it reflects, exploits and engenders hopelessness, resignation to the status quo, and distrust of social freedom, as its history makes clear. One hundred years ago, social feminists acquiesced in the consignment of women to child care and domesticity, in deference to biology and popular ideas about natural divisions of labor. They tried to broaden the domestic sphere, by "making the world a home," but never challenged the ideology that shaped it. Their efforts to feminize or domesticate society were defensive, antilibertarian—the efforts of biology's victims. They sought to protect women by restricting the freedoms of men—to divorce, drink alcohol, patronize prostitutes, or read pornography—because freedom seemed an exclusively and innately male prerogative. Egalitarians claimed it for women too, along with equal economic and political power and the capacity to define themselves. They imagined equality and fought to achieve it, not by restricting the freedoms of men but by expanding the rights of women.

·5·

A History of Protective Labor Laws and the Equal Rights Amendment

Rights without economic power are often academic. Compare the First Amendment rights of a street-corner pamphleteer to those of a major publisher, or the procreative rights of poor women for whom publicly funded abortions are no longer available to those of their middle-class sisters. The question of women's rights doesn't turn only on the marriage relation, as Elizabeth Cady Stanton suggested; it turns on a matrix of gender relations and roles, in the workplace as well as the home.

Questions about whether and how to integrate the workplace have long divided feminists. Are men and women naturally drawn to different jobs, reflecting their different talents and ideals? Is work outside the home an unfortunate necessity for women or a welcome release? Can or should childbearing women compete and perform in the marketplace as equals, unprotected? The fight for equal rights has always involved a fight over the consequences of pregnancy for wage-earning women.

In the early 1900s protective labor legislation created a sharp and bitter line between protectionist and egalitarian feminists, as it does today; yet no other issue has made it so difficult for feminists to choose sides. In opposing efforts by turn-of-the-century reformers to improve industrial working conditions for women and campaigns by social feminists today for special maternity benefits, egalitarians seem always to be fighting for the right to be equally exploited. But workplace protections are always used against women—to exclude them from traditionally masculine jobs for which they're labeled naturally unfit and also to hamper their hiring and promotion. Special protections for women are never entirely benign; instead they become self-fulfilling prophecies about women's inability to compete that perpetuate the dual labor market.

This is not to suggest that women should be left to fend for themselves in a free market but only that workplace protections should be gender-neutral. There is an important distinction between laws that exclude women from certain professions (like bartending) or limit the hours they may work and laws establishing minimum standards for the treatment of all workers, male and female. Minimum-wage and maximum-hour laws applied to both sexes reflect the egalitarian notion that working conditions unfit for women are unfit for men as well. They don't limit women's employment opportunities, trapping them in a cycle of protectionism and discrimination; they regulate the workplace instead of the worker.

But this has never been an egalitarian society, and fundamental workplace protections, such as wage and hour laws, were extended first to women, presumed weakened by their reproductive roles. In the predominant protectionist view, women wage earners have always been anomalies—despite their numbers, despite the fact that the economy could never have functioned without them. Protective labor laws have always reflected a view of women as deviant, because they got pregnant.

It is a fundamental feminist insight, shared by egalitarians and protectionists alike, that the workplace as well as the legal system has always been ruled by a male norm. The prevailing, contemporary protectionist response to problems encountered by wage-earning women enshrines a separate but equal female norm, ensuring special maternity benefits or mommy-track jobs that implicitly endorse the view of women as weaker, secondary workers. An egalitarian response posits a new androgynous norm, a single standard of law and behavior broad enough to encompass the diverse needs and experiences of both sexes.

This means that instead of writing special rules for women in the workforce, feminists should endeavor to redefine the ideal worker. Who is the worker? The worker is a person with children and child-care responsibilities or aging, needy parents; a person with a part-time, flex-time, or full-time work schedule and a life outside the workplace; a person with a wide range of skills and experiences who may change occupations as well as jobs. The worker is a person whose career is interrupted by the demands of family life.

Egalitarian feminism can thus recast the issues of paid work and motherhood dividing women today: Pregnancy disability coverage is not a woman's issue; it's a worker's issue. So is child-care or dependent-care leave. So is occupational safety and reproductive health. We should protect workers, not mothers, providing a safe and humane workplace for everybody in it. We should recognize that men are vulnerable to occupational hazards and a range of human weaknesses and ills. We should stop penalizing women for having babies and limiting their earning power through the pretense of protecting them. That women's secondary status in the workforce has been shaped by law and biases about feminine fragility, that justice and economic equity require an egalitarian approach to workplace regulation are some of the lessons of history.

Demands for improved working conditions by male and female workers naturally accompanied industrialization and the growth of factories in the early 1800s.[1] There was, however, little solidarity between the sexes in the workplace. If women were welcomed into industry by employers as a large, cheap, and presumably submissive labor force, they were resented by men who feared being displaced from their jobs; by the 1830s male trade unionists were denouncing the hiring of women in the mills.[2] But whatever threats women posed to men were easily and quickly contained by discrimination and the development of a sex-segregated, two-tiered labor force with men at the top. Although women constituted one-quarter of the nation's manufacturing force by 1850,[3] they occupied the bottom quarter, having been relegated to lower-level, lower-paying jobs.

From the beginning, wage-earning women paid the price of chivalry; in the early New England mills, women and girls worked twelve- to fourteen- hour days in poorly ventilated rooms filled with noisy, heavy machinery, under tight production schedules. This was not a life for weak and fragile females, although it did demand some feminine docility. Workers were expected to obey their supervisors, as they would have obeyed their fathers at home, and adhere to strict rules of conduct that prohibited talking to other workers or bringing books (including Bibles) into the mills. Factory work proved to be only a little less restrictive than domestic service. Living in boarding houses that were often company-owned, workers' lives were thoroughly regimented; they toiled, took meals, slept, and attended church at regular intervals, dictated by the factory bells.[4]

Factories provided a puritanical and patriarchal, but hardly ladylike, environment for young, unmarried women who sought some measure of independence. Wage-earning women who ventured alone outside the circle of family life suffered the handicaps of femininity without enjoying any of the privileges. They had no private, familial male protection, and throughout most of the nineteenth century they lacked public protection as well. In the years before the Civil War, employer-employee relations were generally considered private matters, and women workers, although they deviated dangerously from traditional feminine roles, weren't generally perceived as a threat to the social order and so did not arouse demands for protection.

But the number of wage-earning women increased throughout the nineteenth century, and their problems intensified. A growing underclass of women workers was shunted into arduous, low-paying jobs, without opportunities for advancement.* In fact, the entry of women into a field previously dominated by men ensured a lowering of pay scales. Susan B. Anthony reported that women office workers generally made less than one-half as much as their male conterparts.[5] The only professions open to women were teaching and nursing, and in 1890 of the 4 million women working outside the home, only 250,000 were teachers; 40,000 were nurses or midwives. The vast majority of women worked in factories, on farms, or as domestic servants; a growing minority (175,000 women) worked in offices or as shop girls.[6]

By the late 1800s increased anxiety about industrialization and changing social values drew attention to the growing female labor force. After the Civil War leisure-class women reformers began to worry about the health and morals of their working-class sisters and the effect of women working on their children and their family lives. What might once have been considered the private grievances of individual women wage earners, if they were considered at all, were recognized as pervasive, public problems, largely because women wage earners were recognized as mothers. As mothers, they were held responsible for the

---

*Occupations were divided along class and racial lines. White women and girls from native families worked in offices and stores. Immigrants staffed the factories and served as domestics. Blacks, who would not be hired for factory work until the early 1900s, worked as farm laborers, tobacco strippers, domestics, and laundresses.

moral and physical well-being of the working class; society needed them healthy and pure. The ideal Progressive future was partly in their hands.

Progressives adhered to a traditional notion of femininity, but at least they did so a little democratically, extending it to lower-class whites. They too were finally deemed to be inherently virtuous and deserving of protection, not just by but from men: Wage-earning women were shown to be especially vulnerable to abuse. Concern about sexual harassment was rising, and even prostitutes were viewed as sinned against, dragged down into sin by poverty.[7] Working long hours for less than living wages also threatened women's health, as well as their chastity, and, it was feared, undermined their reproductive capacities. In a society becoming obsessed with eugenics, working conditions that were bad for women were bad for the future of the race—the white race.

Progressives and protectionist social feminists concentrated on helping women in industry and retail sales; they thus excluded from their protective umbrella about half of the female labor force and nearly all black wage-earning women. Blacks, who worked primarily in domestic service or agriculture, were invisible to white middle-class reformers or not considered worthy of protection. White domestic workers were invisible too, and protecting them would have meant interfering in the home lives of employers, which reformers were not prepared to do. Shop girls, however, were impossible to ignore. They worked in public, on their feet for sixteen-hour days, waiting on leisure-class women. They also tended to be "genteel" whites, in their late teen or early twenties, considered vulnerable to the advances of male supervisors. Women in industrial trades, working in sweatshops and living in slums, becoming more numerous and more militant, were equally hard to ignore.

Hardship was mobilizing women workers throughout industry, but the same ideals about motherhood and femininity that were generating demands for paternal protections of women undermined their efforts to empower and protect themselves. Women organized sporadically in the years after the Civil War, but their union activities tended to be local and ad hoc, prompted by periodic crises in the various trades. They did not succeed in establishing their own permanent, national federations, largely because they were women.[8] As wage earners women were the victims of their socialization: They tended to be relatively passive or at least less likely than men to demand their rights aggressively. The majority of wage-earning women were also young and unmarried and viewed their stint in the workforce as a temporary one that would end at the altar. Leona Barry, an early union organizer who investigated women's working conditions for the Knights of Labor in the 1880s, lamented these tendencies in women—"the habit of submission and acceptance . . . the hope and expectation that in the near future marriage will lift them out of the industrial life to the quiet and comfort of a home."[9]

The view of wage earning as a last resort for women without husbands was pervasive and readily exploited by male unionists anxious to protect their jobs and wage rates. They regularly invoked the most sentimental biases about women's proper place and advocated a "family wage" for men as heads of families, so that women could fulfill their "natural" roles as wives and mothers. Samuel Gompers, founder and first president of the American Federation of Labor (formed in 1886), declared that "the wife as a wage earner is a disadvantage economically considered, and socially is unnecessary."[10] The *American Federationist*, the union's official paper, printed misogynist diatribes like this:

> The invasion of the crafts by women has been developing for years amid irritation and injury to the workman. . . . Is it a pleasing indication of progress to see the father, the brother, and the son displaced as the breadwinner by the mother, sister and daughter. . . ? The growing demand for female labor . . . is an insidious assault upon the home; it is the knife of the assassin, aimed at the family circle. . . . The wholesale employment of women in the various handcrafts must gradually unsex them, it most assuredly is demoralizing them, or stripping them of that modest demeanor that lends a charm to their kind.[11]

The tendency to view women only in terms of their relationships to men—as wives, sisters, and daughters—was shared by protectionist feminists and Progressives, as well as traditional antifeminists. It helped create the dual labor market by justifying the consignment of women to low-grade jobs and making it look natural. This, in turn, ensured the exclusion from the labor market of all but the poorest, most vulnerable women who had no choice but to work: Cultural ideals combined with a dearth of professional- and managerial-level jobs kept married, educated, middle-class women from even entertaining ideas about working for money, made it imperative for them to marry, and drove them to defend the traditional family, demanding respect for the feminine virtues. The movement to protect women in the workplace effectively imposed middle-class ideals about femininity and family life on lower-class wage earners who could ill afford them.

This is not to suggest that the efforts of protectionists and Progressives were entirely misguided or unwelcomed by wage-earning women, who were, in fact, more vulnerable than men economically, less unionized, and less capable of protecting themselves. Protective labor legislation helped establish the power of the government to intervene in the marketplace and provided some relief for considerable numbers of women. But labor laws protected women because they were mothers, reflecting the assumption that they were ill-suited to work outside the home because of inherent physical frailties, sexual vulnerability, and their practically exclusive responsibility for future generations: "Women are fundamentally weaker than men in all that makes for endurance," Louis Brandeis asserted in his famous brief in *Muller v. Oregon*, the landmark 1908 Supreme Court case that affirmed the power of states to single out women for workplace protection. Quoting expert testimony and an array of statistics, Brandeis persuaded the Court that women were more vulnerable to occupational diseases than men and that this special vulnerability, combined with the demands of maternity, justified state regulation of women's terms of employment.[12]

In *Muller* the Court upheld an Oregon law restricting women factory and laundry workers to ten-hour days. Only three years earlier, in *Lochner v. New York*, the Court had invalidated a New York law establishing a maximum-hour day and work week for male bakery workers, because it interfered with workers' and employers' freedom of contract: "The employee may desire to earn extra money, which would arise from his working more than the prescribed time," the Court noted, "but this statute forbids the employer from permitting the employee to earn it." The Court conceded that freedom of contract was not absolute but was limited by the state's police power (to protect the public health, safety, and welfare); but it held that the public interest was not at all involved in arrangements between employers and male employees: "Clean and wholesome bread does not depend on whether the baker works but 10 hours per day or only 60 hours a week." It also found no evidence that the health of workers was affected by working longer than ten-hour days and stated that male bakery workers were "in no sense wards of the State."[13]*

---

*The *Lochner* case has long been discredited as an unwarranted intrusion by the Court into the legislative process. It also rests on the questionable assumption that male workers could bargain as equals with their employers. *Lochner* is not cited here as a case that was rightly decided, as a matter of law or social policy. It does, however,

That women were wards of the state was the main point of the *Muller* case. What's notable about *Muller* is that instead of overruling *Lochner*, the Court distinguished it because the Oregon law applied only to women. Like children (and other state wards), women's freedom (in this case, to contract) could be restricted for their own good: "Woman's physical structure . . . justify special laws restricting or qualifying the conditions under which she should be permitted to toil."

Motherhood was invoked as the primary source of women's weakness and the basis of her claim for protection: "That woman's physical structure and the performance of maternal functions place her at a disadvantage in the struggle for subsistence is obvious. This is especially true when the burdens of motherhood are upon her." The Court also relied on a tradition of feminine dependency: "History discloses the fact that woman has always been dependent upon man. He established his control at the outset by superior physical strength, and this control in various forms, with diminishing intensity, has continued to the present." As minors, though not to the same extent, woman "has been looked upon by the courts as needing especial care." Woman was not, by nature, man's equal, the Court suggested, and she would always need special legislation "to secure a real equality of right." The state had not just the power but the obligation to protect her:

> Legislation designed for her protection may be sustained, even when legislation is not necessary for men and could not be sustained. It is impossible to close one's eyes to the fact that she still looks to her brother and depends upon him. . . . she is so constituted that she will rest upon and look to him for protection. . . . Her physical structure and a proper discharge of her maternal functions—having in view not merely her own health, but the well-being of the race—justify legislation to protect her from the greed as well as the passion of man.[14]

The Court emphasized that protecting women was in the public interest: Maximum-hour laws for women were "largely for the benefit of all" because they ensured the health of future generations. Concern for "the race" permeates the *Muller* case: "As healthy mothers are essential to vigorous offspring, the physical well-being of woman becomes a matter of public interest and care in order to preserve the strength and vigor of the race." Thus, *Muller* established the state's power to regulate the behavior of women and restrict their freedom of choice in the

make clear the sexist assumptions on which the *Muller* decision was based. Whether it upheld maximum-hour laws or invalidated them, the Court should have reached the same decision in both cases, applying the same laws to male and female workers.

interests of their children and also endorsed the basic principle of sex discrimination, asserting that because of woman's natural inferiority, because she "is not upon an equality . . . from the viewpoint of the effort to maintain an independent position in life . . . she is properly placed in a class by herself."*

Muller inspired a rash of state labor laws protecting women.** By 1920, virtually all the states (forty-seven) prohibited them from working longer than eight-, nine-, or ten-hour days; sixteen prohibited them from working at night.[15] The fight for minimum-wage laws, however, was less successful, and maximum-hour and night-work restrictions, unaccompanied by minimum-wage laws, reduced women's earning capacities, imposing considerable hardships on women who depended on overtime pay. Progressives were not insensitive to this problem and fought hard for laws ensuring women a "living wage." But despite the protectionist trend of the early 1900s, by the mid-1920s, only seventeen states had even prescribed minimum wages for women. (Massachusetts was the only industrial state to do so.) The laws were varied; instead of establishing mandatory minimums, the majority of state legislatures established commissions to investigate working conditions and set or merely recommend wage rates. Wage laws did not always apply to all women in all occupations, nor were they always aggressively enforced. Unpopular and broadly attacked by the business community, minimum-wage laws were repealed by some states (Texas and Nebraska repealed their laws in 1919 and 1921) and invalidated by state courts in others.[16] And in 1923, in *Adkins v. Children's Hospital*, the Supreme Court struck down a District of Columbia minimum-wage law for women, calling it a form of "price fixing."[17] Without overruling *Muller*, the Court declared that "adult women . . . are legally as capable of contracting for themselves as men." The *Adkins* decision derailed minimum-wage legislation for about a decade. A 1927 report by the Women's Bureau of the Department of Labor sadly concluded that "today many States have finished their experiment in setting minimum wage rates for adult women."[18]

The experiment began again during the Depression, which revolutionized attitudes toward government regulation of the workplace. In 1937, in *West Coast Hotel v. Parrish*, the Supreme Court overruled *Adkins*

---

*The special legislative classification of women, based on stereotypes of male and female roles, was finally declared unconstitutional by the Court during the 1970s. See *supra* Chapter 3.

**In 1917 the Court upheld maximum-hour laws for both sexes, in *Bunting v. Oregon*, 243 U.S. 426 (1917), but the trend during these years was to protect women exclusively.

and upheld a Washington state minimum-wage law for women.[19] Four years later, in *United States v. Darby*, it upheld minimum wage and maximum hours for both sexes, prescribed by new federal legislation, the Fair Labor Standards Act.[20] This did not, however, herald the end of special protections for women, which had never been occasioned simply by constitutional barriers to protecting men. (The 1917 Supreme Court decision upholding maximum-hour laws for men did not stop the proliferation of laws restricting the hours of women alone.) Protective labor laws would remain in force until contemporary feminists challenged the assumptions about women's weaknesses on which they were based and Title VII of the 1964 Civil Rights Act prohibited them.* In 1969 the Women's Bureau reported that forty-six states had laws regulating women's working hours; only two years later, according to the Bureau, all but ten states had repealed or substantially revised restrictive-hour laws, primarily in response to Title VII.[21]

Because the protection of wage-earning women generally was left to the states, it was never uniform nationwide. The inconsistencies of protective labor laws were among their greatest failings. Laws restricting women's hours of work applied to selected businesses and industries that varied from state to state (exempting, however, domestic service and agricultural work—two primary women's occupations). Sometimes the laws even discriminated among women in the same business: A New York law upheld by the Supreme Court in 1924, *Radice v. New York*[22] prohibited women restaurant employees from working between 10 P.M. and 6 A.M. (when tips were greater and trays lighter, according to waitresses who sought an exemption from the law). Women needed to entertain male customers, however—singers, actors, and other performers—were exempt from these restrictions; so were cloakroom attendants, because, as the state of New York asserted in defense of its law, "the places of such attendants could obviously not be filled by men at night as can the places of regular employees."[23]

In upholding New York's night-work prohibition, the Supreme Court took note of the dangers of night work for women—the "menaces incident to night life" and the impairment of their "more delicate organism." But in upholding the exemption for entertainers and coat checkers as well, the Court confirmed that women would not be protected from these dangers at any inconvenience to men. Nor would the state protect women from any jobs disdained by men, as the

*Title is discussed *supra* Chapter 7.

National Woman's Party observed: "Women may be found working at all hours of the night, cleaning and scrubbing office buildings."[24]

Protective labor laws effectively protected men by arbitrarily excluding women from a variety of male occupations. Some states passed catch-all prohibitions on women working in any jobs considered harmful to their health or "potential capacity for motherhood"; some barred them from manual-labor jobs.[25] Some states prohibited women, on moral grounds, from working in poolrooms or as bartenders. Years later, in 1948, in *Goesaert v. Cleary*, the Supreme Court upheld a Michigan law denying women the right to work as bartenders, unless they were the wives or daughters of tavern owners. The Court reasoned that the "moral and social problems" caused by women tending bar were lessened when women worked under the watchful eyes of husbands and fathers.[26]

Protective labor legislation thus comprised a patchwork of state laws that protected women unequally and, in the long run, at their own expense. Some women welcomed maximum-hour laws, citing concern for their health or their families or a need for leisure time. Others were unable or unwilling to pay the price of protection—reduced earning capacity, loss of jobs that required night work, and decreased opportunities to enter male professions.[27]

Male workers opposed to integrating the labor force benefited most consistently from laws supposed to protect women and enthusiastically supported them. As early as 1879 Adolph Strasser, cofounder with Samuel Gompers of the American Federation of Labor, endorsed protectionism as a way of keeping women out of the competition for jobs:

> We cannot drive the females out of the trades but we can restrict their daily quota of labor through factory laws. No girl under 18 should be employed more than 8 hours per day; all overwork should be prohibited; while married women should be kept out of factories at least six weeks before and six weeks after confinement.[28]

In the early 1900s the AFL became a staunch and powerful ally of social feminists and Progressives in the fight for protective labor legislation and against the ERA.

Introduced in 1923 by the National Women's Party, four years after women won the right to vote, the Equal Rights Amendment was immediately assailed as a threat to protective labor laws, which, of course, it was. Demands for legal equality sparked a bitter internecine war between protectionist social feminists and egalitarians, whose joint campaign for suffrage had always cloaked two very different agendas and differing views of men and women. In England and the Scandinavian countries, feminists were similarly divided over special protections and equal rights; as Crystal Eastman, a founder of the Woman's Peace Party and the American Civil Liberties Union, observed, the conflict was inevitable:

> Sooner or later in every industrial country where women have won the franchise this vexed question of equality versus protection is bound to arise. The good suffragist, after she has won her vote, takes one long night's rest, awakes refreshed and eager, and begins to look around for equal opportunities in every field of human endeavor. On the very first corner she meets the earnest reformer, who stops her, saying, "My dear you must not ask for Equal Rights in industry. If you do, what will become of this whole body of labor law which I have built up by years and years of patient effort to protect a weaker sex from the extreme rigors of industrial competition? Is all my work to be wasted?"[29]

Social feminists, who dominated the women's movement, had always been dedicated to progressive reforms more than sexual equality, favoring the unequal treatment of men and women in the workplace, because only women get pregnant. The Women's Trade Union League and National Consumer's League mounted a fierce and highly successful campaign against the ERA, with the support of male unionists and a range of mainstream women's organizations, from the newly formed League of Women Voters to local women's clubs.

The National Woman's Party represented a minority of feminists who were ridiculed as sexual deviants seeking to deprive women of the "right to differ from men."[30] The NWP itself was not entirely free of the female chauvinism that had infected the suffrage movement: Edith Houghton Hooker, a member of the national advisory board, argued that women's special maternal virtues made the campaign for equal rights, like the campaign for votes, "of vital moment to the race." When women were emancipated, granted full equality, they would "institute a new order of civilization based upon peace, temperance, co-operation and morality."[31] But despite rhetoric like this, the NWP sought to eliminate the legal disabilities that regard for the maternal virtues imposed on women, recognizing their capacity to abide by the same rules and shoulder the same responsibilities as men. During the 1920s the NWP began an ambitious survey of state laws discriminating against women, publishing periodic reports on them in its journal, *Equal Rights*. This campaign against double standards of law was viewed as a perverse denial of "natural" differences between the sexes: "Women cannot be made men by an act of legislation or even by an amendment to the U.S. Constitution," protectionists declared.[32]

For protectionist feminists, biology was destiny. Motherhood didn't interfere with women's capacity to vote, but it assigned them roles at home and in the workplace that were not and could never be interchangeable with the complementary roles assigned to men: "Sex is a biological fact," Florence Kelley a leader of the National Consumer's League wrote, in an attack on the ERA. "The political rights of citizens are not properly dependent upon sex but social and domestic relations are." Echoing conventional wisdom of her day, Kelley asserted that motherhood made women a weaker sex, more susceptible to occupational diseases: "Men do not bear children, are freed from the burden of maternity, and are not susceptible, in the same manner as women, to poisons now increasingly characteristic of certain industries, and to the universal poison of fatigue."[33]

Fatigue was, in fact, a problem for women because of the double burden of paid work and child care that many still carry today. Dr. Alice Hamilton, a pioneer in the field of industrial health, favored night-work prohibitions for women (among other workplace protections) because "the father of a family, if he works at night, can get his sleep during the day and yet have his meals served to him and his children cared for; the mother cannot." That familial roles weren't written in stone Hamilton conceded and deftly dismissed: "Whatever may be in the future," she was concerned with what "is undeniable at the present."[34]

The power of policies adopted in the present to shape the future was ignored. Advocates of workplace protections for women bemoaned the double burden without attacking it; accepting it as natural, they sought to ease a burden they could not imagine eliminating. Hamilton, an extraordinarily successful professional woman, a feminist, and first woman professor at Harvard, stressed that she had never "wish[ed] for special protections or special favors during [her] own life as a professional woman,"[35] but she saw herself as an exception and, like other prominent professional women of her generation, she never married or had children.

Careerism was a respectable option for a minority of exceptional, educated middle-class women of the early 1900s, as long as they stayed single and sacrificed their claim to family life. "Unexceptional" women—wives and mothers—were viewed as temporary or secondary wage earners, for whom family life would and should always come first.

Biology was held to have made women into a permanent underclass of workers—less committed to wage earning, "less able to organize,"[36] and more easily exploited. "Students of industry recognize that women are an unstable factor in industry, that the majority enter industry to fill the gap between school and marriage," one ERA opponent wrote in 1927.[37] Because social feminists didn't challenge the underlying notion that marriage and paid work for women were essentially incompatible, they accepted inequality in the workplace as a fact of life. Their demands for protection reflected the belief that women never could be men's equals at work because of immutable differences between them: "Women will always need many laws different from those needed by men," Florence Kelley declared, because "inherent differences [between the sexes] are permanent."[38]

Egalitarians, however, were not resigned to playing separate and unequal roles. They viewed inequality as a socioeconomic and not a biological construct, which protectionism helped cause instead of cure. Harriet Stanton Blatch, daughter of Elizabeth Cady Stanton and a staunch supporter of the ERA, accused Progressive and social feminists of foisting an "inferiority complex" on wage-earning women by endorsing tired stereotypes about masculine strength and feminine weakness: "Welfare workers always seem to think of industrial women as spavined, broken-backed creatures, and the sons of Adam as tireless, self-reliant, unionized supermen. Neither estimate is correct. Both need the protective aegis of the state." Men too were susceptible to occupational diseases, Stanton stressed: "The average man is an overworked animal and his fatigue tells upon the race." In response to reformers and eugenicists concerned about the effect of work on women's reproductive capacities, Stanton wrote that "a leading obstetrician in New York declares that in his practice nine times out of ten when he is called upon to diagnose the cause of sterility in the American family he finds the trouble in the overwork of the professional or business man." Stanton called for the extension of protective labor laws to both sexes (as did the National Woman's Party): "The objection to special legislation is not on the ground that no protection is necessary, but because partial laws have not protected men and have thrown women out of employment or crowded them into lower grades of work."[39*]

Social feminists did not, of course, agree that protectionism deprived women of better jobs; they believed instead that women were naturally unsuited to whatever work they were prohibited from doing. A 1928 report by the Women's Bureau, a new division of the Labor Department, confirmed this view. In response to protests of protective legislation by the NWP, the Bureau, a stronghold of protectionist social feminists, set out to document the effect of labor laws on women. It found, not surprisingly, that protective laws had not significantly reduced women's employment opportunities or influenced employment patterns. "In almost every kind of employment the real forces that influence women's opportunities are far removed from legislative restrictions of their hours or conditions of work." The "real" forces shaping the labor market for women included nature — "the types of service at which the two sexes excel" — technological advances, and social attitudes toward women in the workplace. Legislative restrictions applying to women pharmacists, for example, didn't limit opportunities for women nearly as much as the fact that "neither the employer nor the public feels the same confidence in the woman [pharmacist] as in the man." Restrictions on night work for women in industry were characterized similarly as simply redundant: They "chiefly reflected the usual attitude of employers" who harbored "astonishingly strong feelings . . . against the employment of women at night."[41]

The fact that laws not only reflected but enforced "feelings" and opinions was ignored. The Woman's Bureau defended protectionism by describing it as superfluous and reasoning in circles. It accepted as natural the clustering of women in certain jobs and found no need to provide them with others; thus protectionism only codified natural, inevitable occupational segregation.[42]

Some exceptional women might prefer atypical, unfeminine jobs, protectionists conceded, but they were anomalies who should not be permitted to shape public policies. Protective labor laws were said to provide benefits for many women at the possible expense of a few, and while trade union women tended to support protectionism, professionals rallied around the ERA. Egalitarians were accused of elitism—of favoring the interests of educated women eager to advance in the professions over those of the great mass of wage earners, for whom

---

*A 1924 report by the New York State Department of Labor found that male factory workers earned about twice as much as females, underscoring the need to expand women's "choice of occupation."[40]

work was not a path to fulfillment but an essential means of support. The ERA was also condemned as an attempt to return to nineteenth-century laissez-faire Social Darwinism, to an unregulated marketplace in which most women would be cruelly exploited.

The National Woman's Party argued, however, that an ERA could require extending protective laws to both sexes instead of eliminating those that applied only to women. Gail Laughlin, president of the National Federation of Business and Professional Women, asserted that protective laws for women were "shutting the door of opportunity" to them, advocating protective laws "based along lines of industry, not lines of sex."[43] Egalitarians were not opposed to worker protections; but they supported a class- or occupation-, not a sex-based approach to it.

They also advocated public support for motherhood, in the form of mothers' pensions—state laws providing women with stipends for their children. The National Woman's Party was careful to point out that mothers' pensions, or mothers' endowments, were not sex-based protections but child welfare laws that conformed to the ERA. Children were the recipients of state aid that only "passed through" the mother's hands. Mother endowments were, in fact, proposed as an alternative solution to problems of motherhood for wage-earning women.[44]

But public will to assist wage-earning mothers was weak. Mothers' pensions were conceived of as welfare (they were the forerunners of the Aid to Dependent Children program initiated in the 1930s), and welfare has traditionally been conceived of as a substitute for, not a supplement to, wages. The fact that welfare has traditionally been available only to unemployed and not underemployed people, discouraging welfare recipients from looking for work, has long been an argument for welfare reform.

Protective labor legislation did not reflect respect for women as mothers as much as concern for men as breadwinners. The effects of housework on women's health never generated much public concern, and strong support for the family wage militated against equal work and equal pay in occupations, such as teaching, shared by men and women. Women teachers were routinely fired when they married ("A teacher's life is a nun's life," one school superintendent remarked in 1923),[45] and they were routinely denied equal pay. Equal pay for women teachers was condemned as a "bonus to single women" that would "force a cut in the pay of married men."[46]

Throughout the 1920s the ERA campaign was a quixotic one. The ERA threatened both male monopolies on higher-paying jobs and employer prerogatives to maintain unsafe workplaces (protective legislation effectively blamed workplace hazards on women's weaknesses). Neither courts nor legislatures nor the public was ready for equal rights or broad-scale government intervention in employer-employee relations. By 1930 only one state (Wisconsin) had an ERA (with a special exemption for protective labor legislation), and with the onset of the Depression the National Woman's Party went into a decline, while efforts to protect men's jobs from women intensified. In 1932 Congress passed the Federal Economy Act, prohibiting federal employment of the spouses of federal employees and requiring that wives with employed husbands be the first fired in times of cutbacks. Public utilities as well as public schools regularly refused to hire married women.[47]

The ERA didn't quite disappear during the 1930s and 40s, but it was hardly a visible or popular public issue. Feminists continued debating its merits, and it gradually gained political support (by the mid-1940s both the Republican and Democratic parties had endorsed it). But the ERA did not emerge as an important national issue until the early 1970s, when it was passed by Congress and sent on its ill-fated way to the state legislatures, for public approval.

·6·

Equality
and the Sexual
Revolution

The Equal Rights Amendment was almost adopted. When the final deadline for ratification expired, on 30 June 1982, thirty-five states had voted to ratify out of the thirty-eight states needed for ratification. But an initial wave of support for the ERA had waned as early as 1973, and throughout the 1970s egalitarian feminists were either outspent or outsmarted by anti-ERA forces on the right. Their defeat was not simply a matter of public relations: It reflected a pervasive attachment to tradition and concern that equality would leave women and their children unprotected.

Despite polls showing that a majority of Americans supported the ERA, their support for it was shallow, as political scientist Jane Mansbridge has pointed out. Americans who endorsed the abstract concept of equality didn't necessarily endorse the changes equality implies.[1] A 1977 survey showed that a majority of people who expressed support for the ERA also adhered to some traditional notions about male and female roles: Sixty-two percent disapproved of married women working if their husbands could support them and the number of jobs was limited; 55 percent agreed that helping her husband's career was more important for a woman than helping her own.[2]

This puzzling split between support for equality in principle and opposition to it in fact is emblematic of American attitudes toward civil liberties. People profess support for First Amendment freedoms but favor the censorship of obscene material or advocacy of atheism.[3] This dissonance about rights is less a reflection of hypocrisy than self-delusion and misunderstanding about what rights entail. It also reflects considerable self-absorption. In their capacity to garner popular support, individual liberties are like tax preferences: People believe in the ones they're aware of enjoying. If some conservatives are liberals who've been mugged, some liberals are conservatives once arrested.

Women tend to support or oppose equal rights accordingly, for practical rather than ideological reasons. Phyllis Schlafly's successful Stop-ERA movement focused on the alleged costs of equality, exploiting women's fears about losing male protection and support and having independence thrust upon them, as well as a traditional feminine distrust of men. The ERA would encourage men to abandon their wives, Schlafly claimed, echoing nineteenth-century opponents to liberalized divorce. Men were philanderers by nature, she said, and women were nesters, which meant that law, not love, was needed to tie them together. The ERA would invalidate men's exclusive obligation to support their families during marriage and after it, through alimony payments, as well as presumptions favoring women in custody disputes. What was at stake in the battle over equality, Schlafly asserted, was a woman's right "to be a full-time wife and mother, in her own home, taking care of her own babies."[4]

But whether full-time homemaking was a right or a privilege or simply a personal preference, it would have been less affected by the ERA than Schlafly claimed. Common law support obligations of men had always been virtually impossible to enforce while couples continued to cohabit. Wage-earner/homemaker statutes "protecting" women were being invalidated by the Supreme Court under the Fourteenth Amendment and amended by the states. State custody laws were changing too, eliminating the protective presumption favoring mothers during a child's early years. In fact, the limited principle of constitutional equality emerging during the 1970s was helping homemakers rather than hurting them. It invalidated state laws giving men exclusive control over marital property, for example, and encouraged judges in divorce cases to recognize that women homemakers often contributed to their husband's earning power at the expense of their own. Equality was empowering for homemakers as well as careerists.

But the homemakers envisioned by Schlafly wanted to be protected instead of empowered because they didn't consider themselves the equals of their husbands. Men are better suited to "strenuous, hard, unpleasant, dirty and dangerous jobs," Schlafly wrote. They're more competitive, ambitious, and more interested in professional life (and less interested in domesticity) because they're "more aggressive, rational, mentally creative [and] analytical minded." Women are "more personal," she added, anticipating Carol Gilligan's assertion that women speak in a different, more personal moral voice. Women also have better control of "their sexual appetites. . . . The sexual drive of men is much stronger than that of women." Laws taming men and upholding traditional family life were thus essential to civilization: "Man's role as provider gives him the incentive to curb his primitive nature. . . . If he is deprived of this role, he tends to drop out of the family and revert to the primitive masculine role of hunter and fighter."[5]

This quaint vision of men as hunters implies that women are prey. Underlying the anti-ERA movement and the feminist discontent of the 1970s that led to a revival of protectionism was a shared belief in women's sexual vulnerabilities, expressed most clearly in the antipornography movement. Heightened concern about protecting women by restraining men was partly a reaction to the sexual revolution, which always had a conflictual relationship with feminism. It stood for both the pill and pornography—for sexual automony and sexual exploitation. The sexual revolution freed women by giving them increased control of their reproductive lives. The trouble was, from a protectionist view, that the sexual revolution freed men too.[6]

Protectionism has always demanded restraint of male sexuality and relied on presumptions of female chastity. Since nineteenth-century antivice crusaders invoked their "moral superiority" to protest pornography, prostitution, and contraception, some feminists have sought sexual repression as a form of protection for women. In the 1960s and 1970s, birth control, the displacement of chastity as a feminine ideal, and the notion that sexual inhibitions were "unhealthy" (even "unnatural"), deprived women who needed them of excuses to say no. To protectionist feminists, expanding sexual freedom for women meant expanding sexual vulnerability. To protectionist feminists, the sexual revolution was a kind of male conspiracy—a license for women's objectification and abuse.

To protectionists on the right, the sexual revolution was feminism. It was abortion, contraception, homosexuality, a breakdown of traditional values, and an attack on family life. This conflation of social issues was partly a hysterical reaction to change and partly political (it was an effective organizing tool); but it was also partly correct. It reflected the fact that both the sexual revolution and egalitarian feminism challenged prevailing ideals about the most basic differences between men and women. Free, or freer, to become pregnant only by choice, women were free to enjoy sex, and men were not the only ones with "urges" they were expected to satisfy. The sexual revolution turned on a revisioning of female sexuality, so it sparked antifeminist social issue movements of the 1970s and helped shape the feminist debate about sexual difference and special protections or equal rights being conducted today.

The sexual revolution was a revolution in ideals about men and women perhaps more than a revolution in behavior. At least, the behavioral changes it wrought are difficult to quantify; ideological ones can be gleaned from the popular press, particularly the women's magazines. The sexual revolution wasn't quite a product of the media, but it did attest to the media's power to shape ideals.

The press defined and popularized the sexual revolution, which started with the Pill. Approved by the Federal Drug Administration in 1960, by 1967 oral contraception was being used by 6 million women. Rules of courtship and seduction were revolutionized, giving women new options and responsibilities and men a new fear of rejection: The question for men was no longer "Does she want to have sex?" She was allowed to want it. The question was "Does she want to have sex with me?"

This was the essence of the "new morality" that emerged in the mid-1960s, perceived by commentators at the time as a shift from communal to individual standards of sexual behavior.[7] Concepts of right and wrong, it was said, were being subjectified. Young people supposedly stopped asking, "Is it right?" Instead they were asking, "Is it right for me?" In the popular view, this new individuality was at the root of the "permissiveness" that characterized the 1960s and was decried by some as "sexual anarchy."

Particularly controversial was the dispensing of contraception—diaphragms and birth control pills—to unmarried college women. One doctor at Brown University created a small scandal by admitting that he prescribed the Pill to students over twenty-one.[8] "College girls everywhere are talking about the Pill," *U.S. News & World Report* warned in 1966. "Is the last vestige of sexual restraint to go out the window . . . will mating become casual and random as among animals?" One religious leader worried that in easing "limitations and restrictions on the use of sex," especially among young people, the Pill threatened our existence "as a civilized people."[9]

Was the Pill simply a license for promiscuity, as many suggested? Looking back, its actual effect on the sexual behavior of young people is difficult to discern. There is no conclusive statistical evidence that the incidence of premarital sex rose during the 1960s, although it was becoming more acceptable. Vance Packard concluded, on the basis of "circumstantial evidence," that it was indeed on the rise. At least, he ventured, his own survey of American college students indicated that "the traditional ideal of chastity until marriage for both males and females did not command majority support from either sex."[10] Premarital sex did not, however, necessarily equal promiscuity in everyone's eyes. Andrew Hacker, writing for the *New York Times Magazine* in 1965, suggested that college students were essentially monogamous. The Pill did not encourage promiscuity: Its use was, instead, part of a trend toward establishing relationships. Sexual intimacy in the context of a primary relationship would be an antidote for the identity crisis of a "mass age . . . sex as a meaningful liaison with another, becomes the route to discovering and maintaining one's sense of self."[11]

Whether it was called intimacy or promiscuity or a process of self-discovery, sex was a ubiquitous topic of polite conversation. One common view of the sexual revolution was that it didn't involve more sex as much as less discretion. "In my day, we did it and no one talked about it," people proudly said.

What was the effect of the new openness about sex? Men had a tradition of bragging about sexual exploits—and real men were supposed to have many. Mores changed most dramatically for women. Sexual sophistication replaced chastity as a feminine ideal, and by the late 1960s the Pill was a campus status symbol. Now not only were young men talking their girlfriends into having sex; young women were talking each other into sleeping with their boyfriends. Sex was becoming a proving ground for women too.

For those who could handle it, the added pressure to be sexually active was well worth the freedom not to marry. With the availability and respectability of birth control, fewer women were forced into marriage by pregnancy or strictures about single women and sex. The sexual revolution weakened the double standard and offered sexual liberation to women. "Like men, [women] are free to take sex, education, work, and even marriage when and how they like," Gloria Steinem explained in 1962. The sexual revolution created a new "autonomous girl"; no longer "forced to choose between a career and marriage," she was free to "find fulfillment in a combination of the two." If she did not seek her identity "totally without men," neither did she seek it "totally through them"[12]

A new generation of women journalists and a nascent genre of feminist journalism mediated the revolution for American women, popularizing a changing ideal. One early, influential, prefeminist advocate of change was Helen Gurley Brown, founder of *Cosmopolitan*, which is neither a feminist magazine nor a traditionally feminine one. In 1963 Brown started writing a nationally syndicated newspaper column, "Woman Alone," with what was then a revolutionary message: Marriage was not the only path to fulfillment for a woman, she suggested; it was an option. In fact, "A woman who either by choice or circumstance has not involved herself in domesticity may have unwittingly worked out a better life for herself than her married friends." Single womanhood was not a "miserable, pitiable state."[13]

Although she persisted in calling them girls, Brown promoted a new image in the media of sexually active, self-supporting, satisfied single women: "The way to convince them you aren't a hardship case is to go around living the most exciting, enviable, useful single girl life you possibly can." This meant having a career, sex outside of marriage, and developing a new etiquette for single women in a world devoted to couples. "Woman Alone" columns offered advice on work ("When to Date and Not to Date the Boss"), on relationships and cohabitation ("Love with a Younger Man" and "Do You Let Him Move In?"), and on socializing without a male escort, instead of staying home ("When You Have No Beau").[14]

None of these issues were being addressed by the women's magazines, Brown complained. The concerns of single women, all 24 million of them, were being ignored by the popular media. As an example of the pervasive marriage bias, she cited an entire issue of *The Ladies' Home Journal* devoted to "the fourth dimension of a woman's life, her career." It was "excellent," she conceded, as far as it went. "The trouble is that like nearly all issues of women's magazines, this particular one ignores the woman who doesn't have the first three dimensions in her life—husband, children, and homemaking."[15]

"The *Journal* and other women's magazines take it for granted that a woman has those—just as she has legs and eye sockets, and anybody who doesn't have them (they must figure) can't read or isn't worth talking to. . . . A career girl I know . . . who happens to be minus her first three dimensions tells me *Playboy* is her magazine. 'I don't know whether I'm the Playboy type,' she said, 'over 30, and 32-27-38. . . . At least everybody on the magazine isn't married, with several children, and baking peach pies and papering cupboards.'"[16]

Of course, the freedom not to marry was dependent on the expansion of economic opportunities. Economic and sexual independence for women have always been tied, and while Helen Gurley Brown was extolling the single life, sex discrimination in employment was beginning to be recognized by the federal government and the states; feminists were beginning their drive for equality. Social issue conservatives had reason indeed to identify the sexual revolution with feminism. If having money obviated a woman's need to marry well, having control of her reproductive life broadened her professional choices.*

It's likely too that sexual freedom was making women more assertive or at least making assertiveness in women more acceptable. With the decline of the double standard, the value placed on feminine passivity declined too "from bedroom to boardroom." Change was reflected in the women's magazines, which began promoting a less genteel, more openly sensual woman. Ten years after Helen Gurley Brown observed that single girls had nothing to read but *Playboy*, the women's magazines were beginning to devote as much space to sex as domesticity. They relentlessly explored sexual fears and fantasies, telling women how to be sexier, how to make their men sexier, and how to deal with the anxiety of not being sexy enough.

Mademoiselle, a magazine for young single women, was one of the first to uncover sex. In 1967 it reported on "The Pill and the Girl Next Door" and in 1969 on "Sex: The New Status Symbol." *Redbook* wrote about sex for its readership of young married women. In 1969 it was examining "Sex Research and Unhappy Wives," and by the early 1970s it featured a monthly column by Masters and Johnson. In 1975 the *Redbook* report on "Pre-Marital and Extra-Marital Sex" reviewed the "end of the double standard."[17]

A preoccupation with sex preceded but was soon joined by a preoccupation with work. Sex and success became the fashions of the 1970s, displacing love and marriage. *Harper's Bazaar* wrote about the "Sex Life of a Working Wife" and asked, "Are Working Women Sexier?" "Can Success Ruin Your Sex Life?" it wondered conversely, while *Mademoiselle's* monthly column, "An Intelligent Woman's Guide to Sex," asked "Can Sex Ruin Your Work Drive?"[18]

Work was glamorized and power feminized. A special feature on "You and Your Job" in a 1977 *Harper's Bazaar* included guides to "great

---

*For a review of employment discrimination laws, see Chapter 7. For a discussion of the relationship between equality and reproductive freedom, see Chapter 12.

looks," "good health," and "big success." The success guide focused on "manipulating your way to the top" and "debunking myths about women in positions of power."[19] By 1980 powerful women had their own magazine; *Savvy* (for executive women) premiered in January 1980, alternating articles about networking and corporate success stories with layouts of expensive lingerie.

Conflicts between work and family were noticed during the 1970s, but without the sense of urgency with which they're discussed today. "Can You Work and Be a Good Mother?," Dr. Lee Salk asked *Harper's Bazaar* readers in 1977. Yes, he assured them, "as long as you're willing to work hard and plan carefully and always put the child's needs first." Three months later, a special section on "The Working Mother's Dilemma" announced good news about child-care alternatives (children fared well in day care, studies showed). The news for wage-earning mothers was upbeat. If careerism was a dilemma for women, it was not yet a crisis. A *Harper's* fashion layout on "The New Working Mothers" made it look easy. *Redbook's* "Working Women's Guide," published in 1978, advised women simply to "set up a message center" and "avoid shopping" during the busiest store hours to save time at home.[20]

Problems of wage-earning mothers were taken more seriously in the 1980s, along with a "crisis" in family life, and both the sexual revolution and feminism lost some of their appeal. As the 1970s came to a close, the same questions about what *Glamour* called "The New Sexual Triangle—Women, Sex, & Men" had been asked and answered enough already. "Sex: Is It Time to Shut Up about It?" pondered *Mademoiselle*. Too much talk about sex was finally sufficient.[21]

It was time, at least, to say something new about it, something negative, and to reexamine the benefits of sexual freedom. Before fear of AIDS beset the heterosexual community, therapists, talk show hosts, and magazines were discovering the costs of the sexual revolution for both sexes. By the early 1980s *Harper's Bazaar* may still have been writing about "High Energy Sex Foods" (eroticism by now had been domesticated), and *Mademoiselle* was telling you "How to Get Your Way in Bed," but the new theme for the 1980s was sexual burn-out or "limited sexual desire" (lsd). Major news, life-style, and women's magazines and films heralded a return to intimacy, romance, and relationships (the market for romance novels blossomed), and there was talk of rising birth and marriage rates, June brides, and women in their thirties having children. America was supposedly settling down. In 1984 *Time* magazine administered last rites to promiscuity and permissiveness, declaring that the sexual revolution was over.[22]

Still, people kept on fighting it, divided over "social issues"—pornography, sex education, abortion, and civil liberties for homosexuals. The revolution in women's attitudes and expectations that began in the 1960s continued disrupting social and economic relationships between the sexes. The 1980s could not be a re-run of the '50s. Sexual mores had irrevocably changed. (When condom machines were installed in the basement of the Harvard University houses in 1988, complaints were voiced about their price, along with concern about their shelf life and the effects of humidity on rubber; but no one talked about "moral decay" or the end of civilization.) Women's professional expectations had changed too, and men were supposed to be changing with them. The ideal Yuppie husband was comfortable around diapers and dishes and Cuisinarts. As feminism suddenly and inexplicably gave way to post-feminism, it also gave birth to a mythic new man.

It has always been clear that a successful role change by women depended on complementary changes by men. Social attitudes would have to be repealed along with laws, and new roles for men began emerging as a major social theme in the mid-1970s. Machismo was out; the new man was "sensitive," "caring," and not ashamed to cry; he even had his own consciousness-raising group. *Newsweek* took note of him in 1978, in a cover story describing "How Men Are Changing." "Men are volunteering to express emotions once anathametized as 'feminine.' . . . They are finding it may be acceptable to express fears, to touch other men, even to weep." Professional, white-collar men were also said to be reassessing their consuming commitments to work and becoming more involved with family life, discovering the "joys of male nurturing." Men were also becoming aware that the "goodies" they had enjoyed were not without cost—stress-related diseases and shorter lifespans than women.[23]

Feminists were also beginning to pay more attention to men's problems, stressing that liberation would benefit both sexes. In a review of "How Men Are Changing" for *Redbook*, Betty Friedan outlined equality's economic and emotional "pay-offs" for men: They would be relieved of the pressure to be strong, silent, and the sole support of their families. Feminism opened a "new American frontier" for men, "a new adventure . . . living and sharing life on equal terms with women." But in the meantime, in the struggle to get there, men were "isolated" from each other, frightened of change, and unsure of how to proceed.[24]

"Many young American males today are in crisis," *Glamour* reported in 1979. They were "plagued with disappointment, loneliness, and confusion," afraid or "in awe" of the new woman, and confused by her demands; they did not know how to behave toward her. Would a woman respect a man who cried? An increase in complaints about impotence and premature ejaculation was attributed to new levels of performance anxiety engendered by feminism and the sexual revolution. The consensus in the popular press was that on his way to liberation, the new man needed help.[25]

Although men's liberation shared several feminist ideals, it also mounted some subtle opposition to the feminist movement, rejecting the underlying notion that this is a sexist society in which men oppressed women. The men's movement promoted an alternative view of men as victims, particularly in divorce court. As fatherhood became fashionable, child custody became an important "men's issue," involving allegations of reverse discrimination. In some ways, the men's movement was a form of backlash; U.S. News & World Report characterized it as a new skirmish in the "Battle of the Sexes." It was largely economic: Men were complaining of token job promotions for women as well as the burden of alimony. "Men fight back," U.S. News declared. "This time it's male grievances that are becoming a focus of attention."[26]

Critics of equality focus alternately on whom it harms most—men or women. The feminist as man-hating, child-hating virago has been held responsible for male sexual dysfunction, the diminution of men's jobs, and an increase in the suicide rate among men. ("Two paychecks can mean one suicide, usually the husband," according to one right-wing journal.)[27] Feminists are also portrayed as "bad" women who threaten the security of good, true women who are happy keeping house. ("Elimination of the role of 'mother' is a major objective of the women's liberation movement," Phyllis Schlafly warned.)[28] Finally, their more sympathetic critics have portrayed feminists as self-deluded women who primarily hurt themselves.

By the late 1970s the image of a feminist as a poor, unhappy imitation of a man began appearing in the moderately profeminist women's magazines. A 1978 Glamour editorial raised what were becoming familiar questions about the "woman as man syndrome. . . . We have been passionately freeing ourselves from one mold and all the while locking ourselves into another," Glamour declared, with less originality than conviction. Women had fooled themselves into believing that "anything he can do, we can do as well"; adopting a male role model, they mistakenly sought "success by imitation."[29] In the popular feminist community, equality came to be commonly identified with the belief that women should be the same as men, not with a commitment to giving men and women the freedom to be what they chose.

The struggle for a free and egalitarian society had resulted in a profusion of mixed messages about male and female sexuality and feminism. As the women's movement prospered in the 1970s and gained acceptance in the middle class, so did the sex industry. As women doctors and lawyers began appearing on television (as well as in real life), so did women prostitutes and porn stars. If feminists increased their numbers, Total Women did too. So did *Cosmopolitan* girls, who were either feminists cloaked in Total Womanhood or Total Women cloaked in feminism. And while Woody Allen was becoming a new male sex symbol, Clint Eastwood was gaining intellectual credibility. No wonder we're confused.

·7·

Equality
in the Workplace:
Title VII of the
1964
Civil Rights Act

In the early 1960s, when the contemporary feminist movement began, old ways and what the United States Supreme Court called "old notions" about male and female roles still prevailed. Marriage was still the most respectable job for a middle-class woman, who was not supposed to compete in the marketplace with men. The family wage, making possible the one-income family, was still a predominant ideal, and career women were likely to be chastised for selfishly usurping men's jobs and depriving their appropriately dependent wives of support. (I had no right being in law school, one woman told me in 1972; I was taking the place of a man, like her son, who would have to support a family someday.)

Women's rights—to enter law or medical school, serve on juries, determine their families' domiciles, or perform "men's jobs"—were not self-evident, even in the 1960s. Today the first problem for wage-earning women may be day care or maternity benefits or answering the overarching question of whether equality will be achieved by treating women the same as men or differently. Twenty-five years ago, the first problem was establishing women's underlying right to equality and self-determination, in the workplace and the home. The principle that men and women should have equal rights and the equal autonomy that went with them was "radical," if not quite revolutionary. Marital rape was not a crime, and sex discrimination was not unconstitutional.

Egalitarian feminism hasn't achieved equality, but it has secured some justice for women and expanded opportunities in the workplace. If the majority of female wage earners remain in lower-paying, female-dominated jobs, a significant minority have entered the male enclaves of law, medicine, and business and improved their status in academia and industry. Sexual harassment and gender stereotyping at work may still be common, but at least they're no longer legal. Women may not legally be refused jobs or promotions because they're too feminine to do a "man's job" or not feminine enough to meet social expectations about women: A woman may not be denied a managerial position because she wears make-up and nail polish and is considered too attractive to be competent and smart, or because she's aggressive and competitive and not enough of a "lady" to be liked. On the job, women are supposed to be treated and evaluated as workers, not women, largely because of legal reforms wrought by the equal rights movement.

The drive for economic equality was slowed during the 1980s, not by nature, as protectionist feminists claim, but by politics. Opposition to expanding the rights of women and minority males hardened and became respectable during the Reagan years and has shaped recent employment discrimination decisions by the Supreme Court. Much protectionist or "postfeminist" dissatisfaction with egalitarianism is misplaced; it overlooks the effects of social service cuts on women, the Reagan Administration's antagonism to civil rights, the fact that discrimination is systemic and slow to change, and the failure of Congress and the federal courts to address pay inequities; it also ignores the progress made by equal rights feminists during the 1960s and 1970s in prohibiting discrimination in the workplace. Equality in employment became a possibility for at least some women and an accepted social ideal.

Feminist reforms began in the 1960s with the modern equal rights movement. In 1963 the first Presidential Commission on the Status of Women, appointed by President Kennedy, urged the Supreme Court to demonstrate that the Constitution ensured sexual as well as racial equality. (Torn by controversy over an Equal Rights Amendment, the Commission intimated that the Court might obviate the need for one by recognizing women's rights under the Fifth and Fourteenth Amendments.)[1] The Court would not begin to grant women constitutional equality until 1971, but in 1964 Congress struck an unexpected blow for women's rights when it included in Title VII of the landmark Civil Rights Act a prohibition of sexual discrimination in employment.

The Civil Rights Act was originally intended to remedy racial, not sexual, discrimination. By the mid-1960s the disparate treatment of racial minorities was beginning to be recognized as a civil and moral wrong; but the disparate treatment of women was still considered natural, along with sex discrimination in the workplace.* Only two states outlawed employment discrimination against women, and want ads were routinely divided into columns of male and female jobs. It was only by chance that Congress extended to women the new federal prohibition of employment discrimination (Title VII of the Civil Rights Act). The word *sex* was added to the law by a white Southern Democrat in an attempt to retard its passage or, according to some observers, as a joke. Congress managed to take it seriously, and the sex discrimination provision was passed, "to almost everyone's surprise."[2]

The early 1960s may have looked like the 1950s at first glance, as any Doris Day or Sandra Dee movie shows; but times were about to be changing. Feminism was percolating. Politically active women were becoming dissatisfied, demanding change, and building a feminist lobby. They made their presence known, both in Congress (a small network of women activists helped secure passage of Title VII) and in the states: In 1962 Michigan established the first state commission on the status of women; five years later, in 1967, commissions had been established in all fifty states. The National Organization for Women was founded in 1966 by a group of activists attending the Third National Conference of State Commissions on the Status of Women.[3]

Passage of Title VII, with its sex discrimination amendment intact, was a landmark victory for equal rights feminists. In deciding Title VII cases, federal courts developed new theories of workplace equality and extended new rights to wage-earning women as well as minority males. No analysis of egalitarian feminism is complete without an analysis of Title VII.

It began effecting change slowly. The Equal Employment Opportunity Commission, established by Congress to administer and enforce Title VII, was at first a doubtful champion of women's rights. Its first chairman, Franklin Delano Roosevelt, Jr., was "lukewarm" about sex

---

*It was not until 1967 that the executive order requiring affirmative action and non-discrimination by federal contractors was amended to protect women as well as racial minorities. (See discussion, pp. 126–128).

discrimination, and his executive director dismissed the sex discrimination amendment as a fluke, questioning its legitimacy: It was "conceived out of wedlock," he said.[4] Congresswoman Martha Griffiths, who had been instrumental in passing Title VII, charged that "the whole attitude of the EEOC toward discrimination based on sex is specious, negative, and arrogant."[5] Griffiths was responding to the Commission's approval of sex-segregated want ads, despite clear statutory language prohibiting them. The Commission would soon change its mind on this issue, thanks to protests by equal rights feminists; in 1968, in response to a lawsuit by NOW, it outlawed the long-standing practice of classifying job ads by sex.[6]

It was a small, if highly symbolic, victory, the effect of which is difficult to gage: Maybe it expanded women's sense of possibilities; maybe it weakened the habit of sex-typing jobs. Twenty years later it's hard to remember that jobs for cab drivers, machinists, and midlevel managers were once listed only for men, while jobs for secretaries, receptionists, and administrative assistants ("Gal Fridays") were listed for women. It's clear today, or at least generally accepted, that these jobs should not be restricted by sex. Whatever the differences between men and women, they don't dictate ability to use a car, typewriter, or other machinery or manage an office. It's equally clear that sex is relevant to at least a few jobs: Men can't be wet nurses or prostitutes for heterosexual males and probably shouldn't be attendants in women's locker rooms. What is still controversial, however, is the relevance of sex to jobs that don't directly involve it—jobs that don't require special reproductive capabilities or involve issues of sexual privacy but do require "masculine" or "feminine" traits. Should men be flight attendants or day-care workers? Does not bearing children make them less sensitive, supportive, and concerned for the welfare of others? What's still controversial are the secondary effects on men and women of their reproductive roles and the relevance of these effects in the workforce.

Title VII didn't quite resolve the question of when sex matters; instead of absolutely prohibiting men-only and women-only jobs, the law permits hiring decisions to be based on sex when sex is a "bona fide occupational qualification" (BFOQ), when hiring a male or female is "reasonably necessary to the normal operation of [the] particular business or enterprise." Religion and national origin may be BFOQs as well: A French restaurant may hire a French chef, Congress suggested. But there are no exceptions for hiring decisions based on race; race is never a BFOQ. A proposal by a Mississippi Congressman to include race as a

BFOQ was readily rejected, while a proposal to include sex as one was just as readily adopted.

Why? Perhaps Congress was more concerned with promoting racial justice; perhaps it had a clearer idea of what constituted racial discrimination—allegations of general racial difference. Underlying a BFOQ for sex, after all, is a belief that sex and gender differences matter in the workplace.

But when differences between the sexes matter, they need not be enforced by law. Men and women will, in general, not apply for jobs to which they're naturally unsuited, or they won't be able to perform them: We don't need laws to prohibit men from being wet nurses. The BFOQ provision is irrelevant or simply redundant in cases involving biological differences, which suggests that its primary purpose is to enforce cultural ones. Cultural mores may legitimately effect hiring decisions in a very few cases (like those involving male and female locker-room attendants), but they usually reflect cultural prejudice. They subject all women to job restrictions based on presumptions or generalizations about the average woman. The connection between belief in sex as an occupational qualification and employment discrimination against women was clearly illustrated by turn-of-the-century protective labor laws.

Early Title VII litigation brought these issues before federal courts, which had the job of defining BFOQs; by defining them narrowly, the courts proved themselves sensitive to grosser forms of sexual stereotyping. In one of the first landmark cases for women under Title VII, the Ninth Circuit Court of Appeals rejected an employer's contention that a state protective labor law served as a BFOQ and an excuse for not hiring women. This case, *Rosenfeld v. Southern Pacific Company*,[7] involved a company's refusal to hire a woman for a job (as agent-telegrapher) that would have required her to lift more than fifty pounds and work a ten-hour day, in violation of California law. The court held that the state labor law conflicted with Title VII and was preempted by it. The courts also prohibited employers from "protecting" women on their own, in the absence of state legislation. In *Weeks v. Southern Telephone and Telegraph*,[8] the Fifth Circuit held that employers could not bar women from "strenuous" jobs on the basis of assumptions about women's physical frailties. The assertion that sex is a BFOQ may not be presumed, the court held; it must be proved. In this case, the court stressed, Southern Bell "introduced no evidence concerning the lifting abilities of women. Rather, they would have us 'assume,' on the basis of a 'stereotyped characterization' that few or no women can safely lift 30 pounds, while all men are treated as if they can."

Stereotypes about male and female personality traits were also offered and rejected as BFOQs. A leading early case involved a successful challenge to an airline policy of hiring only female flight attendants because women were presumed to be better at reassuring anxious passengers. This case, *Diaz v. Pan American World Airways*,[9] shows how protectionist presumptions about women's superior "interpersonal" skills—presumptions shared by some feminists and unrepentant chauvinists alike—can dictate the allocation of jobs.

It also shows how expectations of feminine nurturance are self-fulfilling. Passengers preferred women stewardesses, Pan Am argued, and were more likely to be soothed by them: "Passengers of both sexes . . . respond better to the presence of females than males," according to a psychiatrist testifying for Pan Am. He explained that "many male passengers would subconsciously resent a male flight attendant perceived as more masculine than they, but respond negatively to a male flight attendant perceived as less masculine, whereas male passengers would generally feel themselves more masculine and thus more at ease in the presence of a young female attendant. . . . female passengers might consider personal overtures by male attendants as intrusive and inappropriate, while at the same time welcoming the attentions and conversation of another woman." The psychiatrist concluded that "there are sound psychological reasons for the general preference of airline passengers for female flight attendants."[10]

In rejecting this defense and invalidating the woman-only policy, the court did not challenge Pan Am's psychiatric testimony as much as declare it irrelevant. Without deciding whether women were, in fact, better at soothing passengers then men, the court held that providing nurturance was not "reasonably necessary to the normal operation" of Pan Am's business—"transporting passengers safely from one point to another." Since women's arguable ability to provide a "pleasant environment" for passengers was tangential to airline business, it could not justify a preference for women flight attendants.

This requirement that a sex-based hiring preference be a reasonable business necessity is expressly included in Title VII's definition of a BFOQ. It means that the courts must ask two questions in a BFOQ case: (1) Is the presumption of sexual difference justified? (2) Is it relevant? The question of relevance is sometimes more important than the question of difference, as the pregnancy disability cases show. Only women get pregnant, but all workers, male and female, are subject to being temporarily disabled. Is the cause of a disability (pregnancy or a bad back) as relevant as its effect on the worker? Relevance may be the only answerable question when the differences asserted involve intangibles—character instead of biology. Only women get pregnant, but we may never know whether the possibility of becoming pregnant makes women superior nurturers. What we do know is that superior ability to nurture and please airline passengers is not relevant to the task of safely transporting them.

Questions about sexual difference are especially difficult to answer under Title VII because they may not be answered in general. Facts about the "average" man or woman may not determine the treatment of men and women as individuals. This is a basic principle of due process that was applied by the Supreme Court to Title VII cases in *City of Los Angeles Department of Water and Power v. Manhart*.[11] In *Manhart* the court invalidated an employee pension plan exacting larger pension fund contributions from women because they lived longer on average, raising the average cost of pensions for women retirees. The difference asserted in this case—a generalization about male and female mortality—was "unquestionably true," the Court noted, but it was "equally true" that mortality rates for individual men and women would always vary. The Court stressed that Title VII focuses "on the individual" because discrimination is a matter of judging people by class characteristics rather than individual ones. "Even a true generalization about the class is insufficient reason for disqualifying an individual to whom the generalization does not apply."

An "unquestionably true" generalization may also reflect social rather than biological differences, the Court in *Manhart* observed: "Separate mortality tables are easily interpreted as reflecting innate differences between the sexes; but a significant part of the longevity differential may be explained by the social fact that men are heavier smokers than women." The mere habit of generalizing perpetuates prejudicial stereotypes: "Practices which classify employees in terms of religion, race, or sex tend to preserve traditional assumptions about groups rather than thoughtful scrutiny of individuals."

Of course, Title VII generally invalidates explicit sexual and racial job classifications; that much has always been clear. But the job market remains sex-segregated in fact, if not by law, because men and women are steered to different jobs by custom, conditioning, and education. Jobs are gendered: Men drive trucks, while women type. Nearly three-quarters of all full-time women wage earners are clustered in occupations in which over three-quarters of all employees are female, and female-dominated occupations pay less than those dominated by men. Full-time women wage earners are paid about 30 percent less than their male counterparts, and the wage gap increases with age, suggesting that men advance in their careers midlife, while women stagnate.[12]

Traditional ideas about equal pay for equal work, embodied in the Equal Pay Act of 1963, haven't closed the wage gap precisely because men and women tend not to perform "equal" or identical jobs. They do, however, perform comparable ones, which is the basis for women's claims to comparable worth.

Comparable worth, or pay equity, involves the use of job evaluation programs to weigh such things as workers' skills, responsibilities, working conditions, and the value of jobs to employers, in order to equalize pay scales in comparable male and female jobs. (Job evaluations will vary and may consider a range of factors other than gender in considering what jobs are worth.) Comparable worth can result in a redistribution of wages, meaning pay cuts in male occupations and raises in female ones; or if male wages are used as a standard, wages for women's jobs will rise while wages for men's jobs remain the same.*[13]

Comparable worth is a controversial theory. Some critics point to factors other than sex, such as women's relatively erratic work patterns and relative lack of training or experience to explain the wage gap. (Similar arguments are used to explain lower wages for minority males.) The relation of these factors to discrimination and traditional gender roles—the way in which women's careers are interrupted by familial responsibilities—is ignored. Or it's called natural and therefore good. Some conservative protectionists still support the family wage, in an effort to bring back one-income families headed by men. Some condemn comparable worth as a threat to the male breadwinning role and traditional family life.[15]

Comparable worth has critics on the left as well. It doesn't propose a radical restructuring of the market and an entirely egalitarian workplace, because it doesn't challenge the assumption that jobs have intrinsic values that ought to be measured and ranked. It addresses "horizontal" inequities (pay differentials between maintenance men and women clerks) but not "vertical" inequities—differentials between dentists (almost all of whom are male) and dental hygienists (almost all of whom are female).[16] Comparable worth doesn't threaten to dismantle the

---

*The federal government has been quite hostile to comparable worth (Clarence Pendleton, former chair of the U.S. Civil Rights Commission, called it crazy, but most states have taken it seriously enough to conduct comparable worth studies, and nearly half have made some sort of comparable worth payments to state employees).[14]

hierarchical market; it does, however, promise to raise women's place in it. It promises that if the allocation of jobs continues to be determined by traditional gender roles, at least the distribution of wages in similar jobs won't reflect the traditional devaluation of women's work.

Are horizontal wage differentials a form of employment discrimination? Does Title VII mandate comparable worth? Federal courts have generally held that it does not.

That Title VII requires the nondiscriminatory setting of wages is clear, but there have been questions about whether, like the Equal Pay Act, it simply requires equal pay for equal work. Feminist advocates of pay equity have argued that wage discrimination is not as simple and as easily cured as the Equal Pay Act implied, and the Supreme Court has essentially agreed. In *County of Washington v. Gunther*,[17] the Court held that Title VII goes beyond the Equal Pay Act in prohibiting employers from depressing women's pay scales because they are women, whether or not substantially equal jobs are performed by men for more money. Still, this decision stopped short of mandating comparable worth.

Gunther involved a pay discrimination claim by female jail guards who were paid substantially less than male guards in the same county jail, for performing different jobs. Males supervised considerably more prisoners, and females performed what were characterized as less valuable clerical duties. In upholding the right of female guards to sue under Title VII, the Court carved out a narrow victory for feminists. It expressly declined to endorse a theory of comparable worth, stressing that the case was not based on a comparison of the "intrinsic worth or difficulty" of male and female jobs. Instead, women plaintiffs were claiming that they were paid less than market rates for their jobs because they were women; the Court simply gave them the right to try proving it.

How do you prove that lower pay scales for women are intentionally discriminatory? With great difficulty, according to at least one federal appellate court that has considered cases following *Gunther*. In *Spaulding v. University of Washington*[18] the Ninth Circuit dismissed a pay discrimination claim by members of a university nursing faculty who were paid less than faculty members in other departments with similar jobs. Wage disparities alone did not establish discrimination, the court of appeals held, nor did the university's reliance on market pay scales that were said to have a discriminatory impact on women. One year later, the Supreme Court rejected a similar wage discrimination claim in *AFSME v. State of Washington*,[19] a comparable-worth case involving state employees. A study by the state of Washington had confirmed that jobs performed primarily by women were lower paying (by about 20 percent) than jobs of equal value to employers performed primarily by men. The Court held that this was not evidence of discrimination because the state's intent to discriminate could not be inferred from its use of discriminatory pay scales established by the "market system." It added that Title VII was not intended to "abrogate fundamental economic principles such as the laws of supply and demand or to prevent employers from competing in the labor market." In other words, if the market values women less than men and sets sexually discriminatory pay scales, so can employers. Employers are allowed to discriminate against female workers as long as discrimination is systemic.

If this is true, Title VII is a nullity; market forces have primacy over equal rights. If Title VII was intended to do anything at all, it was intended to interfere with discriminatory market practices—a preference for female flight attendants or white middle managers. Recognizing that not all discriminatory practices are overt, the Supreme Court has held that Title VII prohibits employment practices that appear neutral toward women or minority males (like market pay scales) but operate to keep them in their place. In a landmark Title VII case, *Griggs v. Duke Power Company*,[20] the Court invalidated facially neutral job performance standards that effectively excluded black employees from all but lower-level jobs.

Griggs held that courts would look beyond the face or apparently neutral intent of an employment practice to its effect, in Title VII cases. In *Griggs* the Court held that screening applicants with a standardized job test that has a "disparate impact" on blacks violates Title VII if the test is not shown to be "significantly related to job performance." Courts must thus ask two questions in evaluating the impact of a facially neutral rule: (1) Does the rule hurt women or minorities disproportionately? (2) Is the rule necessary to the operation of business? *Griggs* involved a requirement that employees have a high school diploma or pass a general intelligence test; the test requirement had been instituted on the day Title VII became effective (which should have made this a relatively easy case), but use of this test was not construed as intent to discriminate. Instead, the Court held that ability to pass the test was unrelated to ability to perform any particular job. The Court also observed that blacks in North Carolina, the site of the Duke Power Company, had "long received inferior education in segregated schools," suggesting that the job test perpetuated the effects of prior discrimination.

Standardized tests and other "neutral" practices and procedures can "operate to 'freeze' the status quo of prior discriminatory employment practices," the Court observed. In other words, they can serve as subterfuges for intentional discrimination. Height and weight requirements or physical endurance tests are commonly used to exclude women from what have traditionally been men's jobs, as police officers, firefighters, or airline pilots.[21] Determining whether physical fitness tests are, in fact, related to job performance is a difficult question for trial courts. It's also a difficult question for women asserting their capacity to compete as equals with men and a question that provokes some confused resentment about special treatment and the principle of affirmative action.

The disparate impact rule does not require affirmative action by an employer (job tests that are shown to be related to job performance need not be waived for women or minority males). It does, however, challenge the way affirmative action is popularly perceived—as a lowering of standards that benefits women and minorities at the expense of better-qualified white males. The disparate-impact cases show that "high" standards may not be high as much as they are biased and inappropriate, like the standards at issue in *Griggs*. In the context of a history of segregation and inferior education for blacks, the high school diploma requirement and intelligence tests were hardly "color-blind"; they continued an earlier pattern of racial discrimination.

The problem of inherently discriminatory standards is illustrated clearly by highly publicized disputes about admissions standards for law and medical schools. Take the *Bakke* case.[22] In *Regents of University of California v. Bakke*, decided under the Fourteenth Amendment and Title VI of the Civil Rights Act (prohibiting racial discrimination in federally assisted programs), a divided court invalidated a University of California policy holding open sixteen medical school places for disadvantaged minorities who could not meet the usual test scores and grade point requirements. Writing for a plurality, Justice Powell managed to elude questions about the fairness and appropriateness of these requirements by not asking them; he didn't question the possible built-in biases of tests, the effect of prior discrimination on minority test scores, or the accuracy of tests as predictors of performance in medical school. The plurality in *Bakke* held that, in principle, universities could consider race in making admission decisions, under affirmative action plans (although it invalidated the University of California plan at issue here); but its failure to question apparently neutral admission standards confirmed both the notion that minority students simply weren't smart enough to compete and a distorted view of affirmative action as a lowering of standards. It is a lowering of standards for a university to admit minorities with lower test scores only if the tests themselves are fair.

Standards and tests that aren't fair don't need to be lowered; they need to be changed.[23]

How do you prove a standard is unfair? Under the Fourteenth Amendment, it is difficult to virtually impossible: A rule or practice must be shown to be intentionally discriminatory. Under Title VII it may be shown to have a discriminatory effect (a disparate impact) and no legitimate business justification. Pursuant to the 1971 decision of *Griggs v. Duke Power Company* and the cases that followed it over a period of eighteen years, employers had the burden of proving that a practice effectively excluding women or minority males was a business necessity—a way of ensuring "safe and efficient job performance."[24] Title VII thus extended considerably more protection to victims of employment discrimination than the Constitution did and was a potentially powerful agent for economic change.

It has much less power today. A newly conservative Supreme Court, including three Reagan appointees, has changed long-standing rules in disparate-impact cases, which may make them nearly impossible for employees to win. Under a five-to-four 1989 decision, *Wards Cove Packing Company v. Atonio*,[25] a case involving minority males that applies as well to women, employees now have the burden of proving that an exclusionary employment practice is *not* a legitimate business necessity: Employers are no longer required to justify discriminatory practices, simply by proving a positive—that the practices are necessary to the operation of business. Employees victimized by discrimination have the very difficult task of proving a negative.

Wards Cove Packing Company v. Atonio was a fifteen-year-old lawsuit by a group of Alaskan native and Asian workers in Alaskan canneries who charged they were shunted into unskilled jobs on the cannery line while skilled, noncannery jobs went to whites. They were also housed separately (canneries were in remote regions of Alaska and workers lived in company dorms), and they ate in separate mess halls. The case presented a classic instance of a racially bifurcated workforce (what the dissent called a "plantation economy"), but the Court used it to undermine the principle that even gross racial imbalances make a prima facie case of discrimination, requiring employers to justify their practices. (A prima facie showing of discrimination has never been conclusive; it simply gave employers the burden of proving justification.) The Court held that the racial composition of the company's skilled and unskilled workforce was irrelevant: Disparate-impact analysis required a comparison of the pool of qualified applicants to hirees because racial imbalances might be caused by a "dearth of qualified nonwhite applicants."

Of course, defining the pool of qualified applicants was precisely at issue in the case: Nonwhite employees charged that their qualifications were overlooked because of their race, citing such practices as "nepotism, a rehire preference, a lack of objective hiring criteria, separate hiring channels" (skilled jobs were advertised by word of mouth; unskilled jobs were filled by an agreement with a predominantly nonwhite union), and "a practice of not promoting from within." But the Court held that employees would have to do more than identify practices like these to make a case of discrimination; they would have to establish a direct causal link between each specified practice and workforce imbalances. This is a new requirement in disparate-impact cases, and as Justice Blackmun pointed out in dissent, it may be impossible to meet. The precise means of discrimination are often invisible to employees, as are employers' motivations, which is partly why the disparate-impact rule was devised. Under the *Wards Cove Packing* case, employers who discriminate subtly and covertly, eschewing such crude measures as the job tests involved in *Griggs*, may discriminate with impunity.

Title VII's requirement that courts look beyond the face of a rule to its effect is particularly important when the rules themselves are unwritten. When standards are subjective, when employees are judged not by tests but by individual supervisors, intentional discrimination is particularly difficult to prove. (No one admits to being a bigot; not all are aware of their bigotry.) The Supreme Court itself recognized this in the 1989 case of *Watson v. Fort Worth Bank and Trust*,[26] when it applied the disparate-impact rule to subjective employee evaluations. *Watson* preceded *Atonio* by several months; it may have been the last in a series of cases expanding the Title VII rights of employees.*

The plaintiff in the *Watson* case was a black woman, Clara Watson, a bank teller who was turned down four times for promotion to a supervisory position in her bank. Promotion decisions were made by white supervisors on a subjective, individual basis. Each position for which Watson applied was given to a white employee with less experience in the bank. In the absence of admissions by bank supervisors that they hadn't promoted her because of her race, Watson relied on statistical evidence that blacks had been hurt disproportionately by

---

*The decision to apply disparate-impact analysis to subjective employment processes was unanimous (eight to one; Justice Kennedy did not participate in the case), but the Court split over important questions about evidentiary standards, anticipating its decision in *Wards Cove Packing Company v. Atonio*. Justice O'Connor, writing for a plurality in *Watson*, held that plantiff employees should meet higher standards of proof than had previously been imposed in disparate-impact cases.

the bank's hiring and promotion policies: Black applicants had one-fourth of the chances white applicants enjoyed of being hired for any bank job; blacks were paid less for comparable work and rated lower in job evaluations.[27]

She lost the first two rounds in federal court. The district court and the court of appeals held that statistical disparities did not establish discrimination, because they declined to apply disparate-impact analysis to a promotional process that was entirely subjective. Watson's claim was considered a "disparate-treatment" case—one involving intentional discrimination—and not a disparate-impact case—one involving apparently neutral employment practices with a discriminatory effect. The Supreme Court has called disparate treatment "the most easily understood type of discrimination,"[28] but it has also tended to be the more difficult to prove. While a disparate-impact case might have been established with statistical evidence of an unbalanced workforce (before *Wards Cove Packing Company v. Atonio*), a disparate-treatment case generally involves evidence of an employer's specific discriminatory intention.

Lower federal courts had divided over the use of disparate-treatment and disparate-impact analysis and the use of statistical evidence in cases involving subjective performance evaluations. In *Watson* the Court held that the disparate impact rule should be extended to subjective decision making. The Court stressed that the rule was meaningless if applied only to objective job tests: Employers could add job interviews to a selection process involving standardized tests, call the process subjective, and use subjectivity as an excuse for discrimination. As Clara Watson successfully argued, "Subjective selection criteria present an almost unparalleled opportunity for bias. They conceal the most difficult and evasive form of discrimination: the hidden, subtle, and possibly subconscious preferences of decisionmakers to select others with their cultural backgrounds and experiences."[29]

The *Watson* case should extend the reach of Title VII in white-collar cases, in which subjective, merit-based hiring and promotion are common (but *Wards Cove Packing Company v. Atonio* may make this extension moot). Title VII has not been broadly applied to the white-collar job market, partly because courts have tended to defer to employer evaluations of merit and to the process of credentialing—a process with which judges, as white-collar professionals, are familiar. Major Supreme Court decisions of the past decade upholding affirmative action plans have involved blue-collar jobs.[30] So have major sex discrimination cases brought under Title VII.[31] Equal rights feminists are often accused of aiding professional women at the expense of blue- and pink-collar workers, but, in fact, discrimination at the professional level has been harder to prove, or even discern, because it's cloaked in subjectivity and evaluations of "merit." Congress, as well as the courts, was slow to attack white-collar discrimination, and for several years the professions were legally shielded from judicial scrutiny: The Equal Pay Act was not extended to professional and academic employees until 1972, nearly a decade after it was passed. Title VII was first extended to academics in 1972, as well.

The underrepresentation of women at executive levels in the corporate world, at the partnership level of major law firms, or in tenured faculty positions has been described by protectionists as the natural result of women voluntarily placing families before careers or as a reflection of their relatively recent entry into professional life. But it also reflects the difficulty of confronting subjective expressions of bias and the reluctance of courts, and legislatures, to address them.*

Judges were especially reluctant to intercede in academic cases that required questioning the judgment of well-credentialed scholars and administrators. "Of all the fields which the federal courts should hesitate to invade and take over, education and faculty appointments at a university level are probably the least suited for federal supervision," the Second Circuit Court of Appeals held in *Faro v. New York University*.[32] In *Faro* the court declined to examine the university's "recruitment, compensation, and promotion" procedures, suggesting that courts were not equipped to second-guess faculty committees. The court also worried about subjecting universities to lawsuits by "unsuccessful and disgruntled candidates," who, it implied, were victims of their own incompetence.

If colleges and universities have had a license to discriminate, they've used it freely. The proportion of faculty positions held by women nationwide actually declined from 1930 to 1970. In fact, women held a higher proportion of faculty jobs in 1879 (when they constituted one-third of the nation's faculty) than they did in 1970, when their participation rate was less than one-fourth. At prestigious private universities in 1970, women held only 10 percent of all faculty jobs. (Two percent of Columbia University's tenured faculty were women; there were no women on Harvard's tenured faculty in the graduate school of

---

*Title VII was not applied to a law firm partnership decision until 1984, in *Hishon v. King and Spaulding*, 467 U.S. 69 (1984). It was recently applied in an important case involving a partnership decision by the accounting firm Price Waterhouse. See discussion pp. 110–112.

arts and sciences.) Jobs that were awarded to women tended to be low ranking and nontenured. Pay discrimination was common (and legal).[33]

Until 1972 when Congress passed Title IX, of the Civil Rights Act prohibiting discrimination in education and extended the Equal Pay Act and Title VII to academia, women's only weapon against academic discrimination was Executive Order 11246, which prohibits discrimination by federal contractors (colleges and universities commonly receive money from the federal government, which makes them federal contractors). By January 1970 the newly formed Women's Equity Action League filed formal charges of sex discrimination against more than 100 universities and colleges under this order. WEAL described an "industry wide pattern of sex discrimination in the academic community," citing statistical evidence of women's underrepresentation in high-ranking faculty jobs and employment practices such as advertising for male professors. By the end of 1971 complaints had been filed against 350 institutions. In response, the federal government conducted reviews of discrimination at about 200 institutions and delayed funding to about 40. The most serious sanction—terminating federal contracts—was not invoked.[34]

WEAL led a small feminist movement by academic women that, like most feminist movements, enjoyed partial success. Congress recognized sex discrimination on campus and made it illegal in 1972, but by the mid-1980s, women still constituted only about 25 percent of the nation's full-time faculty and only about 10 percent of all full-time professors.[35] Throughout the 1970s some things changed for women in academia, but others stayed the same, as they did for women throughout the job market. Looking back in 1980, Dr. Bernice Sandler, former president of WEAL, characterized the 1970s as a decade of "paradox": Consciousness was raised about sex discrimination on campus and women were "energized"; the number of women students increased along with the number of women's studies programs; women in academia acquired important new civil rights. But they still occupied lower-level, lower-paying faculty jobs and few high-level administrative ones (less than 7 percent of all college presidents were women). Patterns of discrimination remained essentially unchanged, as Dr. Sandler observed: "The higher the rank, the fewer the women."[36] Sexism on campus is being eroded slowly but not eliminated. In 1987 a federal district court in Boston found Boston University guilty of discrimination in denying tenure to a woman English professor, Julia Brown. BU's English Department contained twenty tenured males and seven tenured females, making it, according to university president John Silber, a "damned matriarchy."[37]

Protectionist stereotypes of women scholars retard their progress; they are vulnerable to being considered "soft" or "school marmish," a term used to describe Professor Christine Sweeney when she was refused promotion at a New Hampshire college in 1974. Professor Sweeney sued under Title VII and was promoted after filing suit. She eventually won her legal battle as well as her promotion when a federal appeals court observed that the refusal to promote her was based largely on personal reasons (dislike for her prim, "spinsterish" ways) and that these appeared to be reasons the male members of her review committee "would not have fastened upon had Sweeney been a man."[38]

The discrimination encountered by Julia Brown at Boston University and Christine Sweeney is relatively common; what's unusual about their cases is the fact that they won. Sex discrimination on campus is still hard to prove; an inestimable number of women don't even try—or don't know they have good reason to. Gender stereotypes are effectively cloaked in subjective standards of merit, which the victims of discrimination themselves have been taught to respect.

Discrimination is insidious, partly because it's not always apparent, even to its victims. Sometimes people don't recognize the refusal to hire or promote them or treat them with respect as discriminatory. They take it personally, considering it a personal failure rather than a reflection of prejudice toward their sexual, racial, or ethnic group. Sometimes courts don't recognize discrimination either because they share the biases it expresses or prefer blaming the victim to admitting that the system is unfair.

Sexual harassment is particularly insidious because it copies socially acceptable or at least socially routine behavior. Harassment begins for women in girlhood; men and boys leer at them on buses or subway trains and in the streets. Before feminism "raised consciousness" about the sexual intimidation and abuse of women, harassment was considered a compliment rather than a threat.

It was not until the mid-1970s, a decade after Title VII was enacted, that sexual harassment was recognized by federal courts as a form of sexual discrimination. Courts had hesitated to "interfere" in harassment cases, as they had in other cases involving subjective hiring and promotion decisions: One court characterized a harassment claim as a "controversy underpinned by the subtleties of an inharmonious personal relationship."[39] Whether an employee was being harassed or whether she was simply supersensitive, whether sexual advances were provoked or entirely unwanted, were questions judges could answer only in the context of their own cultural biases.

To find sexual harassment a violation of Title VII, judges also had to find that it was, in part, impersonal—that it was directed against an employee not just an individual but as a member of her sex. A common early defense to harassment claims was that other women employees were not being harassed, that the plaintiff was complaining about an individual relationship and not group discrimination. "She was discriminated against, not because she was a woman, but because she refused to engage in a sexual affair with her supervisor," the district court in *Barnes v. Costle* suggested, which is a little like saying the differential treatment of pregnant wage earners is legal because it's based on pregnancy, not sex.[40]

But *Barnes v. Costle* was reversed on appeal, and the case became an important early victory for women. (It involved a woman who was denied a promotion and eventually had her job abolished after she refused to sleep with her supervisor.) On appeal, the Court of Appeals for the District of Columbia stressed that gender need not be the only cause for the differential treatment of an employee in a Title VII case: "On the contrary," the court held, "it is enough that gender is a factor contributing to the discrimination in a substantial way." The court recognized that Paulette Barnes "became the target of her superior's sexual advances because she was a woman. . . . No male was susceptible to such an approach."[41]

In this view, sexual harassment is a social or a public wrong, not a private, personal one. It happens to women as a class. It's an expression of stereotyping that reflects ingrained cultural biases about women as sexual provocateurs and sexual prey. It's a form of intimidation that reinforces their inequality. When overt discrimination against women and minority males is clearly prohibited, sexual and racial harassment are ways of blocking the schoolhouse door.

Harassment occurs in two basic forms, recognized by EEOC guidelines issued in 1980: Sexual favors are demanded in return for favorable job treatment (quid pro quo harassment), or employees are subject to generally hostile or offensive workplace conditions (hostile environment harassment). The Supreme Court recently confirmed, in *Meritor Savings Bank, FSB, v. Vinson*, that employers may be held liable for maintaining a hostile environment, even if they have a stated policy of nondiscrimination and grievance procedures for employees, which suggests that employers must take positive steps to "address sexual harassment in particular."[42] The Court also confirmed that a hostile environment claim need not include a showing by the employee of economic harm. The harm in these cases is sometimes intangible—pornographic slides are shown at video presentations or photographs of nude models are pasted next to biographies of women employees in a company newsletter. "Blatant good-old boy sexism still thrives in the corporate workplace," according to a recent *Wall Street Journal Report*.[43]

The extent to which it thrives in all sorts of workplaces is difficult to discern; much of it is subtle and unreported, and much is in dispute. Men and women tend to disagree about what constitutes harassment: "They're not in the same universe at all," Eliza Collins, editor of the *Harvard Business Review*, remarks.[44] But men's failure to realize or acknowledge that sexually suggestive remarks or the circulation of pornography is threatening or, at least, discomfiting for women and a challenge to their authority is part of the sexism that harassment expresses. If the testimony of women wage earners is evidence of harassment, it is indeed pervasive: In a 1976 *Redbook* magazine survey, 88 percent of women respondents reported being harassed.[45] (It's likely that women who suffered harassment responded at a higher rate; the survey didn't measure the problem but did indicate it was widespread.) Forty-two percent of female federal employees reported being harassed in a recent federal survey, which showed that harassment was commonly encountered by women working in predominantly male environments in nontraditional jobs.[46]

The professions that have been most closed to women and most expressive of sexual stereotyping have also been the most hostile. Harassment has been a serious problem for women firefighters and police officers and for women in the military. Two recent Pentagon reports charged the U.S. Army, Air Force, Navy, and Marine Corps with tolerating severe harassment of servicewomen. The problem is particularly acute for women based overseas. Abuses in the Pacific ranged from informing women that sleeping with their superior officers "would make life 'easier' for them," to calling them "Honey," to an offer by a ship captain to sell female sailors to Koreans. In both the Navy and Marine Corps according to the report, "Leadership condones discriminatory behavior, in part, as a means of perpetuating the 'male mystique' that is traditionally associated with military forces."[47]

Sexual harassment is a particularly brutal defense of the male mystique and traditional ideas about sexual difference; it provides an important perspective on the equality debate, partly by pointing out how sexual stereotyping expresses itself indirectly. If effecting justice for women means treating them as individuals, it also requires recognizing the ways in which they're mistreated as a class.

Remedying the indirect effects of stereotyping is an important challenge for courts and the EEOC today in second-generation Title VII cases—cases involving covert discrimination.[48] The Supreme Court handed down an important "second-generation" victory for women in 1989 in *Price Waterhouse v. Hopkins* when it held that evaluating a woman employee on the basis of conventional standards of femininity may constitute sex discrimination.[49] *Hopkins* involved a claim by Ann Hopkins that she was denied a partnership inthe prestigious accounting firm of Price Waterhouse because she didn't conform to stereotypes of feminine behavior.

She won the first rounds, and Price Waterhouse appealed to the Supreme Court. It argued that even if Hopkins established that gender bias played a role in the partnership decision, she should be required to prove that "but for" that bias she would have made partner. The Supreme Court disagreed, holding that Price Waterhouse had the burden of proving it would *not* have made her a partner even if it had not considered gender. The fact that Price Waterhouse may have had legitimate reasons for denying Hopkins a partnership, the fact that stereotyping may have been only a part, not the whole, of the process by which she was evaluated did not doom her case. "We take [Title VII] to mean that gender must be irrelevant to employment decisions," the Court declared. Prohibiting discrimination that occurs "because of" sex does not mean prohibiting discrimination that occurs "solely because of" sex. For this reason, the Court explained, the employer who has relied on gender stereotypes has the burden of proving the stereotypes were essentially irrelevant to the employment decision.*

Hopkins had a strong case; there was little question that stereotypes were involved in the rejection of her partnership bid. She had brought more new clients into the firm than anyone else in her partnership class and had generated business estimated at $35 million to $44 million. But she was aggressive—"unfeminine" and "unladylike," according to the all-male partnership committee that evaluated her. It was said that she

---

*This was a plurality opinion. As it did in the *Watson* case, the Court split over important procedural questions about standards of proof, or persuasion, on employer and employee. The dissent in *Hopkins* would have kept the burden of proving causation on the employee. A plurality essentially placed a burden of proving noncausation onthe employer, but it held that the court of appeals had imposed too high a burden on Price Waterhouse. On this basis, the judgment was reversed, and the case sent back to the lower court for reconsideration under a lower evidentiary standard.

"overcompensated for being a woman," that she was "macho." One relatively favorable comment praised her for having "matured from a tough-talking somewhat masculine hard-nosed mgr. [manager] to an authoritative, formidable, but much more appealing lady ptr [partner] candidate." Still, she wasn't "ladylike" enough: Her use of "foul language" offended male partners because "it's a lady using foul language." She was advised by one partner to "walk more femininely, talk more femininely, dress more femininely, wear make-up, have her hair styled, and wear jewelry." Another advised her to take "a course in charm school."[50]

It's clear that Title VII prohibits Price Waterhouse from following a male-only partnership rule. It should be equally clear that the personality test applied to Ann Hopkins was the equivalent of one. Refusing to promote her for being unladylike is tantamount for refusing to promote her for being a woman. Male partners are not required to be ladylike, although they are probably expected to be at least as aggressive as Hopkins. (Male candidates would, no doubt, like being called hard-nosed and tough-talking.) The irony for Ann Hopkins is that the qualities valued and required for success in the highly competitive, mercantile world of Price Waterhouse were the qualities that doomed her partnership bid because they weren't tolerated in a woman.

This should have been an easy case, which should not have split the Court. It's been fifteen years since the Supreme Court recognized that men and women don't necessarily fulfill traditional male/female roles and shouldn't be expected to do so: Wage-earner/homemaker laws are clear violations of the Fourteenth Amendment, the Court held. Employment practices requiring women to fulfill traditional feminine roles, by behaving in traditional feminine ways, ought to be clear violations of Title VII.

But understanding the discrimination Ann Hopkins encountered requires an understanding of gender stereotyping and a willingness to stop it, which the federal government has lacked. In fact, the Reagan Administration essentially sided with Price Waterhouse, suggesting that Hopkins had not proved her case.[51] Feminists are sometimes guilty of stereotyping too, and the *Hopkins* case has a lesson for feminist believers in women's superior nurturing, compassionate, and less competitive nature. That vision of womanhood was shared by the male partners at Price Waterhouse and used to measure Ann Hopkins. It condemned her as sexually anomalous, or "unladylike"—what some feminists might call "male-identified."

·8·

Equality in Education: Title IX of the 1964 Civil Rights Act

Gender stereotyping begins well before women enter the job market; it begins at birth and is firmly reinforced in school.[1] The protectionist notion that males and females should be educated differently, according to their different natures, is one that helped shape America's educational system. From the beginning, women were educated because they were mothers, responsible for turning out well-informed, active male citizens. The ideal of educated motherhood took hold in the first years of the republic: Democracy required an informed citizenry. It was the guiding ideal for early nineteenth-century pioneers of women's education like Catherine Beecher and Emma Willard, who established two of the first female seminaries in the United States. It was again invoked, toward the end of the 1800s, as an excuse for providing women with college educations.

Women's advance into higher education did not begin in earnest until the years after the Civil War, when the colleges now known as the Seven Sisters were founded and both new and established universities began admitting women. Providing women with an equal "male" education was quite controversial; experts warned that strenuous intellectual activity would impair female reproductive functions.[2] At the turn of the century, a drop in the birth rate was blamed on higher education for women, and surveys showed that college women were less likely to marry or, at least, more likely to marry later than the general population of women.[3] Not all of them used their education at home; some pursued careers. College had given women access to the masculine sphere of professional activity, and the first generations of women professionals tended to remain single. In the 1920s and 1930s, when marriage within a few years of graduation was a norm, college women were still debating the possibility of combining marriage and careers.

When the contemporary feminist movement began in the mid-1960s, middle-class women were routinely attending college (and working outside the home). In 1960, 37.9 percent of all college students were women; in 1970 their participation rate was 41.9 percent.[4] But admission standards were higher for women because many colleges limited the number of female applicants accepted. Cornell maintained a three-to-one ratio of males to females and Harvard-Radcliffe a four-to-one ratio. In 1969 the University of North Carolina at Chapel Hill admitted one-fourth of its female applicants and one-half of its male applicants, pursuant to a stated policy of admitting only women "who are especially well-qualified."[5]

Discrimination against women increased with the level of education; graduate and professional schools provided very limited access to female students. In 1968 only 12.6 percent of students receiving doctorates were women; in 1970 women constituted only about 10 percent of law and medical students. These numbers did not reflect a scarcity of qualified women applicants. Between 1935 and 1970 the number of women applying to medical school increased more than 300 percent, while the number of men applying increased 29 percent; during the same period, the number of men accepted to medical school rose and the number of women accepted fell. According to a 1969 survey, admission officers at nineteen (of twenty-five) northeastern medical schools acknowledged that they "accepted men in preference to women unless the women were demonstrably superior."[6]

Throughout the 1960s protectionist ideals of education still prevailed; women were still educated to be mothers (and college was not uncommonly considered a good place to find a husband). At virtually every level of schooling, women and girls were encouraged to develop different skills and pursue different paths: "Unequal treatment [was] the rule in education, not the exception," an HEW (Department of Health, Education and Welfare) Task Force Report stated in 1973. "Although women are close to half of the working population, education is still preparing them to be housewives."[7] Preparation began early. A 1973 report by the Carnegie Commission noted that barriers against females who might gravitate toward masculine fields of medicine, science, and engineering were erected in childhood.[8] (Today computer science is a male preserve.)[9] A 1974 report by the U.S. Civil Rights Commission observed that a popular vocational guidance plan provided males and females with different questionnaires (blue for boys, pink for girls). Vocational choices varied according to sex: Although boys were asked whether they wanted to be doctors, girls were asked about being nurses or veterinarians for small animals. Boys were allotted forty-seven occupational choices, nearly twice the number of choices offered to girls.[10]

What parents teach their children about gender roles and how they discriminate between sons and daughters is their business; what schools teach and how they treat male and female students is the business of government too. The federal government acknowledged women's rights to equal education in 1972, when Title IX was added to the Civil Rights Act. It prohibits sex discrimination in federally assisted educational programs, from preschools through institutions of higher education. Private and public schools are included, although there are exemptions for religious and military schools and for undergraduate colleges that have traditionally been sex-segregated. Men's and women's colleges were not effected by Title IX (they did not have to integrate), but the law did have a significant effect on coeducational schools. Title IX applies to curriculum, recruitment, financial aid, athletics, health care, employment opportunities, and a range of other programs: Junior high school girls would no longer take home economics while boys were assigned shop. College health services would hire gynecologists.

Title IX was another landmark for the equal rights movement, but it was not an unequivocal endorsement of equality. With an exemption for single-sex colleges, Congress validated a separate-but-equal model of education for women, leaving them the choice between separatism and assimilation. Title IX straddled the debate about the relevance of gender to education and the benefits of single-sex and coeducational schools. It also allowed for some segregation in athletics, in deference to notions of sexual difference and some protectionist concern about women's relative physical weakness and vulnerability. Disputes about the right to "equal play" that followed Title IX and the equal rights movement involved deeply held beliefs about the inability of "average" women to compete with men on the playing field and the dangers of letting them try.

Title IX did however have a dramatic effect on high school and college sports. Within one year of its enactment, the percentage of girls participating in high school athletics rose from 7.5 to 25 percent. In ten years the proportion of female varsity athletes (in institutions belonging to the National Collegiate Athletic Association) nearly doubled, to 31 percent.[11] Title IX closed a considerable gap between men's and women's athletics, increasing funding for females, expanding the programs available to them, and changing social attitudes toward strong, athletic women. It is widely credited with sparking the women's sports revolution that began in the 1970s.

Expanding women's access to athletics challenged cherished protectionist ideas about sexual difference—the belief that females are naturally less aggressive, less competitive, and more physically fragile than men. But what was considered unnatural in women some fifteen years ago—strength and athletic prowess—has become a source of pride: Muscles are now "sexy" for women as well as men. What was most remarkable about the sports revolution was its rapid revisioning of the natural.

But it has been only a partial revisioning. Title IX does not mandate integration of contact sports—boxing, wrestling, and football—and it requires only "substantial proportionality," not equality, in funding for male and female programs. Segregated athletics have also been upheld under the Fourteenth Amendment. Federal and state courts have generally agreed that schools may maintain separate male and female teams as a protective measure, because of presumed differences between male and female athletes. Although, like most protective rules, this denies a top female athlete the right to play on a top male team, it is intended to protect the majority of women, at the expense of a few: In a case denying a girl the right to play on a boy's basketball team, Supreme Court Justice Stevens suggested that teams could be sex-segregated on the basis of average differences between the sexes, even if the exclusion of girls "appears arbitrary in an individual case . . . . Without a gender based classification in competitive contact sports, there would be substantial risk that boys would dominate girls' programs and deny them an equal opportunity to compete in interscholastic events."[12]

What if there are no comparable programs for girls or boys in a given sport? Courts are more likely to strike down rules allowing single-sex teams in the absence of teams for each sex.[13] In 1979 the Supreme

Judicial Court of Massachusetts invalidated a rule barring a boy from playing on a girl's softball team, when a boys' team was not available.[14] In 1975 the Washington Supreme Court struck down a rule barring girls from playing interscholastic football, despite assertions about the less-than-equal athletic abilities of a majority of girls.[15]

Each of these decisions, decided under the Massachusetts and Washington equal rights amendments, respectively, suggests that not all males and females run to type; some girls may be stronger and more coordinated than some boys, which means that qualifying rules should be based on performance, not sex. Absolute bars to male or female participation in a sport discriminates against both sexes, the Massachusetts court stressed: Although athletic opportunities in the past have "grossly favored" males, the less athletic ones, who could not compete with their male peers, were denied the right to equal play by being barred from girls' teams. Sex is not a reliable predictor of ability because biological differences "are not so clear or uniform as to justify a rule in which sex is sought to be used as a kind of 'proxy' for a functional classification." The court also noted that differences between male and female athletes were rapidly changing, suggesting they may not be entirely natural after all: "The general male athletic superiority based on physical features is challenged by the development in increasing numbers of female athletes whose abilities exceed those of most men, and in some cases approach those of the most talented men."

Barring girls from boys' teams denies them the right to prove themselves, one federal court stressed, in a Fourteenth Amendment case invalidating the exclusion of a thirteen-year-old girl from a male football team, when no girls' team was available. A federal district court in Missouri observed that the girl plaintiff, Nichole Force, was not

> claiming a legal right to a starting position on the team, since her position would be determined by her abilities: she seeks simply a chance, like her male counterparts, to display those abilities. She asks, in short, only the right to try. . . .
>
> I do not suggest there is any such thing as a constitutional "right to try." But the idea that one should be allowed to try — to succeed or to fail as one's abilities and fortunes may dictate, but in the process at least to profit by those things which are learned in the trying — is a concept deeply ingrained in our way of thinking; and it should indeed require a "substantial" justification to deny that privilege to someone simply because she is a female rather than a male.[16]

These are, however, controversial decisions that challenge social norms, and the right to "try" or play may vary in various state and federal jurisdictions. Excluding boys from girls' teams (when no boys' team is available) may be justified as a way of "redressing past discrimination" against women in sports.[17] Rules providing for separate and unequal play may also be upheld in deference to traditional theories about sexual difference. In 1979, an Illinois court upheld a rule prohibiting a boy from playing on a girls' volleyball team, in the absence of a team for boys, "because of innate differences," as well as "past disparity of opportunity." The court held that boys and girls "are not similarly situated as they enter into most athletic endeavors."[18]

Still, as the dissent in this case pointed out, similar justifications of racial or religious discrimination would never have been offered or accepted by the courts or the public:

> Surely, not even the majority here, nor society generally, would condone the exclusion of blacks from an all-white basketball team on the grounds that blacks generally are more skilled at the game than whites and might tend to dominate it. Nor would we tolerate an exclusion of Catholics from an all-Protestant high school soccer team on the grounds that Catholic elementary schools have traditionally emphasized that sport so as to give their graduates an unfair advantage. . . . There are legally tolerable means of categorizing athletes by size, strength, and ability. To adopt sex as a proxy for more precisely defined means of levelling off competition is both illegal and irrational. It is simply foolish to perpetuate the fear of equality between the sexes. It is more than foolish to justify discrimination upon the asserted basis of protection and allowing "catch-up" time.[19]

This does not deny that men, on average, may be stronger than women or even more skilled in athletics, anymore than a law making both sexes equally liable for alimony denies that it is usually needed and earned by women. It simply suggests that in high school athletics, as in the job market or the divorce courts, justice is best served by gender-neutral rules that focus on factors such as performance, skills, and needs, instead of on sex.

It's possible that in the short run men's superior athletic abilities will effectively limit women's opportunities to play on integrated teams; judged by the same criteria as men, women might make the team in fewer numbers. Gender neutrality in athletics will not immediately benefit all females. Whether it will eventually benefit most is unknowable. Equality is an experiment. The Constitution is an experiment, Oliver Wendell Holmes remarked, "as all life is an experiment."[20]

The belief that single-sex environments are good for women because they perform better and are more likely to succeed in the absence of men has been used to justify sex segregation in academics as well as in athletics. Women are afforded only second-class status in coeducational institutions, advocates of women's colleges argue. They tend to be intimidated and dominated intellectually by male students, with whom they don't like to compete. They're discouraged by social custom and ideals of femininity from excelling academically. Dr. David Truman, former president of Mount Holyoke College (one of four remaining all-female Seven Sister Colleges), has suggested that coed environments tend to encourage sexual stereotyping that is "damagingly restrictive" for the "intellectually able young woman":

> She must moderate her visible academic accomplishments, notably her school grades, if in competing with males she is not to lose out in the competition with females for male attention. More subtly, her intellectual horizons tend to be limited as she learns from the hidden curriculum that some subjects — especially quantitative and scientific ones — are not only difficult but are not the things that "successful" girls are interested in. . . . The young woman needs a school environment in which such stereotyping by sex is minimized, where the boy-girl game is not played as constantly as it is in the usual coeducational setting. Above all, she needs an environment in which she can find herself as a person, measuring her strengths and talents by real criteria and securing confidence in her choices, before she is required to decide how she will live and perform as an adult woman.[21]

Women's colleges produce disproportionately high numbers of women achievers, Truman stressed, suggesting that, at least in college, separatism works better than assimilation.

This is essentially the argument offered by supporters of black colleges, which are said to provide more nurturing and freer environments for black students that encourage them to achieve. It's a sound argument but not a dispositive one, especially for women. Women's schools subtly encourage the sexist stereotypes they purport to challenge. They encourage women to separate their intelligence from their sexuality. In a 1971 poll of Smith College seniors, a majority of students voted against admitting men (Smith remains a women's college today), largely because they did not want to compete with men intellectually or "dress up" for class.[22] That there was something sexist about wanting to be more pretty than smart among men occurred to very few students.

119

Most welcomed the opportunity to be intellectuals during the week and "women" on weekends, as if intelligence and femininity were naturally incompatible.

Congress may or may not have shared this belief that smart females are disadvantaged sexually when it passed Title IX in 1972. Nearly twenty years after the Supreme Court declared racial segregation unconstitutional, Congress exempted single-sex high schools and colleges from Title IX's admission requirements. Two years later, in 1974, it omitted a prohibition of sex discrimination from the Equal Education Opportunity Act, which prohibited discrimination based on race or ethnicity.

Perhaps in a sexist society, women ought to have the choice of attending a woman's institution in which they feel respected. Women's colleges have traditionally nurtured women intellectually; they grew out of a desire to provide the superior liberal arts education that was effectively denied them in coed environments.[23] The trouble is that in a sexist society all female schools may reflect a tacit acceptance of sex stereotyping (why separate males and females if they're not naturally divergent?), and female schools may not be equal to male schools, especially at the secondary school level. Whether single-sex schools (or black colleges) represent separatism that encourages achievement or segregation that stunts it, whether separate schools are a "badge of inferiority" or an opportunity for growth, depends on whether they actively challenge stereotyping or reflect it, on whether students attend them out of choice or compulsion, and on their levels of funding.

The Supreme Court recognized the use of single-sex schools to enforce sex stereotyping in *Mississippi University for Women v. Hogan*, a 1982 case striking down a state law excluding males from a state nursing school.[24] The state of Mississippi provided coed nursing programs that the male plaintiff in this case could attend, but no comparable all-male nursing college. The state characterized its maintenance of an all-female college as a remedy for prior discrimination against women, but as Justice O'Connor pointed out, women had hardly been denied opportunities to be nurses. Instead, nursing had always been women's work; a women's nursing college didn't remedy discrimination as much as perpetuate it, by perpetuating an occupational stereotype: "By assuring that Mississippi allots more openings in its state supported nursing schools to women than it does to men, MUW's admission policy lends credibility to the old view that women, not men, should become nurses, and makes the assumption that nursing is a field for women a self-fulfilling prophecy."

Hogan was decided under the Fourteenth Amendment; it was not a Title IX case because Title IX expressly exempts public, single-sex institutions, if they have always been single-sex, from its admission requirements. The state of Mississippi offered Title IX's exemption as a defense, but as Justice O'Connor made clear, an act of Congress does not supersede the Constitution; Congress cannot limit the scope of the Fourteenth Amendment. Instead, the Court, interpreting the Constitution, limits the power of Congress, which means that the *Hogan* case might be construed to invalidate Title IX's exemption from single-sex schools. The majority carefully stressed that it was not passing on the constitutionality of separate but equal educational facilities for men and women (there were not equal nursing school facilities for men), but as Justice Blackmun pointed out in dissent, the Court's equal protection analysis in *Hogan* could be used to invalidate any public, sex-segregated school.

A case upholding the constitutionality of separate but equal single-sex schools had, however, been affirmed by a divided Supreme Court three years earlier. This case, *Vorcheimer v. School District of Philadelphia*,[25] involved an attempt by a female student to enroll in an all-male high school. The court of appeals declined to order her admission (and was affirmed by the Supreme Court) because a comparable female school was available to her. The plaintiff's primary reason for wanting to attend the boys' school was a simple "personal preference rather than being founded on an objective evaluation," the court of appeals observed. The difference between a preference and an evaluation by the student was not clear. She testified that "I just didn't like the impression [the girls' school] gave me. I didn't think I would be able to go there for three years and not be harmed in any way by it." Had she couched her preference in psychological theories about the effect of single-sex environments would it have been sufficiently objective? The court simply stressed that Ms. Vorcheimer was not claiming she was being deprived of an opportunity "to obtain an education at a school with comparable academic facilities, faculty, and prestige."

The city of Philadelphia could not, of course, maintain separate but equal high schools for black students, as the court in *Vorcheimer* admitted. Racial segregation was virtually always unconstitutional, it observed, but segregation by sex was sometimes reasonable, because of natural sexual differences. "We are committed to the concept that there is no fundamental difference between races and therefore, in justice, there can be no dissimilar treatment. But there are differences between the sexes which may, in limited circumstances, justify disparity in law."

121

The precise sexual differences that justified the maintenance of single-sex high schools were not described. The court simply noted that sex segregation in education was long established and respected by many educators (it might have said the same about racial segregation in 1954) and that separating adolescent boys and girls fostered their academic achievements. Some students, the court added, preferred single-sex schools (suggesting that personal preferences might matter after all).

Some students prefer racially segregated schools too. As the dissent in this case pointed out, the court's reasoning was reminiscent of *Plessy v. Ferguson*, the notorious 1896 Supreme Court case that validated racial segregation, holding that it was not the purpose of law to enforce social as opposed to political equality.[26] Of course, whether or not separate schools for males and females further or retard the struggle for sexual equality is the underlying question of the Vorcheimer case and the larger debate about single-sex education — separatism and assimilation — that has yet to be resolved.

·9·

Federal Resistance to Expanding Civil Rights

The feminist movement for equal opportunity that began in the 1960s was a moderate success. The differential treatment of women in the workplace and in school was generally recognized as discrimination, not an accommodation to nature. The Supreme Court's extension of the Fourteenth Amendment to women, Title VII, Title IX, and myriad state and local human rights laws, in addition to sixteen state equal rights amendments, gave women unprecedented civil rights and a much richer array of choices. Still, poverty was "feminized," and the dual labor market persists; still, women are only potentially equal.

It's tempting to call this the failure of feminists who forgot that only women get pregnant. But wage discrimination and occupational segregation (women becoming nurses and men becoming doctors) are not biologically compelled, as protectionists suggest. Day-care and parental-leave programs and equal male participation in family life would relieve women's double burden—by transferring part of it to their husbands, their employers, or their states. Women's economic and domestic problems are cultural, not natural: They reflect ineffective enforcement of civil rights laws, a lack of consensus on affirmative action, and the intransigence of the dual labor market.

Like most laws, Title VII and Title IX matter only when they're enforced, and in the past decade, the federal government retreated from enforcing guarantees of civil rights. A review of Reagan Administration civil rights policies demonstrates that the one form of protection that ought to be extended to women and minority males—protection from sexual and racial discrimination—was denied them.[1]

Women and minorities made some professional progress during the 1970s, partly because the Supreme Court was generally sympathetic to claims of equality, partly because employers felt pressured by government (and the threat of litigation) into complying with new guarantees of opportunity and instituting affirmative action programs. The Court essentially maintained its position on civil rights until 1989, when President Reagan's three Supreme Court appointments formed the core of a new conservative majority,* but federal agencies ceased effectively enforcing civil rights laws in the early 1980s, once the new administration was in place: The Equal Employment Opportunity Commission, charged with enforcing Title VII, "stopped living up to its rules."[3] The Labor Department slackened enforcement of affirmative action requirements for federal contractors. The Justice Department, which oversees administration civil rights policy and some discrimination cases against state and local governments, took an activist stance against racial and sexual equality, targeting affirmative action programs initiated under previous administrations.[4]

The Reagan Administration was ideologically opposed to remedying systemic discrimination—inequalities resulting from biases built into the job market that affirmative action addresses. The administration shifted the focus of civil rights enforcement efforts from the forest (systemic discrimination) to the trees (discrimination's individual victims). This willingness to correct only individual instances and not patterns of discrimination held back the equal rights movement in a way that critics of equal rights feminists have yet to acknowledge. It was a way of protecting the system, ensuring that little would change.

Title VII and the Equal Employment Opportunity Commission

EEOC chair Clarence Thomas, appointed by President Reagan in 1982, presided over major policy changes governing enforcement of Title VII

---

*One exception to the Court's general, relative support for civil rights was its decision in *Grove City v. Bell*, which limited the reach of several important civil rights laws, including Title IX's guarantee of equal education.[2]

that questioned "fundamental and well-established theories of discrimination as well as the long standing approaches to remedying it," according to a recent congressional report.[5] Under Thomas's direction, the Commission challenged the use of statistical evidence establishing patterns of discrimination as well as the rule that employment practices having a disparate impact on women or minorities violate Title VII. (The disparate-impact rule, announced by the Supreme Court in 1971, has been an important weapon against systemic discrimination; it recognizes that discriminatory intent is often impossible to prove and no more important than discriminatory effect.) The Commission also reversed its support of affirmative action, declining to enforce goals and timetables in existing consent decrees that had been "accepted and endorsed" by employers and announcing its intention not to impose them in the future.[6]*

All these policy changes were related to the EEOC's refusal to recognize and remedy systemic discrimination. Statistical evidence, the disparate-impact rule, and goals and timetables are all ways of attacking a discriminatory system, which had been endorsed by the Supreme Court, the lower federal courts, and EEOC guidelines promulgated by previous administrations. Congress also recognized the need for institutional change: Title VII specifically empowers the Commission to prosecute cases involving pervasive "patterns and practices" of discrimination.

Pattern and practice cases involving racial or sexual discrimination are complicated and voluminous, requiring extensive investigations and negotiations; they generally last for years. (A major suit against General Motors initiated in 1973 was not settled until 1983.) They are cases affecting large segments of the public that demand intervention by public agencies. The Commission never has had an effective systemic enforcement program, but its problems were exacerbated by Reagan Administration policies:** The rejection of goals and timetables left Commission staff without clear, effective remedies for systemic discrim-

---

*Commission policy is set by five commissioners and generally implemented by a general council, all of whom are appointed by the President. President Reagan's nominees for these positions were controversial because they often had little experience in civil rights litigation or were overtly hostile to settled principles of antidiscrimination law. His first nominee for Commission chair, William Bell, was withdrawn. His first general counsel, a former lawyer for General Motors (the subject of a major EEOC lawsuit) resigned after two years, having been criticized for favoritism to employers.[7]

**Statistics, after all, are telling, and statistics show a marked decrease in systemic litigation initiated by the EEOC during the 1980s, as well as the Commission's increasing inefficiency.[8]

ination, and the disavowal of statistical evidence in class action or pattern and practice cases was crippling. These cases are necessarily, almost by definition, based on statistical disparities in hiring and promotion of women or minority males (and the Commission is authorized to initiate systemic, pattern and practice cases, whether or not it has received complaints from individuals). Under the direction of Clarence Thomas, however, systemic cases were required to be based on a showing of harm to individuals, which made them almost impossible to pursue.[9]

The administration's decision to prosecute individual and not institutional discrimination was a political one that reflected its antagonism to change. Individual victim cases have considerably less impact on the job market and pervasive economic inequities. They also require individual victims who are willing and able to contest their treatment and pursue cases, aware of the way in which they've been victimized and able to prove it.

This individualized, anecdotal approach to discrimination cloaked hostility toward civil rights that focused on hostility toward affirmative action and helped set back egalitarian feminism as well as the movement for minority rights. The Reagan Administration exploited the fears and resentments of white men forced to compete with women and minority males, women's own anxiety about equality and desire for protection, popular confusion over goals and quotas, and a misapprehension of affirmative action as a lowering of standards. Standards of performance, in academia and the workplace, are often inherently discriminatory: Women and minority males have traditionally been held to higher standards than white men (law and medical schools maintained their quotas for women until the 1970s), and they have traditionally been denied the education, training, and socialization needed to meet standards designed for white men. Affirmative action acknowledges the awkward truth that a history of sexual and racial discrimination requires sex- and race-conscious remedies. As Justice Blackmun stated in the *Bakke* case, "In order to get beyond racism, we must first take account of race."[10]

Affirmative Action and Executive Order 11246

The primary federal mandate for affirmative action, which was one of the Reagan Administration's primary targets, is Executive Order 11246. This order (a mandate issued by the President) dates back to a 1941 order by President Roosevelt prohibiting racial discrimination by wartime contractors. It was extended and expanded by Presidents Truman and Eisenhower and applied to all federal contractors and subcontractors. (The need for it was underscored by a Committee on Government Contracts established by President Eisenhower, which observed that minority underrepresentation reflected *"the indifference of employers to establishing a positive policy* of non-discrimination."[11]) An affirmative action requirement was added by President Kennedy in 1961 and a prohibition against sex discrimination was added in 1967 by President Johnson. Employment goals were first implemented by the Nixon Administration in 1969 and upheld in federal court.[12] Executive Order 11246 traditionally enjoyed nonpartisan executive support.

The Department of Labor, through the Office of Federal Contract Compliance Programs (OFCCP), administers the order, and in 1983 it proposed easing requirements for the recruitment and promotion of women and minorities by federal contractors, greatly reducing the number of contractors required to file affirmative action plans, disallowing complaints "alleging class type violations" that don't identify "all known victims of discrimination," and denying class action relief, such as awards of back pay, to all but "identifiable victims," instead of all employees within a class affected by discrimination.[13] These guidelines were withdrawn in response to opposition by both civil rights groups and contractors. A subsequent attempt to eliminate affirmative action by a new executive order was aborted as well. But failure to enforce the order effectively accomplished in fact what the administration could not accomplish by law. One measure of this is the decline in awards of back pay to the victims of discrimination. In 1980 over 4,000 people were awarded $9.3 million in back pay. Two years later, 1,133 people received $2.1 million.[14]

Executive Order 11246, although less well known than Title VII, can be a powerful weapon against systemic discrimination.[15] In a recently concluded case brought under the order, a Chicago bank (Harris Trust and Savings), agreed to pay a record $14 million back-pay award to women and minority males and to integrate its workforce.[16] In this case, a formidable array of evidence established that the bank had maintained a two-tiered workforce, with women and minorities at the bottom: The majority of high-paying officer jobs were held by white males; women and minorities, some of whom held college degrees, filled the majority of clerical jobs. They were paid at lower rates and progressed through the organization, if at all, at a considerably slower pace: In 1977, for example, 414 white males were promoted to officer positions after an average of 81.7 months, while 61 white females became officers after an average of 133 months.[17]

The *Harris Bank* case was complicated and costly and took fourteen years to settle (it began in 1974). Individual employees could not have successfully litigated this case on their own. It illustrates both the potential of civil rights laws attacking institutional discrimination and the need for federal enforcement of them.

Discrimination has always been a federal problem, in theory because it's unconstitutional and in fact because it's nationwide. Since President Eisenhower sent federal troops to Little Rock in 1956 to ensure integration of the public schools, the civil rights movement has dramatized the need for federal intervention to secure constitutional guarantees of equality. If the federal government hasn't always been a leader in the fight for civil rights, it has often been an ally. The FBI hounded Martin Luther King, but during the 1960s and 1970s Congress passed important new civil rights laws and the Justice Department enforced them. The Supreme Court provided some moral leadership along with expanded constitutional rights. Feminism and the struggle for minority rights have always had widespread, localized support, but neither has been simply a grassroots movement. They've depended on federal legal reforms that would trickle down and facilitate change, and some—like school desegregation, gender-neutral Social Security rules, and antidiscrimination laws—did. Progress toward racial and sexual equality has always required a federal commitment to it.

The Justice Department

The lead federal agency for pursuing claims on behalf of women and minority males is—or has been—the Justice Department's Civil Rights Division. Throughout the 1970s it initiated or joined in landmark equal employment cases and championed the use of employment goals to remedy discrimination by private employers and state and local governments. It made what the Women's Legal Defense Fund has called "extraordinary contributions" to the fight against workplace discrimination, until the 1980s.[18]

Assistant Attorney General William Bradford Reynolds, who led the Civil Rights Division during the Reagan years, was openly hostile to affirmative action and efforts to achieve what he considered a "radically egalitarian society."[19] Under his leadership, the Justice Department simply switched sides in employment discrimination cases, defending employers charged with discriminatory practices it had previously attacked or challenging employers' efforts to integrate the workplace: In *Johnson v. Transportation Agency of Santa Clara County*,[20] it challenged a plan to promote women into jobs in which they were grossly underrepresented. In *United States v. Paradise*[21] it challenged a federal court order requiring one-for-one hiring of black state troopers by the state of Alabama, until the trooper force was about 25 percent black; this order followed a finding that Alabama had engaged in a "blatant and continuous pattern of discrimination," in a case in which the Justice Department had originally sided with black officers. In both these cases, the Department lost and the affirmative action plan was upheld by the Supreme Court.

Challenging settled antidiscrimination law, the Department reopened cases in which consent decrees had already been signed and affirmative action plans were successfully operating—plans the Justice Department, under previous administrations, had sought and supported. This was consistent with Department policy of focusing on occasional instances of "reverse discrimination" against white males, instead of pervasive patterns of discrimination against women and minorities. It tried to overturn fifty affirmative action consent decrees around the country, while filing an annual average of fifteen cases alleging employment discrimination against women and minority males.[22]

What is perhaps most striking about this campaign is that it did not reflect employer dissatisfaction with affirmative action: None of the cities that had initiated affirmative action programs pursuant to consent decrees joined in the Justice Department's effort to overturn them.[23] The Department was also rebuffed by the federal courts and by the Supreme Court, which upheld the use of race-conscious preferences to remedy a history of discrimination and the provision of affirmative relief to members of a class affected by discrimination, not merely to known, individual victims.[24] The Justice Department did not lose its direct challenges to affirmative action gracefully. It subsequently announced support for collateral attacks on affirmative action programs by people who claimed to have been hurt by them. In other words, it offered support to white males who initiated their own reverse-discrimination lawsuits.[25]

The Department was finally vindicated shortly after President Reagan left office by two 1989 decisions by the Supreme Court that effectively reversed its position on affirmative action. Both these cases involved racial discrimination, but they reflect and will affect the Court's view of sexual discrimination too. Racial and sexual equality have always been tied because they involve similar processes of stereotyping and a similar disregard for history. History is a primary issue in the affirmative action debate, and the irony of the Court's reversal of affirmative action is that it occurred in two cases involving historic discrimination in which the need for race-conscious hiring was particularly clear; they're worth reviewing.

In *Martin v. Wilkes*[26] the Court held that longstanding affirmative action plans by employers with a history of discriminating against minorities may be subject to subsequent challenges by whites. This case involved an eight-year-old affirmative action plan adopted by the formerly all-white Birmingham, Alabama, Fire Department, to settle a 1974 NAACP lawsuit, after a federal district court found the department guilty of violating Title VII; a court-approved consent decree required remedial hiring and promotional goals for black firefighters. In allowing collateral attacks on this plan by white firefighters, the Court went against the well-established principle limiting people not involved in a lawsuit from litigating its issues anew in subsequent actions. But if it is difficult to imagine employers implementing affirmative action programs in the future that may be subject to endless legal claims of reverse discrimination, it is even more difficult to imagine how the Birmingham Fire Department might have been integrated without an affirmative action hiring plan.

Taking account of race and sex helped expand opportunities for women and minority males during the 1970s and changed the way employers and state and local governments did business. Another irony of the Court's 1989 decisions is that, despite popular opposition to affirmative action, private employers and public officials are not necessarily anxious to change back, as reaction to the Court's attack on minority set-aside programs showed. Over two-thirds of the states and 200 cities have instituted remedial goals or quotas or require good-faith efforts to increase the share of minority businesses in public works. If some localities instituted these programs grudgingly, in response to lawsuits and antidiscrimination policies of previous administrations, many have since embraced them. City and state officials throughout the country expressed concern and some dismay over the Supreme Court's recent decision in *City of Richmond v. Croson* striking down a Richmond, Virginia, ordinance requiring that minority businesses receive at least 30 percent of city contracts.[27]

Before the Richmond plan was enacted, the share of black contractors in city contracts was less than 1 percent, although more than half of Richmond's population is black. Minority (and female) firms still suffer from the effects of past discrimination, as the U.S. Civil Rights Commission observed in 1975: Discrimination has left them with "deficiencies in working capital, inability to meet bonding requirements, disabilities caused by an inadequate 'track' record, lack of awareness of bidding opportunities, unfamiliarity with bidding procedures, preselection before the formal advertising process, and the exercise of discretion by government procurement officers to disfavor minority businesses."[28] In other words, minorities (and women) have been shut out of the network of contractors who receive public contracts and enjoy access to working capital, and affirmative action is needed to let them in. When government ignores this and "channels all its contracting funds to a white-dominated community of established contractors," Justice Marshall suggested in his dissent in the *Richmond* case, it endorses and perpetuates racial inequities.

Color-blind guarantees of opportunity alone have not compensated for a history of racial discrimination. In Richmond a ban on discrimination by public or private contractors did not increase the share of minority businesses, as the 30 percent set-aside did.[29] According to one city official, the 30 percent rule also encouraged the formation of black-owned businesses and decreased black unemployment. Was it unfair to white-owned businesses? Perhaps. But justice often requires a balancing of inequities. Affirmative action is less unfair to white males than the present system—discrimination's legacy—is to women and minorities.

Still, fairness is rarely a match for self-interest, and affirmative action pits the economic interests of women and minorities against those of white men. That racial and sexual equality might be in everyone's long-term interest is an idealistic notion with little practical political appeal. But the government is supposed to uphold constitutional rights and ideals of equality, not pander to popular prejudice. One of the great failings of the Reagan Administration that did great harm to women and minority males was its appeal to ignorance and fear of social change.

The Reagan Administration's disdain for egalitarianism, radical or not, was pervasive and destructive of whatever heterogeneous community Americans might imagine they have. It included initial opposition to extending the Voting Rights Act and even support for racially discriminatory schools[30] and affected public attitudes toward integration as well as legal rights. If greed became respectable during the 1980s, so did states' rights (the old code word for segregation), in the form of the "new federalism," and resistance to demands for sexual and racial equality. To suggest that the victims of discrimination should rely on "self-help" instead of the federal government in their fight for relief is to deny that systemic discrimination exists and requires systemic solutions.

Businesses, academia, and the professions didn't begin admitting women and minority males during the 1970s because it was the right thing to do. It was what they had to do, in response to federal law and some concomitant social pressure. (Employers will also institute day-care and parental leave programs when they must, either under federal or state laws or pressure from male and female employees.) The Reagan Administration's hostility to civil rights limited the gains made by women and minorities during the 1980s. That the equal rights movement hasn't yet achieved equality is hardly the fault of egalitarian feminists nor does it disprove the justice or feasibility of equality as a goal. It reflects, instead, the extent to which discrimination is systemic and difficult to eradicate, as well as the federal government's willingness to tolerate it. Feminists ought not to be blamed for the failures of the system they're attacking.

·10·

Pregnancy, Child Care, and the Workplace

Egalitarian feminists are routinely blamed for overlooking the problem of pregnancy for wage-earning women. Support for equality is routinely mistaken for an unwillingness to accommodate the indisputable, inescapable differences between male and female reproductive roles—instead of a refusal to continue exaggerating them. Assertions that not all women are generally weakened by pregnancy (or the mere possibility of it, as protectionists imply), and challenges to the use of pregnancy as an excuse for denying women jobs do not suggest that men and women are "the same." No two people are the same, of course, but some are comparable. And, as the pregnancy disability cases have shown, equality may require comparable and not identical treatment of male and female workers, just as it requires comparable pay.[1] If women who are disabled by pregnancy are granted disability leaves and a guarantee of reinstatement in their jobs, so should men who are disabled by heart attacks or hernias. All workers, male and female, may suffer a range of disabilities, which in an ideal workplace would be covered by worker disability plans.

The same logic ought to govern our approach to occupational hazards, to which men and women may be equally exposed. But because only women get pregnant, they have always been considered frailer than men and more "susceptible" to "industrial poisons," as Florence Kelley stated some sixty years ago, in defense of special workplace protections.[2] Because they get pregnant, women's health determines the health of "future generations," the Supreme Court stressed in 1911, when it upheld protective labor laws for women.[3] Female wage earners, pregnant or not, have always been protected at least partly for the sake of the fetus, while during the first period of industrialization men were not protected at all.

Laws limiting women's working hours or excluding them from masculine jobs are history, but questions about protecting pregnant or potentially pregnant women workers remain. Jobs involving exposure to harmful chemicals or radiation may pose risks of birth defects and miscarriages, risks employers have addressed by firing or transferring women workers exposed to them, pursuant to "fetal protection policies."

Fetal protection policies are today's analogue to turn-of-the-century protective labor laws. The term "fetal protection" is only a subterfuge for discrimination at a time when female-protection policies would be prohibited by Title VII. It also reflects the recent development of "fetal rights" theories that limit women's reproductive freedom.* Fetal protection policies evince about as much concern for women's welfare and women's rights as traditional protective labor laws and antiabortion prohibitions. They're founded on similar presumptions about female frailty and a similar disregard for male health problems and male susceptibilities to occupational hazards. They similarly limit women's access to jobs, deny them reproductive choice, and endanger men. Labor policies "protecting" women's reproductive health and ignoring men can easily be abused, with horrific results.

The worst-case scenario for women occurred in 1978 in an American Cyanamid Company plant in West Virginia. The company adopted a fetal protection policy excluding women of childbearing age from most of its jobs because they involved exposure to harmful chemicals. Only women who had been surgically sterilized were exempt from this policy. Forced to choose between losing their jobs or their capacity to bear children, five women underwent sterilization. The department in which they worked was eliminated one year later, and the women employees eventually went to court. They charged that the woman-only fetal protection policy violated Title VII's prohibition of sex discrimination

*For a discussion of reproductive rights, see *supra* Chapter 12.

and the Occupational Safety and Health Act (OSHA), arguing that forcing women to choose between sterilization and employment violated the employer's duty to maintain a safe workplace. The Title VII case was settled, and the OSHA case lost by the women employees, in the United States Court of Appeals. In an opinion by Judge Bork, the court characterized their decision to undergo sterilization as an "employee reaction to the employer policy," for which the company could not be held liable. "No statute redresses all grievances," he added.[4]

This was a notorious case but not an entirely anomalous one. According to Joan Bertin, of the ACLU Reproductive Rights Project, "Many of the Country's largest corporations," including General Motors, Gulf Oil, Dow, and Du Pont, have at one time adopted fetal protection policies applying only to women. Exclusionary policies are depriving women of "hundreds of thousands" of jobs, often on the basis of inconclusive information, Bertin stresses: Instead of facts, they tend to rely on assumptions about maternal and fetal vulnerability and a fixation on feminine frailty. They ignore occupational hazards posed to male reproductive health—sterility and birth defects due to a father's exposure to toxic substances.[5]

Lack of evidence about the special reproductive harm occupational hazards pose to women, and not men, should invalidate fetal protection policies under Title VII, as some federal cases suggest. In *Hayes v. Shelby Memorial Hospital*[6] the firing of a pregnant X–ray technician was struck down as a violation of the Pregnancy Discrimination Act (an amendment to Title VII). The Court of Appeals held that the exclusion of pregnant women from the workplace could be justified only by proof that workplace toxins presented a substantial risk to the fetus and to female (but not male) reproductive health. *Zuniga v. Kleberg County Hospital*[7] invalidated the firing of a pregnant X–ray technician on different grounds, as a "mere pretext" for discrimination. *Wright v. Olin*[8] held that a restriction on jobs available to fertile women (all those between the ages of five and sixty-three not certified as sterile) was a prima facie violation of Title VII, leaving employers to prove its necessity. This approach to fetal protection policies does not, however, insure their demise: *Auto Workers v. Johnson Controls, Inc.*[9], a recent federal court decision, upheld a policy similar to the one involved in *Wright v. Olin*, holding that the exclusion of fertile women from the workplace was necessary and that employees failed to prove there were less discriminatory alternatives available to their employer.

Courts have not generally held that fetal protection policies constitute intentional sex discrimination, but neither have they required women

135

employees to prove that these policies reflect discriminatory intent. Fetal protection has a clear "disparate impact" on women, highlighting the importance of Title VII's requirement that the effect of a rule be considered in addition to its intent. A theory of equality that requires laws or employment practices to affect women equally can't help but take account of pregnancy.*

But if Title VII can help preserve women's jobs, it can't compel correction of a workplace hazard. Occupational safety laws should be amended to prohibit dangers to male and female reproductive health.[11] Workplace safety has not kept up with workplace technologies. The manufacture of microchips has been associated with miscarriages and birth defects among women workers; so has the use of video display terminals. The risks associated with microchips have been addressed by excluding women from "hazardous" jobs (men are available to replace them).[12] The risks associated with VDTs have been ignored or denied by some employers and by the federal government, perhaps because VDTs are used in clerical jobs that are usually filled by women:[13] When Suffolk County, New York, passed a landmark bill regulating the use of VDTs, over employer opposition, the president of one computer company observed that this bill, which made Suffolk a good place for computer operators to work, made it a "bad place to do business."[14] A federal study undertaken in 1986 by the National Institute for Occupational Safety and Health of the connection between VDTs and miscarriages was "significantly weakened" by the President's Office of Management and Budget (OMB), which required deletion of important questions about fertility and stress.[15]

If the hazards believed to be posed by VDTs are eventually confirmed, employers will be faced with a problem: They'll have to find a way to protect women workers without firing them because no army of male clerical workers stands ready to replace them. Men who use VDTs may have to be protected from them too: VDTs have been associated with eye strain and back trouble as well as miscarriages. Whether they also endanger male reproductive health is a question no one seems to be asking.

There's an important link between failure to provide a safe workplace for both sexes and the traditional, protectionist concern for women's special vulnerabilities. Fetal protection policies make this clear; so did a

*Title VII rules regarding discriminatory effect have been considered weakened by the Supreme Court's recent decision increasing employees' burden of proof in disparate-impact cases.[10]

1977 Supreme Court decision, *Dothard v. Rawlinson*, allowing the exclusion of women from jobs as prison guards because of the risk of rape from male inmates.[16] In an overcrowded, underfunded prison, male guards are subject to assaults as well. Firing women was a way of avoiding, instead of addressing, the need for penal reform.

Blacks have suffered too from the tendency of employers to blame employees for "susceptibilities" to workplace hazards. Congressman John Conyers has pointed out that blacks are assigned to the "dirtiest and most hazardous jobs" (and exposed disproportionately to toxins in the home because of their relative poverty). Yet their resultant health problems, such as a high cancer rate, are blamed on their life styles or "immoderate personal habits."[17] Racist presumptions about the irresponsibility of black people and an obsession with female sexuality, reflected in fetal protection policies, allow employers to turn problems with the workplace into problems with workers—women and minority males.

Blaming the victim justifies the status quo. If women are naturally handicapped, less than equal workers, then occupational segregation is natural, not the contrivance of discriminatory employment practices. The current debate about equality and protectionism is, in part, a debate about the causes of the dual labor market. Most feminists agree that motherhood is a primary obstacle to equality. Pink-collar women and professionals alike end up in de facto "mommy-track" jobs because despite the emergence of a few "new men," women still bear primary responsibility for child care. But it's not clear that in a feminist world women would still be society's primary caregivers. Do nurturing and domesticity come more naturally to women because they're the only ones who get pregnant? Do they place themselves in less demanding, lower-paying jobs out of a natural, freely chosen, prior commitment to home and family?

The question was put before the federal courts in an unsuccessful discrimination case brought by the EEOC against Sears, Roebuck, the nation's largest retailer of general merchandise.[18] Initiated in 1973, this case charged Sears with excluding women from "big ticket," commissioned sales jobs, which generated big commissions. To prove patterns of discrimination, the EEOC relied heavily on statistical evidence (the case was brought before the Commission eschewed the use of statistics): Between 1973 and 1980 the number of women applying for sales jobs was nearly double the number hired for commission sales; women constituted about 61 percent of full-time sales applicants and 32 percent of commissioned sales employees.[19]

Confronted with evidence of statistical disparities in hiring and promoting women, Sears argued that women tended to be interested only in lower-paying, noncommissioned sales work because it was easier—less competitive, less "dog-eat-dog"—than commissioned sales. They exhibited "discomfit or unfamiliarity with most product lines sold on commission at Sears," which included such "male-oriented" products as hardware and heavy appliances, automotive parts, and installed home improvements, and they believed that "the increased earning potential of commissioned selling was not worth the additional responsibilities, problems, pressures, and uncertainty."[20]

Sears won this case in 1986; the district court questioned the use of statistics to prove discrimination and was pursuaded by the stereotypic portrait of women drawn by Sears. Women applying for sales jobs were "most often interested in selling soft lines of merchandise, such as clothing, jewelry, and cosmetics items generally not sold on commission at Sears," the court held. It then offered some familiar, general observations about women wage earners: "Women tend to be more interested than men in the social and cooperative aspects of the workplace. Women tend to see themselves as less competitive. They often view noncommission sales as more attractive than commission sales, because they can enter and leave the job more easily and because there is more social contact and friendship, and less stress in noncommission selling." The court adopted the characterization of women as contented second-class workers: "Noncommission saleswomen were generally happier with their present job at Sears, and were much less likely than their male counterparts to be interested in other positions, such as commission sales."[21]

Because it turned on the relationship of women's "nature" to their place in the economy—the notion that an individual's professional ambition is determined by sex—this case raised crucial questions for feminists involved in the sameness/difference debate. Sears charged the EEOC with making assumptions about "male/female sameness with respect to preferences, interests, and qualifications," but the EEOC might have responded that it was only challenging a historic presumption about male/female difference. The difference involved in this case was not even biological: It was a personality difference, a difference in ambition, skills, and, as Sears said, "preference."

According to Sears, commissioned sales work requires "aggressiveness, desire, 'hunger,' or more generally motivation," and a "burning desire to succeed," traits that men apparently exhibit more often than women. A hiring guide used by Sears described an ideal commissioned salesperson as someone who is "active and has a lot of drive," "considerable physical vigor [and] a liking for tools," along with "work which requires physical energy." This guide, written in 1953, originally referred to the ideal commissioned salesperson as a man. Sears amended these references so that the guide appeared gender-neutral, without amending it in substance. As the EEOC charged, the manual continued to describe a commissioned salesperson as a stereotypical male.[22]

Whether or not women are, by nature, less aggressive and competitive than men, they are conditioned to be so and discouraged from applying for jobs said to require aggression and an overwhelming hunger to succeed. Sears exploited their conditioning by masculinizing what should be a gender-neutral job. Underlying the masculine description of an ideal salesperson is the questionable assumption that "feminine" qualities—sociability and a sensitivity to emotional nuances—are not relevant to sales work. Good salespeople, after all, describe themselves as amateur psychologists who rely on their ability to "read" customers. The irony about the Sears case for women was that the higher-paying jobs that were denied them included the sort of jobs culture had equipped them well to do: Surely women have an edge over men in selling washing machines.

The EEOC didn't press the argument about the inherently discriminatory standard for commissioned sales work used by Sears; nor did it question the fairness of a system that offered higher wages in departments that tended, for whatever reason, to be dominated by men. Why weren't women selling "softer" merchandise compensated in some way for not receiving commissions? (Was the retail mark-up on automotive parts so much higher than the mark-up on jewelry?) The division of noncommission and commission departments, the characterization of an ideal salesperson on which Sears relied, and its two-tiered wage system reflected a judgment about the relative value of male and female workers. Women were less valuable, less committed to their jobs, according to Sears, partly because they were more committed to family life.

There are divergent feminist theories supporting both sides of the underlying debate about women, work, and family, and two prominent feminist scholars were enlisted as witnesses by Sears and the EEOC, respectively. Historian Rosalind Rosenberg of Barnard College, testifying for Sears, confirmed that "women tend to place family commitments ahead of career aspirations" and to be "more relationship centered. . . . Men tend to be more work centered."[23] Historian Alice Kessler Harris of

139

Hofstra University disagreed with Rosenberg's contention that women's job choices are determined by the "values they have internalized."[24]

Women's choices depend on the opportunities with which they're presented, Harris argued, as a history of female labor force participation demonstrates. Office work was originally considered masculine until employers discovered women could type. During wartime women proved themselves adept at performing men's jobs, and in 1917, Harris observed, clerical and low-level management jobs in banking were opened to women because of a labor shortage. Women were then said to be "exceptionally fitted for work of this character—their neatness, deft handling of money and papers, tact, and a certain intuitive judgment all [counted] in their favor." When men became available for bank jobs during the Depression, women were suddenly considered poor candidates for them, "because they were poor at figures, and because the public would not accept the notion of handing their money over to women." Sexual divisions of labor are "malleable"; they're determined by economics and labor shortages, not nature.[25] (They're also determined by culture; the fields of law and medicine were once considered even more masculine than commissioned sales.)

"Choice can only be understood in the framework of available opportunity," Alice Kessler Harris stressed. "Where opportunities have existed, women have never failed to take the jobs offered. When opportunities have been closed to them, women have rationalized their inability to participate fully in the world of work with notions of domesticity."[26]

It's fair to say opportunities are still closed to women because a dual labor market will take time to dismantle and because equal opportunities have not been effectively enforced or supplemented by child care and a new division of domestic responsibilities between men and women. Recent critics of the equal rights movement who have focused on alleged feminist disregard for women's commitment to family life or child-care needs have underscored the irrelevance of expanded opportunities for wage-earning mothers without day care or helpful spouses. But in blaming feminists for the dearth of day care, they have exploited, or been exploited by, the most regressive stereotypes of independent, self-supporting women.

Of all the charges leveled against equal rights feminists in recent years, the most mean-spirited and misguided involve their alleged indifference and even hostility toward children and wage-earning mothers. "The modern women's movement has not just been anti-men," according to one popular, protectionist feminist tract. "It has been profoundly anti-children and anti-motherhood."[27] Another recent protectionist attack on the equal rights movement charges that child care has been given only "casual" attention by feminists, partly because they "have clung to the myth" of the private, "self-sufficient family."[28]

Feminists who bravely banged their heads against the walls of familial privacy that shielded family violence for so many years would be surpised to hear they cherish the private autonomous family. So would early feminist advocates of day care along with right-wing antifeminists like Phyllis Schlafly, who accused "women's libbers" of trying to "replace mother care with government care." According to Schlafly, feminists fought to make federally funded child care available "for 'all socioeconomic groups' regardless of means," in a conspiracy to destroy the nuclear family.[29] In fact, twenty years ago, feminists were more often condemned for promoting day care than not and spreading the vaguely communistic ethos it was thought to imply. Ellie Smeal, former president of NOW, recalls being "red-baited" on the subject of day care, pointing out that President Nixon vetoed a federal child-care assistance bill passed by Congress in 1971 (the Comprehensive Community Child Care Development Act) because it would "sovieticize" American children.

This act, supported by feminists, would have established federally assisted educational, nutritional, and health services for preschool children. Services were to be funded jointly by federal, state, and local governments and made available to children of all socioeconomic backgrounds, for a fee, which was waived or greatly reduced for poor families. Child-care programs were to be designed at the "community level" with "full involvement of parents and other organizations in the community interested in child development."[30] In vetoing this program, President Nixon cited the "family weakening implications of the system it envisions." It was "the most radical piece of legislation to emerge from the 92nd Congress," and it "would commit the vast moral authority of the National Government to the side of communal approaches to child rearing over the family centered approach."[31]

Social issue activists on the right still associate day care with communism, the decline of family life, and the ruination of children (along with drug abuse, teenage pregnancy, and other ills blamed on feminism and the sexual revolution). Day care is the "thalidomide of the 1980s," according to the Rockford Institute Center on the Family in America. Right-wing, profamily groups are organizing against "nefarious" federal family leave and child-care proposals, which are still condemned as items on a "radical feminist" agenda.[32] Ideological opposition to day care and parental leave policies has been marginalized by demographic changes—the increased labor force participation of young mothers. But in the early 1970s, when President Nixon vetoed the Child Care Development Act, day care was primarily a feminist issue, not a hot popular one: Wage earning was not yet considered normal or respectable for middle-class women with young children. The dream of the one-income family still prevailed and dictated attitudes toward child care.

Until middle-class white families began demanding day care, it was viewed as a response to something gone wrong—a remedy for troubled families or troubled times. Federal child-care assistance was welfare or an emergency wartime measure, associated strictly with poverty and the absence of a male breadwinner. The most widespread and long-standing form of child-care assistance in this country has been the Aid to Families with Dependent Children program that began during the Depression as Aid to Dependent Children. Aside from Head Start programs, part of the 1960s War on Poverty, the only significant federal preschool programs were instituted during the Depression and World War II: In the 1930s Works Progress Administration nurseries were established "not so much to meet the child care needs of working mothers [but] to furnish wholesome environments for children from low income families and to provide jobs for teachers, nurses, and dieticians."[33] By 1938, 1,900 nursery schools served an estimated 200,000 children. According to a federal report on the WPA, nursery programs demonstrated the value of nurseries as "an efficient and beneficial mode of child care," which had a "special usefulness" during the war years.[34] During World War II federal nurseries provided care for the children of working mothers, war workers, and men in the armed services. Funding for these nurseries ended with the war to ensure that women would give back their jobs and go home.[35]

This grudging willingness to provide day care only for "abnormal" families (poor or fatherless ones) persisted through the 1970s, shaping child-care policies. It both reflected and reinforced popular disapproval of mothers who worked outside the home and a rejection of "welfare state" policies. It helped protect men's jobs and male-headed, hierarchical families. Day care has always been essential to the economic emancipation of women and the welfare of children in single-parent and dual-income families, and it has always been a feminist issue.

The reversal of popular attitudes toward day care that occurred in the 1980s was as dramatic as the increase of wage-earning mothers. In 1970 about one-fourth of all women with children under three years old worked outside the home; by 1985 one-half of them did.[36] Over one-half of all new mothers remain in the workforce, and in over one-half of all two-parent families with children under six, both parents hold jobs.[37] Economic changes have normalized the need for day care in a way that feminist ideology never could. *Time* magazine has called day care "the most wrenching personal problem facing millions of American families."[38] Politicians on all sides promise to solve it. Venture capitalists seek to exploit it.[39] Magazine artices about the "crisis in day care" abound.

Day care is widely proclaimed to be *the* issue of the 1990s, perhaps because it was barely addressed in the 1980s. According to a 1988 U.S. Labor Department report, about 10 percent of the nation's employers provide child-care assistance but often in the form of counseling, referral, or information services. Only 5 percent of all business and government employers sponsor day-care centers or provide financial aid for day care to employees.[40] Less than half (40 percent) of the nation's women wage earners receive maternity leaves and job reinstatement guarantees from their companies.[41] Only about one-fourth of states provide child-care assistance to state employees, and during the 1980s,[42] while the need for child care was rising, the Reagan Administration reduced day-care subsidies to low- and middle-income families.[43] The meager child-care programs offered by business, the federal government, and the states provide American families with considerably less assistance in raising children than their counterparts in almost all other industrialized countries enjoy. Equal rights feminism didn't doubly burden women; their governments and employers did.

Government and business will probably attempt to ease women's burdens in the future in order to make them more productive. The number of corporations providing child-care assistance is rising, along with the number of wage-earning mothers. Child care is being recognized as a source of stress for wage-earning fathers too. Parental leave is as "hot" an issue as day care, and Congress has been considering parental leave legislation since the Family and Medical Leave Act was introduced in 1986. States are beginning to provide leave for state employees and to mandate it in the private sector.[44]

Solutions to the child-care "crisis" will be formulated soon, and they ought to be gender-neutral. Parental leave ought to replace maternity leave, encouraging men to stay home with their children. Comparable disability benefits ought to be extended to pregnant and nonpregnant workers and flexible work schedules made available to men and women. Domestic divisions of labor will not change quickly (women may long take more parental leaves than men), but only egalitarian approaches to child care will facilitate their changing at all.

143

·11·

Equality in the Home: Divorce, Child Custody, and Surrogacy

Change is hardest for women who least expect it—women raised under prefeminist rules to marry and stay home with their kids and remain forever one-half of a wage-earner/homemaker couple. For women without the ability or desire to shoulder them, equal responsibilities were too high a price to pay for equal rights, and egalitarian feminism was not a promise but a threat, as the Stop-ERA movement showed. The Equal Rights Amendment questioned men's "natural" obligation to support women, on which so many wives depended, and posited a world in which homemaking would be one choice for women instead of their only calling.

The ERA also posited expanded career opportunities for women; it looked ahead to what Elizabeth Cady Stanton called a "new regime" of emancipated, educated women capable of supporting themselves. Still, some preferred the old regime and relied on their husband's promise of support. Some were caught between the new and the old—the displaced homemakers of the 1970s and 1980s—living proof, it was said, of feminism's failures.

Rising divorce rates, lax enforcement of child-support laws, and the job market's inhospitality to women whose only work experience was in their homes or communities hurt many more homemakers than feminist visions of equality ever could. But right-wing traditionalists for whom marriage depends on feminine subservience blame feminism for the incidence of divorce, while mainstream protectionist critics blame feminists for no-fault divorce, the reform of alimony laws, and an erosion of presumptions favoring mothers in custody disputes, all of which are considered bad for women.

Rules about divorce changed dramatically during the 1970s and 1980s, along with ideals about marriage, child custody, wage earning for women, and sexual behavior. Attributing these changes to feminism exaggerates its power. Feminism was only part of the context in which change occurred. Economics, birth control, and the sexual revolution are as much to "blame" as feminism—if assigning blame is an appropriate response to social change that may have helped more people than it hurt. Still, gender-neutral, no-fault divorce laws, spousal maintenance, and paternal custody awards reflect egalitarian feminist ideals, and the debate about divorce and custody is, in part, a debate about equality and protection for women.

Elizabeth Cady Stanton proposed no-fault divorce a century ago, "to open the doors of escape to those who dwell in continual antagonism . . . . The freer the relations are between human beings, the happier," she wrote.[1] Imagine people staying married out of choice, not compulsion, she suggested. Imagine women enjoying equal professional opportunities and being able to move in and out of marriage as readily as men.

Stanton was further ahead of her time than even she realized. The nation's first no-fault divorce law was passed by California in 1970. Supported by a mix of feminists, liberal reformers, and divorced men who resented paying alimony, it allowed either spouse to end a marriage without alleging grounds for divorce or obtaining the other spouse's consent. In other words, it allowed men or women to end their marriages unilaterally, for no particular reason. This is a pure no-fault law. Modified versions of no-fault divorce allow for divorce by consent of both parties and mix no-fault with traditional fault-based divorce, so a spouse who doesn't agree to a divorce can be sued for one, if he or she has committed some marital transgression. All the states now have some form of no-fault.[2]

No-fault divorce doesn't simply loosen the bonds of matrimony; it privatizes them, by giving people permission to divorce as they choose, without meeting conditions set down by the state. This tacitly challenges the traditional protectionist view of marriage as a trap set by women, from which the law won't let men escape, and the traditional view of men as philanderers. The notion that American family life depends on men's legal obligations to stay with and support their wives and children, not their willingness to do so, underlies much opposition to liberalized divorce. No-fault divorce idealizes marriage as a voluntary union of equals.

New laws governing the distribution of marital property on divorce also reflected this changing view of marriage as a partnership. Divorce reforms (and emerging constitutional standards of equality) expanded women's property rights on divorce, giving them a share in what had previously been owned solely by their husbands, as heads and masters of the household. The experience in New York State is instructive. In 1980 New York adopted an equitable distribution law, defining marriage as an economic partnership and requiring the equitable distribution of marital property on divorce. The concept of marital property was new to New York law. Until 1980 New York had been a title state: Each spouse retained ownership of separate property by retaining title to it; divorce was simple and hard on women. As primary titleholders, husbands got most of the property and wives got alimony, leaving them as dependent on their husbands after divorce as they were during marriage. Now title is irrelevant. With few exceptions, essentially all property acquired during the marriage is shared, or marital property, which includes not only houses, co-ops, and cars but also intangibles such as professional degrees and pension rights. A wife now can claim a share in her husband's law or medical degree and practice.

Equitable distribution was intended to be good for women, and compared to New York's old law, it hasn't been too bad. It gave wives unprecedented rights in what had long been considered their husband's property. When title determined ownership, women had no right to share in "his" business, "his" law practice, "his" stock portfolio, and other property in his name until he died. What they had was a right to be supported during marriage, which was difficult to enforce, and a derivative right to alimony, which was difficult to collect. The old law was based on a view of women as dependents in a hierarchical relationship. Equitable distribution made them partners in a marital enterprise.

But it did not necessarily make them equal partners, and the charge that wives are not getting their rightful share (half) of the marital property is a primary basis for complaints about reform by feminists on both sides of the sameness/difference debate. New York's equitable distribution law, for example, does not entitle women to one-half of the marital property; it entitles them to whatever share of it the judge deems fair, under the circumstances, considering the length of the marriage, the contributions of each spouse, their "probable future financial circumstances," and ten other factors listed by the legislature. The equitable distribution law vests considerable discretion in the courts; it's a law that's as good as the judges applying it.

According to the 1986 "New York State Task Force Report on Women in the Courts,"[3] New York's judges have not been fair or good to women. They tend to undervalue a homemaker's role in her husband's career; they underestimate the work involved in keeping house as well as the struggles facing women trying to enter the working world after many years at home. As a result, in long-term marriages, women have been receiving up to about one-third, not one-half, of the marital property, which, depending on your view of the marriage relation, is either small recompense or a windfall.

They've also been receiving relatively short-term maintenance awards instead of long-term alimony, intensifying protectionist critiques of reform. But equitable distribution and the expansion of women's property rights were supposed to obviate alimony by giving women new financial independence. In New York, courts are empowered to award maintenance to the needier spouse (instead of alimony) "as justice requires"; the amount and duration of maintenance, like the distribution of marital property, is left to the discretion of the court, considering the circumstances of the case.

But according to the "New York State Task Force Report," judges have not been sensitive to the economic circumstances of women or cognizant of a wife's contribution to her husband's earning power. In long-term marriages, women with little earning potential of their own have been awarded short-term maintenance, generally appropriate only in short-term marriages when the dependent spouse can reasonably be expected to become self-supporting. For middle-class women, this can be devastating, as the report points out: Maintenance awards are often more important to women than the distribution of property because the income of the family breadwinner is often the primary marital asset.

Women have a case against divorce reform, as it has been construed by judges. It's fair to suggest that these reported abuses—inappropriate rehabilitative maintenance awards and denial to women of a fair share of marital property—are the fault of courts applying the law, not the legislature that wrote it. They're not the fault of egalitarian feminists who envisioned marriage as a partnership, not a hierarchy. Judges have the power under New York's law to order long-term maintenance for homemakers who need and have earned it or to award women half shares in their marital estates. What they apparently lack is the inclination to do so.

Divorce laws can be highly discretionary; to have faith in them, you have to have faith in judges. Awards to women in New York State are said to be increasing, but whether the law should mandate a fifty-fifty property split as a general rule, leaving either spouse to prove it's unfair, in any particular case, is a controversial question for husbands, wives, lawyers, and feminists. How you answer it depends not just on your conception of gender roles but on your view of judges.

In her landmark study of California's new no-fault divorce law, Lenore Weitzman points out the tendency of judges to underestimate women's financial needs, as well as their contribution to the marriage;[4] male judges tend to side, in effect, with the husband. In carrying out California's new legal mandate to make women self-sufficient after divorce, Weitzman found that judges "are applying minimal and unrealistic standards of self-sufficiency and denying support to most divorced women."[5] These standards are even being applied to women who are supposed to be exempt from them—custodial mothers, women needing transitional support, and older homemakers for whom self-sufficiency isn't feasible. Judges still tend to consider a husband's income "his" income, not the income of his family, and they don't like separating him from much of it. Judges "rarely" require men to support their former wives and children half as well as they support themselves, even when they can afford to do so.[6]

It's possible to infer from this not just gender bias but vindictiveness on the part of judges applying the new divorce laws in what they may consider to be a postfeminist world. It's as if they were paying back feminists for demanding equality by thrusting it on women who were raised to be content with inequality and shaped their lives around it. A full-time homemaker who has sacrificed her professional opportunities to her family is not the economic equal of her husband and ought not be treated as such. Homemakers, male or female, generally have legitimate financial claims on the spouses whose homes they've made—claims that are consistent with egalitarianism. The right of a homemaker to continuing support has less to do with gender than with agreed-on divisions of labor within a family—the bargain made between husband and wife. Spousal support is a matter of fundamental fairness, as the California Court of Appeals stressed in a 1977 decision overturning a "niggardly" alimony award to a homemaker and charging the lower court with using the alimony statute as a "handy vehicle for the summary disposal of old and used wives."

> In those cases in which it is the decision of the parties that the woman becomes the homemaker, the marriage is of substantial duration, and at the separation the wife is to all intents and purposes unemployable, the husband simply has to face up to the fact that his support responsibilities are going to be of extended duration—perhaps for life. This has nothing to do with feminism, sexism, male chauvinism, or any other trendy social ideology. It is ordinary common sense, basic decency, and simply justice.[7]

Judges do not always exhibit sense or decency or mete out justice to women, as the California court observed, and that is not the fault of feminists. Egalitarian feminism recognizes that egalitarian marriage is still only an ideal, not a fact, for many women. It does not advocate denying homemakers the support they've been promised or imposing standards of self-sufficiency on women who have been denied the training and experience needed to meet them. It does require that maintenance awards and property divisions be gender-neutral, so as not to validate the principle of feminine dependency or accept it as an unalterable fact of life: A housewife deserves maintenance because she's a housewife, not because she's a woman. Egalitarianism also questions the good of a system that encourages women to be housewives and provides relatively few opportunities and little support (such as assistance with child care) to women who want to be something else.

Despite the injustices judges sometimes visit on women in the name of equality, divorce reforms have, on balance, benefited women by creating new rights to marital property and setting forth a new ideal of marriage as a partnership, an ideal future generations may enjoy. The failures of reform have generally been failures in the ways the new laws are applied, not in how they were conceived; they're more judicial than legislative failures. They don't discredit the concept of no-fault divorce (and can't fairly or logically be blamed on feminism), and they don't make the old laws look good.

Divorce has never been the boondoggle for women that Johnny Carson's alimony jokes imply. Even under traditional laws, alimony was awarded to a "small percentage" of women, in small amounts that were notoriously difficult to collect.[8] There were also systematic failures by the states to enforce men's obligation to pay child support, which new federal legislation addresses.[9] Divorce has always been a financial disaster for women homemakers; they've almost always been left with their children, maybe their house, and less work time, fewer marketable skills, and less experience than their husbands. No-fault divorce didn't make being divorced any harder, in general, for women.

It did, however, make getting divorced easier for their husbands. In a traditional fault-based system, people couldn't obtain divorces unless their spouses gave them grounds, such as adultery, mental cruelty, or abandonment. Innocent spouses could stay legally married forever, if they chose, or they could agree to a divorce, for a price. Fault-based divorce gave them a bargaining chip. A stereotypical philandering, wage-earning husband who wanted to "trade in" his stereotypical faithful, long-suffering wife might be made to pay for the privilege of doing so. He might also have to pay for his marital transgressions. But in a pure no-fault system, fault affects neither the underlying right to get divorced nor the distribution of marital property, and people are allowed to violate their marriage contracts with impunity.

This failure to hold people accountable for the sufferings they inflict on their spouses, which has nothing to do with feminism, is one of the most controversial aspects of no-fault divorce. Denying an injured spouse the right to revenge (or what some prefer to call retribution) violates a common sense of fairness; revenge, after all, is some justice. Being betrayed by a spouse is devastating and, as divorce lawyers say, so is learning the law will not recognize, much less exact a price for, your betrayal.[10]

One solution to this is a hybrid system in which no-fault principles govern the basic right to get divorced but not the distribution of property: People would be free to divorce, unilaterally, regardless of fault; their marital behavior, however, would help determine the divorce settlement. But no-fault laws were adopted partly because judges wanted to get out of the business of deciding who did what to whom—assessing the guilt and innocence of warring spouses—and avenging their wrongs. No-fault was supposed to dignify the process of divorce by shielding it from marital squabbling. And in an ideal world, it would: No-fault would be a rational, just way of evaluating the needs of each spouse and their contributions to the marriage and dividing their property accordingly. Ideally, each side would be equally well represented, courts would make fair property settlements, uneffected by gender biases, and injured spouses would find more appropriate forums in which to vent their rage.

But in this world, women tend to be poorer than men and less able to afford the cost of litigation. The spouse with a higher income and control of more property, usually the husband, can effectively force a settlement in his favor by delaying litigation, blocking discovery proceedings aimed at determining the extent of his holdings, sitting back and letting the meter run. Like most laws, no-fault and equitable distribution work best for people who can afford to make sure they're effectively enforced. Women are disadvantaged on divorce not by feminism but by the poverty and dependence that accompany traditional feminine roles.

The irony of protectionist feminism is its support for tradition, which underlies much current dissatisfaction with divorce reforms. Laws about divorce, like laws about marriage, help define the roles men and women are expected to play. The divorce debate is, in large part, a debate about femininity and child rearing, and it rages most intensely around the issue of child custody.

One casualty of the equal rights movement and changing ideals about family life has been the tender-years presumption that required courts to award custody of young children to mothers unless they were shown to be unfit. By 1981 that presumption had been abandoned in about two-thirds of the states. Now custody is generally determined by the "best interests of the child." The demise of the maternal presumption should be welcomed by feminists: Equality requires gender-neutral custody laws that treat men and women equally, presuming them to be equally fit parents. It requires eliminating sexual stereotypes epitomized by laws that pay deference to women's "superior" parenting skills, compassion, emotional sensitivity, and capacity for nurturance. It recognizes that not all mothers are better parents than all fathers.

This does not ignore the fact that women tend to spend more time with children and bear primary responsibility for raising them, nor does it suggest that familial roles should not effect custodial rights. Justice may require gender-neutral laws favoring "primary caretakers" in custody disputes. Women who stay home with their children should probably be awarded custody of them, as a general rule, because they've stayed home with them, not because they are women.

Still, protectionist feminists and other defenders of women's superior parenting instincts oppose even a primary-caretaker rule because it exposes women to custody challenges from which they should, in this view, be legally protected. Although the great majority of women retain custody of their children on divorce (partly because their husbands don't demand it), increasing numbers of them are said to be losing custody in disputed cases.[11] Whether or not custody disputes are being fairly decided is impossible to discern. In the popular feminist view, women are "losing their children" because judges impose higher standards of parenting on them and punish them for being sexually active, for example, or for violating other codes of feminine behavior. Judges are also said to favor the parent with more money, which is usually the father. The decline of the maternal presumption is blamed too for facilitating bad-faith custody challenges by men intent on blackmailing their wives into unfavorable divorce settlements.[12]

The use of a custody challenge as a negotiating tool is a common problem in divorce cases and a serious one for women. But it does not justify a presumption that all custody challenges are merely legal ploys or an across-the-board rule denying equal custodial rights to all men. It may best be addressed by educating judges and imposing sanctions on spouses who bring frivolous custody cases in order to extort settlements. The judicial process is often abused by litigants in a wide range of civil and criminal cases (it's not a problem unique to divorce courts); curbing that abuse is one of the judiciary's primary responsibilities.

The "problem" of judges' holding women to higher standards of parenting is less clear. Charges of discrimination against women are supported primarily by anecdotal evidence and movies like *The Good Mother*. Countercharges of discrimination against men are becoming nearly as common and are supported anecdotally as well. The maternal presumption may have been erased from the statute books, some matrimonial lawyers suggest, but it's engraved in the hearts and minds of judges. ("The ghost of everyone's mother walks the courthouse corridors," one prominent New York divorce lawyer claims.)[13] All that can finally be said is that perhaps judges in local divorce courts across the country are discriminating against men and perhaps they're discriminating against women. But women who believe they're being victimized by male judges with traditional ideals about mothering and femininity ought to understand that these are the underlying ideals of the maternal presumption. The notion that a good mother is not sexually active is bound to the view of a good woman as sweet, sensitive, and instinctively parental. Alleged double standards of parenting for men and women provide a compelling argument against the maternal presumption, which enshrines stereotypes and double standards—and for gender-neutral custody rules. If charges of discrimination against women are true, then female chauvinists are being victimized once again by the same stereotypes they're advancing.

Men are occasionally victimized by protectionist stereotypes too, especially when they seek parental rights in relation to children born out of wedlock. Unwed fathers do not enjoy the same rights as unwed mothers. Adoption laws in many states provide that in order for an unwed father legally to contest an adoption, he must first have declared his paternity, offered financial support to the child's mother, and lived with her for a stated period. Mothers, however, are automatically required to consent to adoptions, whether they're married or not, by virtue of their motherhood. Women must act affirmatively to give up their children; men must take action to retain them. One justification for these distinctions is practical; expanding unwed father's rights will introduce uncertainty into adoption proceedings and may discourage adoptions by couples fearful of facing custodial challenges from fathers who unexpectedly turn up and want their babies back. But adoption laws also reflect gender biases and the common presumption that men who want their children will marry the women who bear them; the image of an unwed father as an irresponsible, untrustworthy philanderer is one of our most resilient stereotypes.

But mores about marriage and cohabitation are changing, and principles of sexual equality are encouraging courts to reexamine double standards of parenting within and outside of marriage. Family law is changing, and challenges by unwed fathers are increasing and opening up a new area of law.[14] In some states, fathers are slowly winning new rights in adoption cases. In a recent New York case an unwed father was granted custody of a seven-month-old girl after the mother had given her up for adoption at birth.[15] The father in this case (identified simply as Gustavo) was a highly sympathetic plaintiff who had done all that state law required of him in order to win the right to contest the adoption: He had offered to marry the mother, wanted to live with her, asked her not to give their baby up, and filed for paternity shortly after her birth; the adoption was completed without his knowledge. That this case awarding him custody was treated as groundbreaking is an indication of how limited the rights of unwed fathers have been.

The notion that sex-based limitations of parental rights might constitute discrimination dates back less than twenty years, to the 1970s, when the Supreme Court announced new standards of sexual equality. In 1979, in *Caban v. Mohammed*,[16] the Court struck down a New York law denying unwed fathers the right to contest adoptions under any circumstances; a mother was generally required to consent to an adoption; a father's consent was irrelevant. (The father in the *Gustavo* case owed his award of custody to *Caban*, which required New York to rewrite its adoption statute.)

Caban involved an adoption claim by a father who had acknowledged his paternity, contributed to his family's support, and maintained a relationship with his children after separating from their mother. He didn't fit the stereotype of an unwed father on which New York's law was based, but that didn't matter; the law's denial of fathers' rights was absolute. There was no action Caban could take to win his parental rights, no proof of fitness that could even be offered.

The law's failure to provide for exceptions was critical, given the facts of this case. Caban demonstrated "that an unwed father may have a relationship with his children fully comparable to that of the mother," the Court observed, rejecting the law's presumption that "a natural mother, absent special circumstances, bears a closer relationship with her child than a father does."*

Caban was not the first case in which the Court struck down an absolute presumption of an unwed father's unfitness. In 1972, in *Stanley v. Illinois*,[17] it invalidated an Illinois law denying an unwed father the right to contest state action removing his children from his custody. Stanley was a particularly grievous case, involving the forced break-up of an apparently stable unwed family. The state separated a father, Peter Stanley, from his three children (declaring them wards of the state) after the death of their mother, with whom he had lived intermittently for eighteen years. Despite the fact that he had helped raise his children and wanted to retain custody of them, Stanley was presumed unfit because he was unwed and denied a hearing to determine his fitness, on account of sex. Mothers, married or not, were essentially presumed fit—at least, their children could only be taken from them after a hearing and proof of neglect.

The unfairness of this, however, was not clear to all members of the Court, who were persuaded by stereotypes of unwed fathers. Two justices (Burger and Blackmun) dissented in this case, asserting that "a State is fully justified in concluding, on the basis of common experience, that the biological role of the mother in carrying and nursing an infant creates stronger bonds between her and the child than the bonds resulting from the male's often casual encounter. . . . Most unwed mothers exhibit a concern for their offspring either permanently or at least until they are safely placed for adoption, while unwed fathers

---

*The fact that Caban was denied the opportunity to establish his parental rights may distinguish this case from *Parham v. Georgia*, a 1979 case in which the Court upheld a Georgia statute denying an unwed father the right to sue for wrongful death of a child he had failed to "legitimate." Still, these cases are difficult to reconcile. Perhaps the Court simply considered a custody claim more important than the right to initiate civil litigation. But as the dissent in *Parham* forcefully observed, an underlying presumption of the Georgia law—that fathers who lose their children don't suffer—was simply "incredible."

155

rarely burden either the mother or the child with their attentions or loyalties." The dissent noted that these generalizations about mothers and fathers, "like most generalizations, are not without exceptions," but held that exceptions did not undermine the law's essential fairness, given its intent to serve the "best interests" of children.

Of course, the principle of nondiscrimination reflects the view that the inequities of generalizations—the hardships they inflict on nonconforming men and women—outweigh the good intentions or interests of administrative convenience they serve. And as the Court has noted in a series of cases during the 1970s, generalizations are often self-fulfilling. Presuming that fathers are unfit or less fit parents encourages them to be so. Denying fathers their rights gives them an excuse for evading their responsibilities.

Fathers' legal responsibilities for their children have, in fact, generally been contingent on their rights. Traditionally, women have had virtually exclusive parental rights to children born out of wedlock (and relatively few rights in relation to children born in it). Women were also, in effect, solely responsible for their nonmarital children. Most states imposed on men a general support obligation, but it was minimal, left to the discretion of courts, and difficult to enforce, and nonmarital children had limited inheritance rights. They could not, in general, inherit from their fathers, except by will (not intestate), unless they had been formally acknowledged.

Laws discriminating against children born outside of marriage began changing in 1968, when, in Levy v. Louisiana,[18] the Supreme Court struck down a Louisiana law denying nonmarital children the right to sue for wrongful death of their mother. Following Levy, state and federal courts began reviewing laws limiting the rights of nonmarital children in relation to their fathers. (Although Levy involved a mother-child relationship, discrimination was "most common and serious" in cases involving fathers.)[19] Three years after Levy, in 1971, the Court seemed to reverse itself by upholding a Louisiana law denying a nonmarital child the right to inherit intestate, even though her father had acknowledged his paternity.[20] A year later, however, the Court held that nonmarital children are entitled to workers' compensation benefits on the death of their father,[21] and in 1977 the Court essentially overruled its earlier decision on intestacy when it struck down an Illinois law denying a nonmarital child the right to inherit intestate from her father.[22] Thus, the rights of nonmarital children were expanded during the 1970s, as were the rights of women, but the Supreme Court cases on illegitimacy are somewhat confusing; and the constitutional status of children born outside of marriage is not quite clear.[23]

It is clear, however, that the way society treats nonmarital children depends on the way it treats unwed mothers and fathers and on its vision of the legitimate family. It need hardly be stressed that the mere notion of illegitimacy is a creation of the protectionist, patriarchal family. Traditionally, children who were the "legal issue" of a marriage were their father's heirs; children born out of wedlock were their mother's problems.

Laws defining fathers' rights ought to be seen in the context of laws about children's rights and family relations. As unwed fathers are recognized, their children are too. The legal and social stigmatization of unwed mothers, unwed fathers, and their "bastard" children reflects a single act of stereotyping and a single, sexist vision of family life.

Stereotyping is a process of perception, not a collection of images perceived. Feminists can either challenge that process or contribute to it; they cannot endorse some stereotypes without endorsing others and suffering all their consequences. They can't glorify motherhood and denigrate fatherhood and expect men not to abdicate responsibility for their children. They can't idealize women's superior parenting skills and object to double standards of male and female parenting: Women who believe they're naturally endowed to meet higher standards of parenting can hardly complain when men fail to meet them or when higher standards are used to judge women.

Still, people fighting for their children are not always logical or ideologically consistent, and the feelings that many women share about maternal virtues are stronger than ideas about equality. The tension for feminists between feelings and ideas in matters of maternity was highlighted by the Baby M case and the battle over surrogate motherhood. The commercialization of childbearing raises divisive questions about reproductive choice and the objectification of children, but at the center of the custody dispute over Baby M was a question about the primacy of the mother-child bond.

Baby M's story is practically folklore—the subject of innumerable articles, editorials, talk shows, and books. The plot is familiar (infertile couple hires a woman to bear a child for them and she decides to keep her), but the details of the case and the legal issues on which it turned deserve recounting.

The case began in 1985 when William and Elizabeth Stern entered into a surrogate contract with Mary Beth Whitehead. Elizabeth Stern feared she had multiple sclerosis and that pregnancy posed a serious threat to her health. Her husband, however, whose family had been decimated by the Holocaust, was intent on having a child that was genetically his. Mary Beth Whitehead wanted to give an infertile couple the "gift of life," and she wanted to earn money for her family. For $10,000 she agreed to conceive a child with William Stern, carry it to term, and turn it over to the Sterns at birth, waiving all her maternal rights.

But as everyone knows Whitehead changed her mind. She "realized almost from the moment of birth, that she could not part with this child. She had felt a bond with it even during pregnancy." At first, she tried to uphold the contract, turning the child (whom she called Sara) over to the Sterns. The next day she appeared at their door in despair: "She told them she could not live without her baby, that she must have her, even if only for one week." The Sterns, afraid Whitehead would commit suicide, surrendered the child (whom they called Melissa) on the condition that she'd be returned. When Whitehead refused to return her, the Sterns obtained a court order; Whitehead and her husband fled with the baby to Florida, and in a series of telephone conversations with William Stern she threatened to kill herself and the baby or accuse Stern of child molestation if he tried to regain custody.[24]

The Whiteheads were eventually apprehended (after three months of living in a series of motels), and the child was awarded to the Sterns pending a determination of custody by the New Jersey courts. The Sterns won the first round; after a two-month trial the surrogacy contract was upheld, Mary Beth Whitehead's parental rights were terminated, and the Sterns were awarded custody. They lost much of their case on appeal; they retained custody, but the surrogacy contract was declared invalid, Whitehead's parental rights were restored, and she was granted liberal visitation rights.[25]

There were then three primary questions before the New Jersey Supreme Court: (1) the validity of the contract, (2) Whitehead's legal status as the parent of her child, and (3) the conflicting custodial claims of the Sterns and the Whiteheads. It was therefore possible for the court to find, as it did, that surrogate contracts violated the laws and policies of New Jersey, including those against baby selling, that Whitehead's parental rights could not be terminated by contract or judicial order absent proof that she was unfit or guilty of abandoning her child, but that Baby M ought to remain in the custody of her father and stepmother because they provided a more stable environment for her. Once the surrogate contract was invalidated and Whitehead's parental rights affirmed, the Baby M case became a custody case, to be decided according to the same standards used in more typical custody cases following divorce.

In New Jersey the tender-years presumption favoring maternal custody had been replaced by a presumption that mothers and fathers are equally fit parents and by a requirement that custody be awarded according to the "health and welfare of the children." Mary Beth Whitehead could not claim in court that, as a mother, she was a naturally superior parent, but a belief in the visceral, sacred bond between mother and child, which develops during pregnancy, underlay her fight for custody and the public support she received from feminists and others opposed to the practice of surrogacy: "My body, my soul, my heart, my breathing, my everything had gone into making this baby," Whitehead exclaimed. "What had Bill Stern done? Put some sperm in a cup?"[26] Feminists who rallied round Whitehead evoked inflammatory images of children being torn from their mothers' breasts, images even of slavery and "the cries of mothers and children taken from each other in the name of creating the perfect race."[27] The custody trial itself was denounced as "a form of child abuse and sex discrimination,"[28] as if a judicial assessment of the best interests of a child whose parents are feuding is always, at best, superfluous, as if fathers have no conceivable custodial claims worthy of consideration.

Mary Beth Whitehead seemed, at first, an unlikely feminist heroine even for protectionists. A high school dropout who was married and pregnant at sixteen, she defined herself entirely through motherhood: "I believed that being a mother and taking care of children was my calling," she explained. "If I gave my baby away, my life wasn't worth anything."[29] But she was a fitting heroine for the tradition-hungry, post-feminist 1980s, and some feminists embraced her with the passion of prodigal sinners or careerists returning to the fold.

If Mary Beth Whitehead, former teenage mother, was the good woman of this story, Elizabeth Stern, childless professional, was the bad one. Her "excuse" for not getting pregnant—fear that she had multiple sclerosis and might be blinded or paralyzed by pregnancy—was questioned and made an issue in the case because Whitehead claimed her belief in Betsy Stern's infertility was the basis of her agreement to bear the Sterns a child. (The Court noted that Stern's anxiety "appears to have exceeded the actual risk," conceding that the anxiety was real nonetheless.)[30] Whitehead's lawyer set up a clear conflict between Whitehead, the nurturing, maternal, natural woman, and Stern, the selfish careerist: "Childbearing would have been an inconvenience for Mrs. Stern," he told the judge. Her claim of infertility was "a lie." The "truth" was "Mrs. Stern thought her career was too important to bear her own children."[31]

Feminists did not attack Elizabeth Stern in this way, though some questioned her "collaboration" with William Stern in what they considered an egotistical quest for an heir, an exercise in "macho geneticism." But neither did they defend Stern's decision to delay childbearing or consider her—a successful woman doctor—an appropriate feminist role model. Support for Mary Beth Whitehead was not diluted by much sympathy for Elizabeth Stern. Feminists who sided with Whitehead tended to do so unflinchingly and with little sense of irony, as an apparent act of atonement for once questioning the rewards of motherhood, out of confusion about equality and gender roles, and because of the way Whitehead was vilified at the custody trial.

Feminists have rightly pointed out that Whitehead was subject to the kind of character assassination traditionally used against rape victims. Character is an appropriate issue in a determination of parental fitness (and not in a rape case), but the attack on Whitehead was vicious and often ill-founded. Psychiatrists testifying for the Sterns accused her of narcissism, evidenced partly by the fact that she dyed her hair. She was said to have a "mixed personality disorder," manifested by her flight from police seeking to take back her baby and her belief that as Baby M's mother she knew "what was best for the baby" and that "the baby belonged with her." (If all mothers who believe this are crazy, no mothers are sane.) The trial judge called Whitehead "manipulative, impulsive, and exploitative . . . a woman without empathy," when he took the extraordinary step of terminating her parental rights.[32]

This was not the most judicious of judicial rulings, and in reversing it (in part), the New Jersey Supreme Court observed that Whitehead had been "rather harshly judged. . . . We think it is expecting something well beyond normal human capabilities to suggest that this mother should have parted with her newly born infant without a struggle."[33] But the Baby M case was a highly emotional one, revolving as it did around the mother-child bond. It was a case inflamed by prejudices —about the advantages of middle-class family life (the Stern's financial stability was a factor in the custody decision) and the natural parental skills of men and women. For some feminists, the Baby M case became a test of their commitment to motherhood, which had long been questioned. Either you were for Mary Beth Whitehead and motherhood or against them.

There are, however, cogent arguments against surrogacy that don't rely on romanticizing motherhood. It can fairly be called a form of baby selling in which the child is simply bought before rather than after her birth. It turns women as well as children into commodities (Dr. Lee Salk called Mary Beth Whitehead a "surrogate uterus").[34] It raises the spectre of poor women being paid to breed for the rich. It may not be fair to children. Whether or not society deems motherhood more sacred than fatherhood, it may decide, as a matter of public policy, that surrogacy is an unacceptable way to bring children into this world.

Is a ban on surrogacy a form of protectionism for women? Is it patronizing to deny them the right to bear children for money? Freedom-to-contract arguments are often used to defend surrogacy, but they ignore the economic disparities between parties to a surrogate contract and the potential for exploitation. We routinely regulate arrangements between people with unequal bargaining power—through minimum-wage and maximum-hour laws, rent control, and consumer protection laws. In an egalitarian society, surrogacy might be permitted in the name of freedom and reproductive choice. Whether this society can find ways to eliminate coercion from surrogacy agreements and ensure that women who agree to bear children for money do so freely, fully understanding the consequences of their decision, are difficult practical questions for state legislatures. Whether the "pain of infertility" and principles of freedom and choice justify the buying and selling of babies is a moral question about which we have no consensus. Whether reproductive technologies and third-party reproductive techniques will result in more or less reproductive control for women depends on how we perceive the relationship of technology to choice and the relationship of choice to equality.

·12·

Equality
and Reproductive
Choice

Only women get pregnant. When we talk about equality, we talk about motherhood and reproductive choice—the right to be pregnant or not. In a society that enshrines double standards of sexual behavior and imposes primary responsibility for child care on women, childbearing has unique social and economic consequences for them. Egalitarian and protectionist feminists who disagree about what causes the limits motherhood places on women's educational and employment opportunities (culture or nature) agree about their effects: Women are kept relatively poor and powerless, homebound, and financially dependent on men.

Of course, if motherhood's restrictions on women are natural, as protectionists claim, then reproductive choice is less central to their welfare than pronatalist measures such as public stipends for mothers and "mommy-track" jobs that enable them to work (for considerably less money than men) and raise children too. If motherhood's restrictions on women are natural, choice is less central than protectionism for women, and in fact, throughout our history protectionism has been essentially incompatible with reproductive choice.

The sterilization of five women at an American Cyanamid plant in 1978 pursuant to a fetal protection policy underscored the relationship between workplace protections and reproductive control. But protective labor laws, based on assumptions that reproduction weakened women whether or not they were pregnant, have always regulated women's work lives partly for the sake of their children, subordinating the interests of women to what were presumed to be the interests of children. As the Supreme Court noted in *Muller v. Oregon*,[1] the well-being of future generations (the future of "the race") depended on the well-being of women, which made childbearing a public as well as a private interest, empowering the state to regulate women's reproductive lives.

The *Muller* case traced a continuum of ideals about childbearing, gender roles, and racism; the romanticization of motherhood combined with protectionism combined with eugenics and concern about "race suicide" to deny all women their reproductive rights. (Childbearing by native-born white women was encouraged and effectively coerced by abortion prohibitions; childbearing by women of color was bemoaned and occasionally controlled by involuntary sterilizations.) Less than thirty years after *Muller*, Nazi Germany showed just how dangerous this continuum of protectionism and eugenics could be. The Nazis' glorification of the feminine sphere ("*Kinder, Küche, Kirche*") was based on the same racist principles of population control that justified systematic forced sterilizations. Stringent, criminal antiabortion legislation (and the establishment by Himmler of a Central Agency for the Struggle against Homosexuality and Abortion) was accompanied by laws prohibiting voluntary sterilization for socially desirable people—Aryans who had a patriotic duty to breed—and mandating it for "invalid" people to prevent the propagation of "lives unworthy of life." Yet the Nazis invented Mother's Day; they combined aggressive pronatalism for the racially "pure" with eugenic sterilization—and genocide.[2]

This does not mean protectionism is inherently fascistic or that another Holocaust is imminent. But the experience of Nazi Germany illustrates with dreadful clarity the way racism and sexism shape laws regulating reproduction and delineates the relationship between abortion prohibitions and involuntary sterilizations. So does the history of sterilization abuse in this country.

By 1932 over 12,000 people in the United States had been sterilized pursuant to eugenic sterilization laws prevailing in about twenty-seven states.[3] The typical law targeted convicts and people considered mentally impaired.[4] Sterilization campaigns reflected anxiety about feeblemindedness and other forms of "degeneracy" considered hereditary. They were also shaped by class biases. Poor people were considered too "stupid and immoral" to practice birth control, and the Depression renewed efforts by eugenicists to solve the problem of poverty by sterilizing the poor.[5] Sterilization movements were also virulently racist. In 1939 the Birth Control Federation of America proposed a "Negro Project," noting that the "mass of Negroes, particularly in the South, still breed carelessly and disastrously, with the result that the increase among Negroes, even more than among whites, is from that portion of the population least fit, and least able to rear children properly."[6]

This unholy trinity of concerns—about poverty, "degeneracy," and "the increase among Negroes"—was linked by the logic of sterilization propaganda: Blacks were considered less "fit" than whites; unfitness or degeneracy was considered a cause of poverty. The notion that poverty—poor education, nutrition, and housing—might make people unfit was an anathema to eugenicists, who essentially blamed poverty on the unfitness of the poor.

Eugenicism declined after the 1930s, partly because of its association with fascism, and in 1942 the Supreme Court struck down a law authorizing involuntary sterilization of convicted felons.[7] But racism and middle-class resentment of welfare programs continued fueling campaigns against the poor and women of color. In the early 1970s coerced sterilization of Medicaid recipients created a small scandal. Sterilization abuses were revealed in *Relf v. Weinberger*,[8] a notorious case involving the sterilization of two black girls ages twelve and fourteen at the behest of a federally funded Community Action Committee. The girls were sterilized after their mother signed a consent form with an X in the mistaken belief that she was authorizing Depo-Provera injections. (Depo-Provera had been administered to the girls as a birth control measure, as it was routinely administered to poor women, until it was discovered to be carcinogenic.)[9]

In *Relf* a federal district court enjoined the use of federal funds for involuntary sterilizations on the basis of "uncontroverted evidence in the record that minors and other incompetents have been sterilized with federal funds and that an indefinite number of poor people have been improperly coerced into accepting a sterilization operation under the threat that various federally supported welfare benefits would be withdrawn unless they submitted to irreversible sterilization."

Blackmailing welfare recipients into being sterilized by threatening to cut off their benefits was not uncommon; in one year alone, 1972, before the *Relf* case brought sterilization abuses to light, between 100,000 and

200,000 sterilizations were funded by the federal government.[10] By the mid-1970s, nonwhite welfare recipients had undergone about one-third more sterilizations than the total number of women not receiving welfare.[11] Native American women were also targeted for sterilization; by 1976 about one-fourth of all those of childbearing age had been sterilized. Puerto Rican women of childbearing age had an even higher sterilization rate, over 35 percent, as a result of an official population control program dating back to the 1940s.[12]

Private doctors treating Medicaid patients sometimes practiced their own form of coercive family planning with legal impunity. In *Walker v. Pierce*[13] a federal appeals court dismissed a civil rights action against an obstetrician, Dr. Pierce, who required Medicaid patients having their third child to agree to be sterilized after delivery; without their consent to sterilization, he refused to treat them. According to one witness, he explained that "he was tired of people going around having babies and my tax money having to pay for it." Dr. Pierce received about $60,000 in Medicaid payments while pursuing this policy, but the court of appeals found that he was not acting "under color of state law," a condition of liability for a civil rights violation. It noted too that he had "publicly and freely announced his sterilization policy" and was entitled to his "personal economic philosophy." The fact that in implementing his personal philosophy Dr. Pierce was acting like a one-man legislature, attaching his own conditions to the receipt of Medicaid benefits, was ignored. So was the uneven balance of power between a doctor and a Medicaid patient that is surely potentially, if not inherently, coercive.

Coerced sterilizations of minority women dating back generations, the racism of some early birth control advocates, and their alliance with eugenicists helped create a rift between black women and white prochoice activists that persists today. Abortion has been associated with sterilization and racist population control and labeled a form of genocide.

The racism that has infected public discourse about reproduction is real, but blame for it is misplaced: Opponents of abortion rights, not advocates of choice, favor coercive reproductive policies. That some white Americans fear being outnumbered by blacks is evident in conservative warnings about a middle-class American "birth dearth" and the decline in fertility among "smart" women.[14] But birth-dearth fears are partly responsible for antiabortion sentiment: White middle-class feminists are condemned for neglecting their womanly duties, notably the duty to nurture and breed. White fears about the black birth rate that underlie abortion prohibitions are also likely to result in a new campaign to sterilize the underclass. At a time when the minority community is disproportionately plagued by drug abuse and AIDS and troubled by teenage pregnancies, new state power to restrict abortion may well be tied to coerced sterilizations of minority women. Indeed, for the past decade, the federal government has provided Medicaid funding for sterilization while denying it for abortion.

The logic is clear: Abortion rights enhance women's reproductive autonomy; sterilization destroys it. Restrictions on the right to bear children are bound to accompany restrictions on the right not to bear them.

Future restrictions on choice may be subtle and insidious, as technology advances, making the history of reproductive racism well worth remembering. Eugenicists may never have perpetrated genocide, and the eugenics movement, like Nazism, may be history, but racism and sexism are not; and new technologies offer unprecedented control of the reproductive process.

Because racism and sexism persist, reproductive technology raises the spectre of a new eugenics (concealed by a new reproductive protectionism) and threatens the reproductive choices of some women as much as it expands them for others. Third-party reproductive techniques, such as egg donations—the transplanting of a fertilized egg from one woman into the womb of another—make pregnancy possible for infertile couples but they may also facilitate the creation of an underclass of "breeder" women.* Prenatal screening can identify untreatable fetal disabilities, helping women decide whether or not to terminate their pregnancies, but they also raise the possibility of coerced or, at least, encouraged abortions for "undesirable" fetuses, as well as the possibility of coerced intervention on behalf of the fetus. Doctors are beginning to obtain court orders authorizing prenatal procedures, such as intra-uterine transfusions, over the objection of the mother.[15] The medicalization of conception may make doctors de facto guardians of women's reproductive rights. The costs of new technologies and routine denial of prenatal care for poor and minority women allocate women's rights along class and racial lines. (Denial of access to technology has been

---

*Of course, the use of women as breeders through surrogate arrangements is pre-technological, even biblical, as several feminists have observed. But the dangers of technology are particularly insidious: Egg donation may be a relatively harmless procedure for which women may only be inconvenienced, at a profit, but it may also encourage their commodification.

called a "corollary" of forced sterilization.)[16] Reproductive choice—including both the decision to be a mother and the decision not to be one—depends on access to health care as well as individual rights.

Who controls the birth process? Who controls the use of new technologies and enjoys access to them? These questions can only be asked, not answered, here, and their importance underscored. In vitro fertilization has already resulted in the birth of an estimated 15,000 babies worldwide.[17] In vitro techniques, embryo freezing, and genetic screening are making "intentional parenthood" inevitable: Prospective parents or doctors or the state will be able to determine the incidence of conception and birth and perhaps the genetic make-up of children as never before. At present, legislation regulating the new technologies is minimal. We have no cohesive public policies governing assisted reproduction. Should women who donate their eggs be paid, as men have always been paid for sperm donations? How do we determine legal parentage when fertilization and gestation have been separated and a child may be said to have two mothers? Should embryo transplants or prenatal screening be publicly funded or covered by private insurance plans? How can we make screening widely available without forcing it on women and without encouraging genetic abortions?

The questions are complex and multiple and require at least some reasoned legislative responses that may be impossible to shape in the context of a war about abortion. But ethical, legal, and political issues raised by the new technologies cannot all be decided in court and ought not to be decided on an ad hoc basis by an often arbitrary, discriminatory, and overburdened health-care system. Nor should reproductive policies be shaped by entrepreneurs in new technologies seeking to exploit the "pain" of infertility, the social pressure to bear children, and the stigma attached to couples who can't.[18]

It should also be recognized that neither technology nor surrogacy are the only solutions to infertility. As Nadine Taub, professor of law at Rutgers University, has pointed out, there are nontechnological alternatives—improved health care, elimination of occupational hazards faced by male and female workers, and workplace policies, such as family leaves that don't penalize or stigmatize workers and allow women to have their children early without impairing their careers. Professor Taub's proposal suggests that what makes technology potentially abusive—social and economic injustice—may also contribute to the problem technology is expected to solve: Health care and safe working conditions are luxuries of the middle and upper clases; intentional early childbearing is an option mainly for women who can afford to work part time or not at all at an early point in their careers and are willing to sacrifice some degree of professional success for motherhood. Whether it focuses on infertility or abortion, technology or social norms, the debate about reproductive choice always leads back to the struggle for racial and sexual equality.

The relationship of reproductive choice to equality has not, however, been recognized by the Supreme Court. From a 1942 decision invalidating mandatory sterilization laws to the 1973 decision of *Roe v. Wade* recognizing women's right to choose abortions, the Court has located procreative rights in the right of privacy.[19] But privacy rights, encompassing the right to use contraception, have been steadily attacked by social issue conservatives, and the Supreme Court has become more conservative. The Court's support for sexual privacy is shallow and inconstant;[20] its support for abortion rights, perhaps, is history.

In 1989, in *Webster v. Reproductive Health Services*,[21] the Court retreated from its fifteen-year commitment to reproductive choice when it upheld a Missouri law imposing significant new restrictions on abortion rights. Beginning with the declaration that life begins at conception and describing fetuses as unborn children—invested with the same rights as people who've been born—the Missouri law prohibits public employees and public facilities from performing or assisting in abortions not necessary to saving the mother's life. The law also requires that women past their twentieth week of pregnancy undergo costly, medically unnecessary, and potentially risky tests to determine viability—the point at which a fetus can live outside the womb, if only with extraordinary technological support.

The Court in *Webster* declined to overrule *Roe v. Wade* in theory, but four justices were sharply critical of it. Chief Justice Rehnquist suggested that the state's "compelling interest" in preserving fetal life is present from conception, not just from viability, as *Roe* held. In upholding Missouri's onerous restrictions on abortion, the Court came close to reversing *Roe v. Wade* in fact, especially for women who lack access to purely private medical facilities. (Chief Justice Rehnquist cavalierly explained that pregnant women in Missouri were simply left with "the same choices" they would have had if the state operated no public hospitals at all, as if a state shut-down of all publicly assisted hospitals might be sound public policy.)

The Court similarly had upheld prohibitions of public funding for abortion in 1980;[22] poor women have long lacked equal access to abortion and equal opportunity to exercise their rights. But the Missouri law went beyond a cutoff of direct abortion funding: Its prohibition of public assistance appears broad enough to prohibit abortions in private hospitals merely located on public land, or dependent on public water and sewer facilities.[23] Missouri may not have established a new principle providing for cutoffs of public abortion funds, but it did extend an existing one.

Missouri broke most clearly with established principles of abortion law with its viability testing requirement. *Roe v. Wade* firmly held that states could not regulate abortions in the interests of fetal life during the first twenty-four weeks of pregnancy, or before the fetus may be viable. It is still a fact of life that fetuses are not viable at twenty weeks, as Chief Justice Rehnquist conceded in *Webster*. He held, however, that the state may presume viability at twenty weeks, because of "error(s) in estimating gestational age." Doctors may then be required to conduct tests to prove that the fetus is not viable before performing an abortion. *Webster* thus imposed new limits on physician autonomy as well as women's rights. In previous cases, the Court held that doctors should be free to determine viability, without interference from the state.[24] By allowing the Missouri legislature to presume that fetuses are viable at twenty weeks, *Webster* effectively holds that the determination of viability is a political as well as a medical question.

Prochoice activists have pointed to *Webster* as the beginning of the end for abortion rights, and avowed opponents of choice have happily agreed. Moderates, however, tend to minimize *Webster's* importance, pointing out that restrictions on public abortion funding aren't new. They characterize viability testing as an insignificant financial burden on women (as it may be for some) and an insignificant infringement of their individual rights. As a violation of privacy rights, intrusive mandatory tests—such as amniocentesis—for pregnant women have been given less consideration than mandatory drug testing of public employees.

Either the sky is falling for women or it's not. The *Webster* decision is a kind of Rorschach test; it means different things to people with different political perspectives. How seriously you take the abortion restrictions it upheld depends on how seriously you take women's rights and women's claim to autonomy.

Confusion over what *Webster* means also reflects divisions within the Supreme Court. *Webster* was not decided by a clear and simple majority; in other words, no one judge spoke for a majority of the Court. Instead five of the nine justices agreed the Missouri law was constitutional without agreeing why.

It is clear, however, that at least four justices are prepared to overrule, or substantially erode, *Roe* (Chief Justice Rehnquist and Justices White,

Kennedy, and Scalia). Justice O'Connor provided the swing vote that barely preserved *Roe*, but she has expressed serious doubts about abortion rights in the past and is hardly a champion of choice.[25] In *Webster* she avoided ruling on the constitutionality of *Roe v. Wade* by qualifying the clear language of Missouri's law, minimizing its restrictions to make them appear consistent with *Roe*.[26] We don't know how Justice O'Connor will vote in a case involving state abortion restrictions that cannot, by any exercise of judicial imagination, be reconciled with *Roe v. Wade*. We don't know what the Court will do next about abortion.[27]

But we do know this: In 1973, in *Roe v. Wade*, the Supreme Court withdrew from states the power to prohibit abortions during the first six months of pregnancy. In 1989, *Webster v. Reproductive Health Services* gave some of that power back. "Who decides," the rallying cry of the prochoice movement, is a question now before the states.

It's important to remember that the Supreme Court is supposed to review the constitutionality, not the morality, of abortions. It decides whether or not women have a constitutional right to choose abortions: If they have that right, state power to restrict abortion is quite limited. Courts are then required to review state abortion laws strictly, as strictly as they review laws involving First Amendment freedoms or racial discrimination. Restrictions on abortion must then be essential to the preservation of a compelling state interest. But if women have no constitutional right to choose abortions, the state is free to restrict or prohibit them reasonably, as it restricts or prohibits residential housing in commercial zones. Women may then have no more legal control over the decision to bear children than building contractors have over local zoning ordinances.

A Supreme Court ruling that women have no constitutional abortion rights thus leaves the states free to enact or not enact abortion prohibitions. (Unless President Bush's proposed constitutional amendment banning abortions is adopted, giving fetuses more legal rights than women, states will not be required to regulate procreation by banning abortions.) Abortion rights were determined by state law until 1973, when *Roe v. Wade* was decided. From a legal perspective, women may be going back to where they were before *Roe*, although the social and political landscape has changed with the rise of the right. As the debate about abortion intensifies, *Roe v. Wade* and the context in which it was decided merit reviewing.

In *Roe v. Wade* the Supreme Court struck down a Texas statute prohibiting abortions that were not necessary to save the mother's life.

171

Similar statues prevailed in about thirty states. The Court recognized a Fourteenth Amendment right of privacy that included a woman's right to choose an abortion. This right, however, was not absolute; rights seldom are. It could be superseded by a compelling state interest either in protecting the mother's health or in preserving "potential life." To determine when the state's interest in the mother or her fetus becomes compelling—to balance the state's interest in the mother or her fetus with the mother's rights—the Court fashioned its much-maligned trimester approach to abortion regulation: It provided that because abortions are relatively safe during the early months of pregnancy, they must essentially be available on demand during the first trimester. During the second trimester, they may be regulated in order to protect the mother's health. During the third trimester, medically unnecessary abortions may be prohibited in order to preserve potential life.

By drawing a line at viability in delineating women's abortion rights, *Roe v. Wade* struck a balance between private, individual procreative rights and public concern about potential life. Even prochoice advocates sometimes become uncertain about the morality of abortions once the fetus is viable, capable of living outside the womb, almost a recognizable human being. Uncertainty about the morality of abortions in some cases, however, does not undermine a belief in the justice of abortion rights. As feminists must repeatedly point out, questions about procreative justice ought not be determined by varying individual ideas about procreative morality or by individual religions. Recognizing a woman's right to decide about abortion doesn't mean endorsing the decision she makes; it means her decision is not ours to endorse.

Still, for many people, the primacy of choice is clearest during the first six months of pregnancy, before the fetus is viable—when practically all abortions are performed. *Roe v. Wade* addressed discomfort about the possibility of late-term abortions, while providing a constitutional framework for the exercise of women's privacy rights. It was an appropriate, arguably essential assertion of judicial authority: *Roe*'s trimester formulation was no more legislative than rules devised by the Court to protect First Amendment rights in libel cases or to review instances of racial discrimination, as Justice Blackmun observed in his dissent in *Webster*.

But in *Webster*, Chief Justice Rehnquist characterized *Roe*'s trimester scheme as "unsound in principle and unworkable in practice," although it worked fairly well for fifteen years and established sound principles of women's rights. *Roe v. Wade* has always been harshly criticized for its detailed, "medicalized" approach: Its validity depends partly on the state of medical technology as well as on the Constitution, as Justice O'Connor suggested when she described *Roe* as a case "on a collision course with itself."[28] While technology was making late abortions safe, undermining the state's power to regulate them to protect the mother's health, she observed, it might also push back the point of viability, strengthening the state's power to prohibit abortions entirely in order to preserve potential life. Her prediction has not come true; the earliest point of viability remains constant at about 24 weeks. But technology—including such routine procedures as sonograms—has humanized the fetus, intensifying emotional opposition to abortion rights.

The extent of that opposition is unclear. In the wake of the *Webster* decision, there appears to be no national consensus on abortion, according to a *New York Times* poll, and polls themselves produce confusing, varying results depending on how questions about abortion are asked. The *Times* reported that 63 percent of people surveyed agreed that "if a woman wants to have an abortion and her doctor agrees to it" she should be allowed to have one. But when queried about the specific circumstances in which abortions should be legal, people qualified their support for choice. Most favored it in limited medical circumstances, to protect the mother from a serious health threat or prevent a serious birth defect. Less than half (43 percent) favored it in cases of poverty. Only 26 percent favored making abortions available to women when pregnancy "interferes with work or education."[29] The notion that women have an obligation to bear children that preempts their need or desire to pursue careers still prevails. Women who prefer professional life over motherhood are still considered selfish.

Public support for the proposition that government should not interfere in personal procreative decisions is countered by resistance to the notion that a woman should be free to have an abortion for whatever reason that seems valid to her.[30] In the views of many people, including some who profess to be prochoice, law should prevent women from having abortions for what are popularly considered "bad" reasons, such as the desire to finish graduate school or the lack of desire to bear children. Opponents of abortion rights can begin eroding support for choice with horror stories about abortion as a method of birth control or sex selection, which is generally condemned.[31] Abortion for other "bad" or "selfish" reasons—notably those involving career decisions—are denigrated as "convenience" abortions, as if children were only inconveniences. There are no convenience abortions because there are no merely inconvenient, unwanted pregnancies, especially for women who take motherhood as seriously as child bearing.

Still, it will be difficult for prochoice advocates to convince voters of this—that abortion is a responsible, "moral," and even "selfless" alternative to bearing a child you cannot care for. Of course, women wouldn't have to justify their abortions if there was a firm public commitment to choice. Relatively few people, and fewer politicians, want to be known as antichoice; but the popular tendency to rank abortions on a moral scale for purposes of legislation, with abortions in cases of rape or incest or serious health threats on the high ground, shows how shallow support for choice can be.

How, or if, the debate about choice will be resolved is not yet clear. Four months after the *Webster* decision (the date of this writing) state-by-state abortion battles have only begun. Prochoice advocates have enjoyed a few early victories: The Florida legislature rebuffed efforts by Governor Bob Martinez to restrict abortion rights. Texas Governor William Clements, an opponent of choice, has postponed putting the abortion issue before the Texas legislature. Antiabortion politicians have been switching sides, or qualifying their opposition to legalized abortion and backlash to *Webster* helped elect prochoice governors in New Jersey and Virginia. Commentators have noted a "shift in the political winds"[32] favoring abortion rights, affecting state and local elections, and prompting Congress to change its longstanding position on federal abortion funding. In October 1989, nearly ten years after the Supreme Court upheld its cut off of abortion funding for poor women,[33] Congress voted to provide funding in cases of rape or incest. President Bush vetoed the measure, reportedly for fear that women would lie about being rape or incest victims in order to obtain abortions. There has been relatively little public reaction to his veto, but it did not affect the rights of middle-class voters.

The prochoice movement was strengthened by *Webster*, because it threatened the rights of middle-class women as well as the poor. But opponents of abortion rights have a stronger hold on state legislatures, thanks to lobbying efforts of the past ten years. The state of Pennsylvania, a leader in antiabortion legislation, recently passed a stringent antiabortion law that clearly violates *Roe v. Wade*. It prohibits abortion for sex selection at any time during pregnancy, requires women to notify their husbands of their plans to abort, and to wait twenty-four hours before abortions may be performed; it requires doctors to discourage women from having abortions by outlining alternatives to it and describing the course of fetal development.[34]

Support for these prohibitions among Pennsylvania voters is difficult to gage. Pennsylvanians are "deeply divided" over abortion, according to a *New York Times* poll: Forty percent of people surveyed said that abortion should be generally available; 40 percent supported restrictions on their availability. Almost two-thirds of Pennsylvanians expressed concern about the prospect of women losing their abortion rights, but 81 percent supported husband notification laws.[35]

In Pennsylvania and throughout the nation, people are confused about abortion, wavering between a belief that government restrictions on procreation are wrong and a belief that abortions somehow aren't right. Prochoice and antichoice activists are liable to be considered "extremists,"[36] and public sentiment seems to favor a compromise on abortion rights, which would leave women with fewer rights and less access to abortion than they were granted by *Roe v. Wade.* There may yet be no consensus on abortion, but there is a growing sense that the rights of women should be balanced with the preferences of their husbands, some undefined public interest in monitoring the morality of abortion decisions, and a concern for fetal life.

Still, there is no consensus on when life begins—how could there be?—or on the value of potential life: Fetuses that are conceived as a result of rape or incest are apparently less "valuable" to many than fetuses conceived consensually in marriage. But widespread support for abortion rights of rape and incest victims is telling; it confirms the fact that we don't generally value fetuses as much as children or infant human life. The suggestion that children born of rapists should be killed would be met, universally, with horror. Our culture reflects a subliminal consensus that fetuses are not human beings, which doesn't necessarily translate into a consensus on when life begins.

Some confusion about the metaphysical value of fetuses and the origins of human life is inevitable, even welcome as a sign of humility, and it is not the business of law. The question of when life begins is a religious one that ought not to be answered by courts and legislatures in a pluralistic society. Still, new theories of fetal rights, shaped partly by technology and some disrespect for women, have become powerful weapons in the fight against abortion rights. If a fetus is considered human, or a potential human endowed prematurely with human rights, abortion may be framed as a conflict between two independent beings, the mother and fetus, a conflict the state has a duty to referee. Fetal rights have been most commonly invoked as a basis for prohibiting abortion, but they are also being used to justify the regulation of a woman's behavior during pregnancy. Pregnant women who use drugs or alcohol have been accused of manslaughter or the crime of delivering drugs to a child.[37] Pregnant women have also been forced to undergo caesareans or invasive prenatal procedures for the sake of the fetus.[38]

While antichoice activists, religious leaders, and some doctors are demanding recognition of fetal rights, based on the arguable assertion that a fetus is a human being, the Supreme Court that decided *Roe v. Wade* has been accused of inventing new constitutional rights for women. As critics of *Roe* never tire of pointing out, the right of privacy is nowhere mentioned in the Constitution. But privacy and procreative rights had been established by the Court in previous cases that generated considerably less controversy. In 1942 in *Skinner v. Oklahoma*[39] the Court struck down a law allowing involuntary sterilizations of convicted felons, describing procreation as a "basic civil right." In 1965 in *Griswold v. Connecticut*[40] it struck down a law prohibiting married couples from using contraception, as a violation of marital privacy. And in 1972, shortly before *Roe v. Wade* was decided, *Eisenstadt v. Baird*[41] struck down a prohibition on the distribution of contraceptives to unmarried people. "If the right of privacy means anything," the Court in *Eisenstadt* declared, "it is the right of the individual, married or single, to be free from unwarranted governmental intrusion into matters so fundamentally affecting a person as the decision whether or not to bear children."

This right, to use contraception whether you're married or not, has been shaken by the antiabortion movement. Opponents of choice have objected to the distribution of contraceptives to teenagers as well as the use of intrauterine devices and "morning after" pills that operate after conception. The Supreme Court that recognized the right to procreate and use contraception was considerably more liberal than the Court hearing privacy and procreation cases today, and public sentiment in the 1960s and 1970s appears to have been more liberal too.

Roe v. Wade was decided during a period of liberalization; in *Roe* the Court was following a trend as much as it was establishing one. The Thalidomide scare, the population control movement, the sexual revolution, and the women's movement were changing popular and professional attitudes toward birth control. The medical establishment, previously opposed to abortion, now recognized it as an accepted medical procedure that doctors, not legislators, should control. Doctors played an important role in the abortion reform movement, partly because they were criminally liable under the typical antiabortion statute. As defendants in criminal cases and plaintiffs in constitutional challenges to restrictions on abortion and contraception, doctors, concerned with their professional autonomy, were involved in much key litigation of the 1960s and 1970s.[42] In *Roe v. Wade* the Court relied on their support for legalization. It relied on the legal establishment too; as the Court stressed, in 1972 the American Bar Association approved a model Uniform Abortion Act, which allowed abortions to be performed by physicians in the interests of the mother's general well-being and in order to prevent birth defects. By the time *Roe v. Wade* was decided, about one-third of the states had adopted similar liberalized laws. Four states—New York, Alaska, Hawaii, and Washington—allowed abortion on demand during the early months of pregnancy. Moreover, both state and federal courts were beginning to question the constitutionality of blanket prohibitions on abortion. The notion that women had a constitutional right to decide whether or not to bear children was gaining judicial credence.[43]

So *Roe v. Wade* was decided in the midst of change. It has been suggested that if the Court had stayed out of the abortion debate, the states would somehow have muddled their way through to an acceptable middle ground, avoiding the acrimony of the past fifteen years.[44] But the Court's brave resolution of the abortion debate in *Roe* may soon be proved to have generated much less acrimony and political upheaval than the *Webster* decision returning the abortion issue to the states. And if one-third of the states had liberalized abortion laws by 1973, two-thirds of them did not. There were still an estimated 1 million illegal abortions a year, and countless women were still being deprived of their reproductive rights. To suggest that abortion laws should be shaped by a process of political consensus is to deny that they involve fundamental rights, to be defined and protected by the courts interpreting the Constitution. It was, in fact, the acknowledgment of reproductive choice as a fundamental right for women that set off much of the backlash to it. The notion that women, not doctors, had privacy rights—of autonomy and self-determination—came as a bit of a shock.

But respect for privacy, especially in the context of family life, runs through the American legal system, and *Roe v. Wade* should be viewed against the backdrop of a line of cases about familial autonomy. The right to marry has been included in the right to privacy,[45] and the Supreme Court has long limited the state power to interfere with family life. It has, for example, struck down compulsory public school attendance laws and laws requiring English speaking in private schools, ceding to parents the right to make decisions about their children's educations.[46] The school law cases involve clashes between parental and state authority when children are not asserting contrary rights of their own. But the Court has recognized that children or minors have rights too, although they're limited. Before the *Webster* decision, the court had struck down laws making parental consent an absolute condition of abortion, holding that minors must at least be given the opportunity to get judicial consent instead, so that "mature" minors can obtain court-ordered abortions.[47]

This substitution of judicial for parental authority occurs when children are at odds with their parents. It reflects another, contrary tradition of state interference in family life, in the interest of children, through such measures as child neglect and welfare statutes and judicial resolution of custody disputes. Familial autonomy is not absolute. It breaks down when members of the family come in conflict with each other, and, of course, you can tell a lot about our culture by looking at which side of what dispute the judicial system chooses to take.

The tradition of familial privacy, or familial autonomy, is not just part of the legal context of *Roe v. Wade*; it's also the source of much feminist dissatisfaction with the Supreme Court's approach to abortion rights.[48] Privacy is an unpopular right among some feminists, precisely because of its association with the autonomous family—that is, the patriarchal autonomous family. To some, protecting privacy and the family means protecting patriarchy and its attendant abuses. Marital rape and other forms of family violence were long considered private, which is partly why so much feminist energy has gone into making the private public, the personal political.

Feminists have always had to contend with the inevitable tension between privacy and social justice, and this tension has affected the abortion debate. Still, it is facile to suggest that privacy rights are bad for women. Even feminists who want child care to be acknowledged as a public responsibility too or those who want an activist welfare state in which mothers are entitled to some form of financial support don't generally want welfare workers inquiring into women's private lives. Nor do they want bureaucrats, much less police officers, in their bedrooms. A recent Supreme Court decision upholding a state sodomy law applied to consenting adults in the "privacy" of the home illustrates the dangers of not respecting privacy enough.[49]

The Court doesn't value privacy when it doesn't value the activity privacy protects, and neither do some feminists. Another source of feminist dissatisfaction with privacy rights is their inclusion of the right to read pornography,[50] and the battle over pornography is related to the battle over abortion: They both involve privacy rights and First Amendment rights as well. The First Amendment is not exactly a source of reproductive rights, but it does protect advocacy of them and education about choice. It has always played an important role in the birth control movement. The first federal obscenity law, the Comstock law, passed in 1873, targeted information about contraception and "contraceptive devices" as well as French postcards, Margaret Sanger was prosecuted for obscenity violations in the early years of this century, and during the 1970s sex education was targeted by antiporn, antichoice activists on the right. In 1983, relying on the First Amendment, the Supreme Court struck down a prohibition on the unsolicited mailing of advertisements for contraceptives. More recently, Reagan Administration regulations prohibiting counseling about abortion by clinics receiving federal funds were struck down on First Amendment grounds.[51]

The third and most compelling feminist objection to privacy as a basis for abortion rights is that privacy rights are essentially negative. The Supreme Court has defined procreative privacy as freedom from government interference with decisions about childbirth. This creates a right that obliges the state to do nothing, which became a problem for women when the Hyde Amendment cut off federal Medicaid funds for therapeutic abortions. In 1980, in *Harris v. McRae*, the Court upheld the Hyde Amendment, reasoning that in respect of women's privacy rights, the state may not prohibit abortions, but neither must it provide them.[52]

But for the Supreme Court this case was as much about money as it was about reproductive rights. The Court has never recognized economic need as a source of constitutional rights, and in *Harris v. McRae* it stressed that due process was a limitation on government power, not an affirmative spending obligation. Had the Court paid more attention to the reproductive rights at issue, it might have concluded that denying money for abortions and providing it for childbirth expenses was indeed a way of punishing poor women for exercising the privacy rights enunciated in *Roe v. Wade*.[53] There were, then, sound privacy-based arguments that should have militated a different result in this case. But it is hard to get past the notion that privacy is a matter of governmental noninterference, especially in a funding case: Privacy is a precarious and somewhat anomalous basis for a claim to public funds.

The feminist critique of privacy was rather perversely vindicated by *Harris v. McRae*. The limited nature of privacy rights, their association with patriarchy, and the failure of privacy theories to address the practical effect of pregnancy on women's lives, and on their status as a class, have revitalized feminist arguments for a new, equality-based approach to abortion.[54] The argument focuses on the ways in which women are disadvantaged by pregnancy, especially when it's unwanted. It denies them equal educational opportunity (pregnant teenagers used to be expelled from public schools) and forces them out of the workplace or into low-paying jobs. The effect of childbearing and child care on women's economic status ought to be clear enough today. After ten years of popular magazine articles about women "juggling" work and family and searching in vain for decent day care, even the Supreme Court could take judicial notice of the fact that motherhood is often a bar to wage earning. It might also note that, from the beginning, in the mid-1800s, the feminist movement has always included demands for reproductive control, whether in the form of "voluntary motherhood" or access to contraception and abortion.

But if the historical connection between reproductive rights and sexual equality is clear, the legal argument linking them is revolutionary—because abortion prohibitions apply only to women. There is no similarly situated group of men to whom pregnant women can be compared, and traditional equal protection analysis requires, fairly literally, similar treatment of groups of people similarly situated. That this approach blinds the Court to discrimination based on reproductive differences was made clear by its decisions in the 1970s upholding the exclusion of pregnancy-related disabilities from employee disability plans, under the Fourteenth Amendment and Title VII.[55] In each case, the Court got stuck on the fact that only women get pregnant; there were no men enjoying greater pregnancy disability benefits than women.

These cases prompted passage of the Pregnancy Discrimination Act, the amendment to Title VII that equates pregnancy discrimination with sex discrimination. It changed the rules by which the Court must decide Title VII cases, but it could not change the Court's interpretation of Fourteenth Amendment guarantees of equality. (The Court, not Congress, is the final arbiter of the Constitution.) The Court has rejected a result-oriented analysis of equality, in both sex and race cases. It is a violation of Title VII, but it is not unconstitutional to discriminate on the basis of pregnancy. In challenging abortion prohibitions under the Fourteenth Amendment, feminists are challenging the Court's approach to larger questions of racial and sexual equality.

Still, it's important to note that restrictions on reproductive freedom violate privacy rights too. The *American Cyanamid* case demonstrated the interplay of privacy and equality for women. The women employees at American Cyanamid who were sterilized in order to keep their jobs had privacy rights to determine their own procreative futures without interference from their employers. They had equality rights to be included in the male workplace despite their reproductive differences.

There is also a point at which privacy and equality rights converge—the point of personal autonomy. Both privacy and equality arguments involve claims by women for control of their reproductive lives. Advocates of equality talk about the effect of pregnancy on women, individually and as a class. Privacy advocates talk about a more abstract violation of individual integrity. An equality argument may seem the "politically correct" one to some feminists, but it is also politically impractical; indeed, the politics of abortion wars today make feminist disputes about privacy and equality seem merely academic. But it is an ideological as well as a political mistake for feminists to dismiss privacy rights as mere property rights or instruments of patriarchy: They include rights of self-determination, and without self-determination, what use is equality?

·13·

Equality in Criminal Justice, Sexual Violence, and Pornography

Rape is the ultimate assault on a woman's autonomy, and as numerous feminists have pointed out, it's a form of political control. Virtually all women live with the threat of sexual violence; like random bombings and other acts of terrorism, it limits freedom through fear. Women even fear images as well as acts of violence, and in the 1970s the movement to end sexual abuse led to a movement to censor pornography. For some feminists, there's no clear distinction between pornography and rape; a pornographic magazine or video is an act of abuse or subordination or sex discrimination. This confusion of images and action (and of freedom to imagine with freedom to act) inspired the most self-destructive form of feminist protectionism: Censorship will silence women too. It tacitly confirmed the most regressive protectionist stereotypes of male and female sexuality that egalitarianism challenged—images of feminine docility, purity, and submission and male aggression. These stereotypes shaped double standards of criminal justice—the differential treatment of men and women accused and convicted of crimes—and double standards of sexual behavior that have always been a part of rape.

Rape is the dark side of chivalry. It demonstrates most brutally the cost of protectionism and sex-role stereotyping for women. Protectionist ideals of "natural" women as pure, passive, nurturing, domestic, and dependent and of "natural" men as lustful, predatory, and aggressive have naturalized rape. It was criminalized not out of respect for women but to protect male property rights. Conversely, the legal conception of a wife as the property of her husband justified marital rape and other forms of spousal abuse. Rape laws codified regressive, protectionist standards of femininity. As victims of rape, women were required to prove their innocence—their chastity and virtue. A victim's sexual history was used against her at trial to impeach her credibility, and she was expected to have strenuously fought off her attacker: Submission was equated with consent; the most credible rape victim was a badly battered one. A nonconforming, "independent," or "loose" woman was commonly assumed to have provoked her attack or not to have been damaged by it.*

"Virtuous" women, however, were deemed to have been damaged irrevocably by rape. What man would want them? If the law trivialized the rapes of "bad" (unfeminine) women, it exaggerated rape's effect on "good" ones. The disproportionately few men who were convicted of rape were subject to draconian punishments usually reserved for murderers. Until 1972, when the Supreme Court revised constitutional standards for capital punishment, the federal government and about one-third of the states prescribed the death penalty for convicted rapists.[1]

The protectionist equation of rape with homicide reflected more patriarchal outrage over the violation of male property rights than respect for women; indeed, it reinforced the view that women were only as valuable as they were virtuous, that a woman who was raped might as well have been killed. The Supreme Court eventually took a more judicious, less sexist view of rape in 1977 when it declared the imposition of capital punishment in rape cases unconstitutional. In *Coker v. Georgia*[2] the Court recognized that rape, however horrible, is not murder, that women recover from it, and life goes on:

> We do not discount the seriousness of rape as a crime. . . . [It is both a violent crime and an expression of] total contempt for the personal integrity and autonomy of the female victim and for [her] privilege of choosing those with whom intimate relationships are to be established. . . . Rape is without doubt deserving of serious punishment;

---

*Attacks on a woman victim's character are not unique to rape cases; Marla Hansen, the New York model whose face was slashed by two men hired by her landlord, was viciously assaulted on the witness stand.

but in terms of moral depravity and of injury to the person and to the public, it does not compare with murder, which does involve the unjustified taking of human life. . . . The murderer kills; the rapist, if no more than that, does not. Life is over for the victim of the murderer; for the rape victim, life may not be nearly so happy as it was, but it is not over and normally is not beyond repair.

The destructive stereotypes that underlay traditional rape laws and the litany of injustices inflicted on rape victims by the criminal justice system are, by now, familiar, thanks to feminists who have brought them to light. Reform of state rape laws, based partly on a revisioning of rape as a sexual crime of violence, has been one of the most notable achievements of the contemporary feminist movement. Virtually all the states have repealed or amended their rape laws since the mid-1970s. (Michigan enacted the first comprehensive rape reform statute in 1974.) Laws vary from state to state, and the process of reform has been piecemeal, but the trend has been a moderately feminist one. The traditional exemption for marital rape has been repealed in about half the states. (That marital rape was legal in every state merely twenty years ago, that it is still legal or a minor offense in some, is a measure of how far feminists have come and have yet to go.) The majority of states have limited the admissibility of a rape victim's sexual history, through rape shield laws. (As a general rule, a prior relationship between a victim and her alleged attacker is admissible; otherwise her sexual history must be proved relevant before being admitted as evidence.)[*] Victims are, in general, no longer required to have strenuously resisted their attackers. Harsher punishments for rape have been softened in an effort to encourage prosecutions and convictions.[3]

The underlying concept of a sex crime, however, has been expanded; no longer limited to rape ("forcible penetration"), it includes as sex crimes a range of acts, such as the rape of a woman with a bottle, that were previously simply considered assaults. The gradation of crimes newly defined as sex offenses—from fondling to rape—means that when sex offenders plead guilty to lesser crimes as the great majority of defendants do, they still plead down to sex crimes, which tracks them as sex offenders.[4]

---

[*]Rape shield laws are controversial because they may conflict with a defendant's Sixth Amendment fair trial rights. The exclusion of relevant evidence about a victim's sexual history would arguably violate the defendant's right to confront witnesses. The problem for women is that a judge's determination of the relevancy of evidence about sexual behavior may well be infected with gender bias.

Expanding the definition of sex crimes—the substitution of terms like "sexual assault" for rape—is also a move toward gender neutrality. Traditional penal laws define rape exclusively as a crime men commit against women. This not only fails to recognize acts such as homosexual rape; it makes only men liable for statutory rape (intercourse with a minor) and perpetuates an ideal of feminine passivity. Whether women are capable of raping men—or men of being raped by them— is merely a semantic question. Women *are* capable of sexual assaults and batteries, as the New York State Court of Appeals observed when it struck down New York's forcible rape law applying only to men.[5] The fact that most acts of sexual violence tend to be committed by men against women (or children) reflects the sociosexual conditioning of which traditional rape laws are part. To cast sex crimes in gender-neutral terms does not lessen the protection the law extends to women or extend their liability unfairly; it simply recognizes that women are actors too. But only women get pregnant. Questions about the constitutionality of rape laws applying only to men have been answered by courts with reference to male and female reproductive differences. In *Michael M. v. Superior Court* the Supreme Court upheld a law making only men liable for statutory rape, characterizing it as a legitimate response to the problem of teenage pregnancy.[6] In *Country v. Parrett* a federal appeals court upheld a forcible rape law applying only to men who chose female victims on the grounds that male rapists impose the fear of unwanted pregnancy on women.[7] The Court in this case rejected as a "dangerously broad rationalization" the state's contention that its law was intended to prevent unwanted pregnancy, but it asserted that "the fact that only women can become pregnant and only if attacked by a man implies that a male assailant can impose a unique harm on a female victim." Only women get pregnant, the Court intoned repeatedly: "A male can impose the fear of and, in some cases, the actuality of an unwanted pregnancy. No woman can impose this harm on a man and no assailant can impose this harm on a person of the same sex. Only women can become pregnant and thus only they can fear an unwanted pregnancy or be forced to undergo the physical, emotional, ethical, and financial consequences of such a pregnancy."

In this view, the primary harm of rape is its possible reproductive consequence, not its assault on individual privacy, autonomy, and well-being. In this view, a male assault of an infertile woman should be as legal as a female assault on a man. Protectionist male-only rape laws reflect the traditional devaluation of women who cannot fulfill or have simply outlived their reproductive roles.

The tendency to view women reductively in terms of their capacity to reproduce that shaped protective labor laws shaped criminal laws as well, at considerable cost to women. Gender stereotypes, based on reproductive differences, subtly encouraged or at least excused a great many rapes, while avenging a few for all the wrong reasons and criminalizing consensual, commercial sex only for women. While rape was defined as a crime that could be committed only by men, prostitution was one for which only women were prosecuted.

Unlike rape laws, prostitution laws aren't generally discriminatory on their face; they don't define prostitution as a female crime. Since reproductive differences don't effect the ability of men and women to have sex for money, even the Supreme Court that upheld male-only rape laws would have difficulty with female-only prostitution laws. But laws have routinely targeted prostitutes and not their customers, and since the great majority of prostitutes are women who service men, a law that punishes the seller and not the buyer punishes only women. If the Fourteenth Amendment served as a prohibition of effective as well as intentional discrimination, it would surely prohibit this: In 1988, in New York City, 4,489 people were arrested for prostitution; 4,136 of them were women.

Statistics like these also reflect the discriminatory enforcement of gender-neutral prostitution laws applying to both prostitutes and their customers. How laws are written is only part of the problem for women; how they're enforced is another. Police routinely single out women prostitutes for arrest, usually with impunity and public approval.

The American Bar Association has condemned the targeting of women prostitutes as "one of the most direct forms of discrimination against women in this country today,"[8] but there is little popular or judicial support for stopping it. Sex discrimination challenges to prostitution laws have generally been unsuccessful. The Pennsylvania courts have rejected a challenge to the disparate treatment of prostitutes and their clients, pointing out that the sellers of drugs are traditionally punished more severely than the buyers (and ignoring the fact that drug dealing does not involve gender relations).[9] The Supreme Judicial Court of Massachusetts, rejecting a broad attack on the Massachusetts prostitution law, dealt with a sex discrimination claim similarly by practically ignoring it.[10] The court held that the exemption of customers from criminal liability was an appropriate exercise of legislative discretion, noting that the law also prohibited the sale and not the purchase of pornography. (Women's bodies were thus considered contraband, like pornography or drugs.) The court also rejected a challenge to police enforcement practices, finding insufficient evidence that the Boston Police enforced the law only against women—despite police testimony that it was department policy to arrest only female prostitutes.

The Supreme Court of California rejected a similar charge of discriminatory enforcement against the Oakland Police Department.[11] The court held that evidence that police employed more men than women as decoys in solicitation operations, ensuring the arrest of more female prostitutes than male customers, was not evidence of intent to discriminate against women. The policy was instead characterized as a "consequence of the department's sexually unbiased policy of concentrating its enforcement efforts on the 'profiteer' rather than the customer of commercial vice." The fact that the relatively few male customers who were arrested were released, and given a notice to appear in court, while female prostitutes were kept in custody and quarantined while being tested for venereal disease was similarly rationalized: Prostitutes were less likely to meet the requirements for release; they often had no identification or permanent address and tended to have prior arrests for prostitution, the Court observed, ignoring the fact that their arrest records, aliases, and general lack of respectability resulted inexorably from the discrimination of which they complained. If male patrons were prosecuted as vigorously as female prostitutes, they'd have arrest records too.

Feminists alternately deplore prostitution as a manifestation of women's sexual objectification or defend it as an assertion of women's sexual autonomy. They argue about the merits of legalizing prostitution (registering prostitutes and regulating their activities), decriminalizing it (letting them alone), or prohibiting it, as a public health and welfare measure. But there is a general feminist consensus that condemns arresting prostitutes while their customers go free. The demand by feminists, egalitarian and protectionist alike, for a single standard of sexual morality dates back to the mid-1800s.

But the feminine ideal propounded by nineteenth-century social feminists and reformers generated the double standard. A dualistic view of male and female nature led inevitably to dualistic models of behavior. As long as women are considered purer and less sexually aggressive than men by nature, they will be held to higher standards of morality and punished disproportionately for moral offenses. The nineteenth-century women's reformatory movement and use of indeterminate sentencing for women (based partly on the notion that women were more amenable to rehabilitation) left a lasting legacy of discrimination. Disparate sentencing for adult men and women convicted of the same or similar offenses was a respected tradition in American penology until some twenty years ago.

In 1968, in *United States ex rel. Robinson v. York,*[12] a federal district court in Connecticut struck down a Connecticut law imposing indefinite, three-year maximum sentences on women convicted of crimes for which men might serve sentences of less than one year. The law applied to women convicted of felonies or of minor morals offenses, such as prostitution and disorderly conduct. It also applied to "unmarried girls between the ages of 6 and 21 who are in manifest danger of falling into habits of vice or who are leading vicious lives."

In striking down this law as a violation of equal protection, the court paid deference to differences between the sexes and to Supreme Court decisions upholding protective labor laws for women or the exclusion of women from jury duty. It did not apply a strict or even intermediate standard of review to the law even though it involved allegations of sex discrimination. *York* was decided before the Supreme Court declared that sex was a slightly suspect basis for legislative classifications. But the court in *York* held that the disparate sentencing scheme was unreasonable; there was no "just relation between the misdemeanors involved here and the inequality in potential punishment." It also rejected the state's contention that disparate sentencing was doing women a favor by offering them a chance of rehabilitation. The court recognized that at least some special protections for women were, in fact, special punishments: The state's characterization of its law as an "attempt to provide for women and juveniles a special protection and every reformative and rehabilitative opportunity" was dismissed by the court as a "way of concealing the abrasive nature of imprisonment under the charming image of an educational institution."

York was complemented by two landmark state court decisions in Pennsylvania and New Jersey striking down similar disparate sentencing laws for men and women.[13] Still, the belief that sex is related to criminal and rehabilitative tendencies didn't quite disappear and didn't always work against women. (In 1970 Maine's highest court upheld a law imposing a higher sentence for prison escape on a man that could have been imposed on a woman.)[14] Men have generally received longer sentences for serious crimes, were more often subject to pretrial detention, and have always constituted the great majority of the prison population. Women may, of course, have been committing fewer felonies, but statistics suggest that they were also receiving less stringent sentences.[15] While chivalry consigned them to reformatories, it spared them from death row.

But the pettiest forms of female criminality have always been viewed by protectionists as uniquely threatening to the social order because of women's role in harmonizing family life. This was reflected in the reformatory movement and the imprisonment of women for "social offenses" that appeared to threaten the family. Miriam Van Waters, a prominent early-twentieth-century penologist, described the "problem" of women offenders in a 1947 speech to the Massachusetts State Federation of Women's Clubs:

> The number of women lawbreakers is small, perhaps one third of the total number of offenders, but the social damages to homes and to community life are great. Children suffer from delinquent mothers and sisters. It used to be said let sin alone and it lets you alone. But this is not true. The community pays a heavy price for the woman delinquent who is by nature and tradition the conservator of family life. It is ironic to consider how slight the offenses of women are in relation to those of men. In Massachusetts, 80% of the women confined in the State Reformatory are convicted not of major offences—but on charges of drunkenness, sex misconduct, desertion, stubborn child, and neglect. These are social derelictions, very serious to family life, but they are not felonies.[16]

The injustice of institutionalizing women for "social derelictions" was lost on Van Waters and other advocates of indeterminate sentencing and rehabilitation for women. Viewing reformatories as essentially benign social (not penal) institutions, she stressed that women inmates needed "self-help," which generally amounted to training as domestic servants.

Social offenses by women generate less concern today, perhaps because the incidence of felonies by women is said to be increasing, a phenomenon for which feminists are often blamed. Female criminality is considered the price or consequence of equality. Arrests of adult women rose 60 percent between 1960 and 1975, while arrests of female juveniles rose 254 percent.[17] Whether these increases reflect an increase in reporting and apprehension rather than commission of crimes, whether the crime rate for women has increased more than the crime rate for men, and whether women are committing different kinds of crimes—robberies and nondomestic crimes associated with men—are controversial questions. Still, feminism, which some consider the masculinization of women, is a popular scapegoat for crime: According to a former police chief of Los Angeles, "The women's movement has triggered a crime wave like the world has never seen before."[18]

The association of liberated women with "bad" women who commit crimes—and of femininity with law-abiding docility—is hardly new. A hundred years ago Cesare Lombroso "proved" that women criminals tended to be masculine. And if femininity is defined as passivity and respect for authority, violent crimes, as opposed to sneaky ones, like shoplifting, are inherently unfeminine. If egalitarian feminism consists solely of an attack on femininity, its success, which we have yet to witness, might logically be linked to an increase in some kinds of female crime. But egalitarianism is an affirmative movement to expand economic opportunities for women and increase their self-esteem and willingness to take responsibility for themselves—hardly prescriptions for criminality. If it were to meet all or some of its goals, the crime rate for women might go down, as their economic and social status goes up (unless female white-collar crime increases in a feminist world).

A feminist analysis of female criminality also suggests that women's crimes are reactive; female domestic violence, for example, is often a defense against male abuse. In other words, "He started it." Of course, any crime from a terrorist bombing to a mugging can be and usually is politicized, attributed to some form of oppression. Sexual discrimination is only one of several injustices that countless people abide. But it's also true that basic definitions of criminality have always been gendered, as prostitution laws demonstrate, and it's likely that feminism and changing ideals of gender are changing the social constructs of crime. It's likely too that feminism is changing the way law enforcement officials perceive and treat women. Preconceived notions linking emancipation to criminality make female offenders look like part of a feminist trend, which may encourage some judges, police officers, or prosecutors to punish women suspects for what are considered the sins of feminism, as some have punished women seeking divorce.

Mandatory differential sentencing for men and women is no longer valid; women generally have equal rights to receive equal sentences for equal crimes. But sentencing is often discretionary; judges often choose between a range of minimums and maximums. Gender-neutral sentencing laws may be applied in a discriminatory fashion by judges who believe they're being fair; gender biases are often unconscious. The unbiased administration of criminal justice has always been difficult to ensure because the enforcement process involves substantial discretion, not just on the part of judges: Police decide whom to arrest; prosecutors decide whom to prosecute on what charges. Probation officers recommend sentences. Laws are as infected with gender and racial biases as the people enforcing them.

Violations of equal rights are especially difficult to prove in the context of subjective decision making. Problems of proving or even discerning ad hoc discrimination have been clearly delineated in employment cases, involving subjective evaluations of merit. Title VII's disparate-impact rule and the use of statistical evidence of racial or sexual imbalances to prove discrimination relieves employees of having to prove their employers intended to discriminate. But the Constitution has no disparate-impact rule and women offenders have no general statutory right to equal treatment in court. (There is no law like Title VII governing the criminal justice system.) Systemic discrimination—like the maintenance of unequal, substandard prisons for women—may be blatant and brutal enough to be considered unconstitutional or create pressure for reform.[19] But random, individual inequities are often invisible.

This highlights the need for social attitudes to change along with laws for women to be treated equally as offenders and victims: Rape reform laws can redefine sex crimes, prescribe their punishments, and regulate the trial process. But they can't ensure that police officers responding to a rape will treat the victim sympathetically or that assistant district attorneys will vigorously prosecute their assailants. Rape shield laws can limit the admissibility at trial of a victim's sexual history, but victims whose sexual histories make them suspect may never see their cases tried at all. Prosecutors screen cases, seeking the most credible witnesses whose testimony is most likely to result in conviction.[20] Of course, in an overburdened system, the great majority of cases aren't tried; most are resolved by pleas. But plea bargains as well as trial strategies are shaped by a prosecutor's assessment of the strength of a case, which in a rape case is shaped by prevailing views of gender relations and roles.

Acknowledging this, feminists have focused on "consciousness raising" about sexual violence, with some success. Police forces, hospitals, and district attorneys' offices have sex crime units or task forces trained to deal sympathetically with rape victims. Television movies periodically "expose" the plight of rape victims and battered wives. Sexual violence persists, but public discourse about it is slowly changing. Few lawyers or judges today would dare suggest that the victim of a rape should lie back and enjoy it.

Feminism has also provided women who "fight back" against abusive men with new theories of self-defense, raising controversial questions about individual accountability and the irresistible effect of gender biases on behavior and about differential standards for men and women accused of homicides or assaults. Should the law blame a women for killing a man who threatened her? Or was he asking for it, as women were once presumed to have asked for their rapes? Is the environment of sexual injustice to blame for crimes committed by women against men? By what standards of reasonableness should we judge male and female fears of assault and responses to attackers?

In 1977 the Supreme Court of Washington considered these questions and expanded a woman's right to self-defense in *State v. Wanrow*.[21] The Court reversed the second degree murder conviction of Yvonne Wanrow, who had shot and killed a man suspected of molesting the daughter of her friend during an altercation at the friend's house. The man, William Wesler, was unarmed, but at 6'2" tall and intoxicated he could conceivably have posed a powerful threat to Wanrow, a 5'4" woman on crutches with a broken leg. Wanrow, who had come to the house with a gun to protect her friend from an anticipated visit by Wesler, claimed she shot him reflexively when he loomed unexpectedly behind her.

She was convicted of second degree murder after the trial judge instructed the jury that in evaluating her claim of self-defense, it could only consider what transpired "at or immediately before the killing." (On appeal the State Supreme Court stressed that settled law required the consideration of circumstances that occurred "substantially before the killing.") The trial judge also relied on a traditional "reasonable man" standard for evaluating Wanrow's perception of danger and her response to it.

In general, the traditional formulation of self-defense in a homicide case requires that a defendant, identified always as "he," have a reasonable basis for believing himself in imminent danger of being killed or seriously injured; his right to use deadly force or a deadly weapon depends on the reasonableness of his fear of a deadly attack. He is not generally authorized to use a gun against an unarmed man. The judge in the *Wanrow* case put it like this:

> When there is no reasonable ground for the person attacked to believe that his person is in imminent danger of death or great bodily harm, and it appears to him that only an ordinary battery is all that is intended and all that he has reasonable grounds to fear from his assailant, he has a right to stand his ground and repel such threatened assault, yet he has no right to repel a threatened assault with naked hands, by the use of a deadly weapon in a deadly manner, unless he believes, and has reasonable grounds to believe, that he is in imminent danger of death or great bodily harm."[22]

On appeal, the Supreme Court of Washington rejected this masculinized formulation of self-defense as applied to Yvonne Wanrow.

193

Reversing her conviction, the court held that a small women on crutches might have been justified in using a gun instead of her "naked hands" on a large, able-bodied, hostile male.

By itself this is a reasonable and not especially radical holding that is not based only on gender; it simply requires juries to be alert to the circumstances of the case before them when considering a claim of self-defense. Presumably a small man on crutches would have had the right to a similar jury instruction. But the Court went on to issue the remarkable mandate that Wanrow's actions be considered not only in light of the circumstances of her case, but in light of her position as a woman in a sexist society: "The respondent (Wanrow) was entitled to have the jury consider her actions in light of her own perceptions of the situation, including those perceptions that were the product of our nation's long and unfortunate history of sex discrimination."*

The establishment of dual standards of self-defense for male and female defendants is highly controversial (and might violate a state or federal ERA). The notion that sex discrimination is an excuse for acts by women that might be considered crimes when committed by men raises questions about our definitions of criminality for all victims of social injustice. Should a history of racial discrimination justify crimes by minority defendants? Should poverty justify crimes by the underclass? How do we sort out the social and environmental causes of crime from the personal ones? When do we absolve defendants because of their circumstances, and when do we blame them for their character defects?

The *Wanrow* case was a discomfiting victory for egalitarian feminists who believe in single standards of law. The court's acknowledgment of sex discrimination and its effect on a woman's psyche was, by feminist standards, enlightened. Its sensitivity to women's fear of men was welcome and long overdue. In some ways, this decision was simply corrective; it wasn't conferring privileges on women as much as it was compensating for a traditional male bias built into the criminal justice system. Rules about self-defense have always been gendered by reliance on a reasonable man standard. The Washington court simply formulated a standard for reasonable women too. Still, its willingness to consider the general circumstances of women's lives as well as the specific circumstances of one woman's case is troubling. Separating the general from the specific causes of crime is a challenge judges and juries in every criminal case ought to meet.

---

*This quote about sex discrimination is taken from the Supreme Court decision in *Frontiero v. Richardson*, 411 U.S. 677 (1973).

Cases involving battered wives that came after *Wanrow* were, in this respect, easier and less controversial. The "battered wife syndrome"— the notion that a woman may be terrorized and emotionally disabled by battering—rests on a very specific prior relationship between a defendant and an abusive mate. (Wanrow had not been battered by the man she killed.) Posttraumatic stress syndromes are becoming popular defenses in a range of criminal cases: Vietnam vets are said to suffer from them too.[23]

Questions of individual accountability are not new to the criminal-justice system, and they're not simply a function of gender. Judges and juries have long struggled to determine when mental incompetence or derangement makes someone not guilty of a crime. But the use of these defenses in cases involving sexual assaults and homicides does raise important issues for feminists, as well as criminal justice professionals. How we define temporary insanity or justification in defining criminal liability when men and women kill each other depends on our view of what's normal and natural in sexual relations and our tolerance for what has long been considered normal and natural violence against women.

Sexual violence is commonplace and only occasionally newsworthy. Occasionally a particularly vicious rape or sex murder galvanizes the public; often the victim is a young, white middle- or upper-class woman who was supposed to have been protected, even immune, from the violence that plagues the underclass. Take the killing of Jennifer Levin by Robert Chambers, the "preppie murder" in Central Park that occurred in August of 1986 and preoccupied New York City for about a year.

Chambers, a nineteen-year-old with a history of behavioral problems and drug abuse was charged with first degree murder, pled guilty to a lesser charge of manslaughter, and was sentenced to five to fifteen years for Levin's killing. He strangled her during what he initially described as sex play but what appears to have been an outburst of sexual rage. Before pleading guilty, Chambers claimed to have killed accidentally and in self-defense, during a rough sexual encounter in the Park. At 6'4", weighing 220 pounds, Chambers had little to fear, reasonably, from an unarmed eighteen-year-old female; but he implied that Levin compensated for her size and relative lack of strength with sexual aggressiveness.

His early account of Levin's death confirmed that she was asking for it. Chamber claimed that on the night of her death, Levin waited for him outside an Upper East Side bar they both frequented that catered to an Upper East Side, college-age crowd. She insisted on walking him home and persuaded him to stop off in the park to discuss the relationship she hoped they might have (they had dated casually in the past). Levin "pleaded her case. . . . When it appeared that she was getting nowhere, she reached out and scratched his face in anger." She then begged for forgiveness and initiated a rough and, for Chambers, painful sexual encounter that resulted in her death.[24]

This story outraged feminists (on both sides of the equality debate) because it so clearly exploits myths about "bad" promiscuous women—and because it wasn't believable. In a culture in which men commonly attack women, it was easier to imagine Chambers agreeably accompanying Levin to the Park and strangling her in a fit of sexual rage.

But feminist voices weren't the primary ones heard in public discussion of this case. It focused on the problems of underage drinking and drug abuse among young men and women of privilege and, to a lesser extent, on the problem of broken homes. (Levin's parents were divorced; Chambers's parents were separated and he had a history of drug problems.) Instead of focusing on gender biases, public discussion of this case focused on "values" and social control of adolescents.

That Levin's killing reflected a current of misogynist rage was clear and beyond dispute to most feminists. That the problem of sexual violence figured much less prominently in coverage of this case than problems of adolescent behavior and contemporary family life only confirmed the hostility or, at best, insensitivity toward women that produces rape/murder.

In some ways, the prevalence of that hostility is what makes it so easy to ignore; it's been normalized. The notion that "bad" girls run risks of being assaulted or even killed by the men they "provoke" is a given that not everybody questions. Like other biases—against racial or ethnic groups—having been internalized, misogyny is ignored. And it's systemic. The extent to which the double standard and its attendant hostility toward women have been institutionalized was demonstrated by the support Chambers received from the Catholic Church—one of the more notable but least noticed aspects of this case.

Five weeks after his arrest, Chambers was released from the custody of the Department of Corrections to the care of his church. Freed on $150,000 bail, he was ordered to report daily to Monsignor Thomas Leonard, his former elementary school teacher, who offered to counsel him and guarantee his future court appearances. The church's support for Chambers was another provocative similarity between this case and the 1978 killing of Bonnie Garland by her boyfriend Richard Herrin, the

"Yale Murder".* Herrin never claimed to have killed accidentally; he smashed Garland's skull with a hammer while she slept. But five weeks after confessing, first to a priest and then to police, he was free on bail, enjoying the sanctuary offered by the Christian Brothers in Albany, New York, and the support of the Catholic community at Yale University, which helped organize his defense fund. Herrin was eventually acquitted of murder, having convinced the jury that his act was mitigated by severe emotional distress: Garland had been trying to leave him. He was convicted of manslaughter and sentenced to eight to twenty-five years.[25]

Perhaps fallen altar boys and other prodigals always should be succored by their church; it's not supposed to turn away from sinners. But the Catholic Church's involvement in these two cases raise questions about its complicity in the abuse of women and illustrates the way traditional ideals of femininity that are supposed to protect women are turned against the female victims of sexual violence.**

In discussing Jennifer Levin's killing, Monsignor Thomas Leonard expressed more concern about female assertiveness (a "new sense of independence among women") than male aggression, implying that Levin was at least partly to blame for her death.[26] Bonnie Garland provoked her killing too, Herrin's lawyer implied, and the jury apparently agreed. Feminism was subtly held to blame for both these deaths, and feminist outrage about Levin's killing was misplaced, Monsignor Leonard suggested. "Anger" made feminists unfair and unwilling to judge the case "on its own merits." It became "a flashpoint for all the other anger in the women's movement." As if feminists have more to fear from their own anger than from the anger of men, the Monsignor warned that "left to fester, anger robs the spirit of a certain freedom."

It's true that the *Chambers* case should have been tried on its own merits, as it was. Chambers was accused of a crime against one woman, not all womankind. Women who kill men ought not be absolved by a history of sex discrimination, and men who kill women ought not to be blamed for it.

But the misogyny reflected by the *Chambers* case and the fear cases like this instill in women rob them of more freedom than feminist anger ever will. This assault on women's freedom was ignored by the

*Herrin and Chambers were represented by the same attorney, Jack Litman, who used a similar tactic of discrediting the victim in both cases.

**Both cases raise questions too about the place of Christian forgiveness in a system of secular justice. Defining criminal liability is not the business of the church anymore than saving souls is the business of law.

Monsignor, who preferred to focus on social issues raised by the case, rather than sexual ones. Both Chambers and Levin were children of broken marriages, he stressed: "A tragic event has happened and part of that tragedy is that there is a whole host of kids abandoned by their parents." He deplored the divorce rate, teenage drinking, and the breakdown in family values, turning the case into a story about adolescent rebellion that trivialized Levin's death. Young people like Levin and Chambers have "no one to rebel against," he said, as if they were two kids who stole a car and went joyriding.

Monsignor Leonard, of course, was one man concerned with providing Chambers with spiritual counseling, who had no apparent intent to interfere in the legal process. It was indeed his business to forgive, or at least understand, and not condemn an allegedly repentant sinner. But his focus on the social issues raised by the case—divorce, adolescent rebellion, alcohol abuse, and promiscuity—was typical and shared by such powerful secular institutions as the *New York Times*. It effectively absolved Chambers and made him a victim too. As Monsignor Leonard said, this was a tragedy that "happened" to Chambers as well as the girl he killed: "He could have had better parental guidance."

Social problems—questions about parental guidance and community values—were also the focus of discussion about the brutal, nearly fatal gang rape of a jogger in Central Park in April 1989. A "posse" of minority teenage boys on a rampage through the park raped a twenty-eight-year-old white investment banker, beating her savagely about the head, leaving her comatose and brain damaged. There was much speculation about the racial motivations for this attack, suggestions that the boys were out "to get" a white woman. There was much concern about "wilding"—sprees of random violence by gangs of teenage boys—and there was wonderment that the suspects in this case came from relatively intact, working-class families, (suggesting that parents can't shield children from the violence that surrounds them). There were cries to reinstate the death penalty and demands that juveniles who commit crimes like this be prosecuted as if they were adults. But in all the outcry over this case, there was relatively little mention of the fearsome rage against women it delineated. Numerous people were attacked by the "wilding" gang that night; only one was sexually assaulted, beaten, and nearly killed—a lone woman jogger with the nerve or incredibly bad judgment to run by herself in a deserted area of North Central Park at ten o'clock at night.

Most women who grow up in this culture know better, which is not to suggest that she was asking for it or bears any responsibility for her attack. It is simply to underscore the pervasiveness of sexual violence and hatred of women. Vulnerability to rape and murder is a fact of life that deters most women from taking lonely, late-night runs. That lesson was lost in all the talk about values and social control inspired by this case.

Like the killing of Jennifer Levin, the Central Park rape was a sex crime that fascinated and repelled and was turned into a parable about many things other than sex. What were clear and vicious expressions of men's rage against women were construed as expressions of social instability and the decline of family values (phenomena periodically blamed on feminists). The moral of these cases was ignored by the moral tales they were said to be telling. But there's a moral in that too.

Despite rape reform laws and increased concern about sex crimes, sexual violence can still go unquestioned because traditional ideals about male and female sexuality run deep. Male domination and female submission are still considered natural, which makes rape and even murder natural expressions of male aggression, especially when turned against an "uppity" woman who gets out of line. Jennifer Levin was promiscuous, Chambers implied; she was demanding and sexually aggressive. His priest questioned her "sense of independence." By rationalizing misogyny, they made it easy to ignore.

But if pathological hostility toward women is invisible to most male chauvinists, it's ubiquitous to some feminists, whose outrage over sexual violence extends to metaphoric as well as actual expressions of it. The feminist movement against pornography was, in part, a movement to open the public eye to metaphors of male domination in the mainstream media—in advertising, feature films, television, and record album covers, as well as hard-core pornography. The outrage was justified and the consciousness raising honorable: Feminists against pornography attempted to show just how acceptable sexual violence was. But in attempting to prohibit mere images of violence, they undermined the integrity of feminism as a civil rights movement: Antiporn feminists sought to make pornography unacceptable, not by social pressure but under law, in order to protect women, arguing that there was a direct, causal link between reading or viewing pornography and beating or raping a woman.*

In demanding the censorship of material deemed harmful to women, antiporn feminists, like other protectionists before them, also relied on the same old vision of men and women that pornography successfully

---

*I was briefly involved in the antipornography movement in the late 1970s and have considerable sympathy for the view of pornography as misogynist propaganda. I have never had any sympathy for efforts to censor it.[27]

exploited. The belief that even subtle images of sexual violence directly lead to sexually violent acts rests not only on the questionable notion that images are viewed objectively, that one picture has the same meaning for many people and effects them in the same way. It rests on a view of men as amoral creatures with urges they can't control. Catherine MacKinnon, a feminist legal scholar and leader in the antipornography movement, claims that prohibiting pornography doesn't raise First Amendment issues because pornography is an act (of sex discrimination) and not an instance of speech. What makes it an act is its effect on male consumers and what she perceives as a clear and simple link between seeing and doing for men.

"Giving a man pornography is like saying 'Kill' to a trained attack dog," MacKinnon explains, which is more a theory of sexuality than speech: Pornography is action because all men are dogs on short leashes.

This rather bleak view of male sexuality is shared by right-wing antiporn protesters and pornographers alike. It's the problem, not the solution, for women. It sets up an irreconcilable conflict between freedom of speech for men and freedom from sexual violence for women that dates back to mid-nineteenth-century antivice movements and undermines the fight for reproductive freedom. Information about contraception and abortion have always been labeled pornography by social issue activists on the right, along with sex education. According to Jerry Falwell, sex education is dangerous: After being taught "the fundamentals of sexual relationships," he reports in a fundraising letter, one class of ninth-graders in a California public school graduated three years later with "one half the senior girls pregnant."[28] Phyllis Schlafly agrees that sex education is a "principle cause of teenage pregnancy." Its purpose is "to teach teenagers (and sometimes children) how to enjoy fornication without having a baby and without feeling guilty."[29]

The New Right answer to the "problem" of sex education, feminism, and other forms of secular humanism has been censorship in public libraries and schools. According to Judith Krug of the American Library Association, the 1980s saw a threefold increase in the number of library censorship cases, over half of which "had something to do with sex." Librarians became more hesitant to fight for books that were labeled pornographic, Krug observed, because of added pressure from feminist protesters: "They were less willing to enter the fray because of a sense that some of our feminist friends were on the other side." Legislative solutions were also pressed. The proposed Family Protection Act of 1981 would have denied federal funds for the purchase of school books that "denigrated the role of women as it has been historically understood," and to any school program that "inculcated values or modes of behavior which contradict the demonstrated beliefs and values of the community."

It's distressingly easy to imagine a feminist version of this—a Woman's Protection Act prohibiting the purchase of school books *promoting* the role of women "as it has historically been understood." Feminists against pornography, with differing beliefs and values of their own, generally support sex education, freedom of choice, and new roles for women and were clearly disassociated from the goals of the New Right. But they adopted some of its basic precepts about sexuality and its fear of speech that advocates ideals or behavior different from their own.

The feminist antiporn movement was readily coopted by the right, as the Reagan Administration's 1986 Commission on Pornography showed. The commission, led by Attorney General Ed Meese, recommended a federal crackdown on pornography, of questionable constitutional validity, based largely on testimony that pornography causes sexual abuse. President Reagan, who was rarely accused of harboring sympathy for feminism, deplored the "link" between "pornography and sexual violence toward women."[30]

Right-wing activists have adopted the rhetoric of feminism: Phyllis Schlafly has said that "pornography really should be defined as the degradation of women. Nearly all porn involves the use of women in subordinate, degrading poses for the sexual, exploitative, and even sadistic and violent pleasures of men." How, she wondered, would pornography "affect a man who is already prone to violence against women?"[31]

This confusion of speech with action, the view of pornography as a form of abuse, reflects the spirit of the 1980s. "Rhetoric is policy," President Reagan remarked. "Words are action." Books make young girls pregnant, as Jerry Falwell and Phyllis Schlafly confirm. Or as attorney Catherine MacKinnon says, "Men have sex with their image of a woman."[32]

Calling pornography a practice of abuse instead of the propaganda of abusers was an ominous shift for feminists. Calling an image an act is Orwellian, but as a justification for censoring pornography it also reflects women's acceptance of their own powerlessness. Feminists today are in a position to counter sexist speech with nonsexist speech of their own, to promote noncensorious protests of material considered dangerous or demeaning to women along with literature and education promoting alternative visions of sexuality.* The short libertarian answer to the problem of pornography is more speech, not less.

Feminist protesters responded to this by arguing that they lacked the resources to challenge a multi-billion-dollar sex industry, raising legitimate questions about First Amendment freedoms in an age of media conglomerates. Feminists have been one of several groups battling sexist, racist, or "secular humanist" biases in the popular media. They complain of insufficient access to the marketplace; civil libertarians complain, in turn, that some large-scale private protests, like consumer boycotts of television shows, are a kind of de facto censorship (suggesting that only unsuccessful protests are constitutional). How can private interest groups and minorities compete in an incorporated marketplace? According to feminist Andrea Dworkin, "The First Amendment . . . belongs to those who can buy it."[33]

This is hyperbole with a kernel of truth that underscores the propriety of purely private media protests. But it does not justify government intervention in media affairs (although some variation on Dworkin's theme is the basis for the controversial fairness doctrine), nor does it acknowledge the success of feminists in making their political statements about pornography. Without invoking the power of government, feminists proved, in spite of themselves, that women need not remain the hapless victims of a behemoth sex industry. Andrea Dworkin has proclaimed that pornography silences women, but it did not silence her.

The antipornography movement has waned in recent years (along with the sex industry). Popular feminist issues are those involving work and family life—child care, maternity benefits, and divorce. Efforts by feminists to prohibit pornography as a form of sex discrimination have been firmly rebuffed in federal court,[34] and AIDS has made sex education a public health imperative. But there is an important lesson to be drawn from the ascendance of the antiporn movement during the 1980s: As a form of terrorism, sexual violence works. It intimidates women, convincing them of their weakness and their need to be protected from men by law. The equation of words with actions, of pornography with sexual abuse, played on ignorance of First Amendment freedoms and the history of the anti–birth control movement, but most of all, on the awful fear of sexual violence. Most women know what it is to be harassed and intimidated, if not abused, but it takes a

---

*They might also focus on strengthening prohibitions of the acts with which pornography is associated, such as the use and abuse of children in pornographic films.

great leap of feminist faith and an overwhelming sense of vulnerability to believe you've been assaulted by a book.

The ironies of feminist movements to censor pornography are manifold. In the 1830s, the time of the Second Great Awakening, the 1880s, the peak of the social purity movement, and the 1980s, feminist pornography protests reinforced reactionary, evangelical crusades to preserve traditional codes of sexual behavior and familial roles. Protectionism made some sense to the disenfranchised woman with no legal rights or worldly expertise; she had reason to believe in her own weakness. Today, this sense of powerlessness is regressive and self-defeating. There is no trade-off of rights and freedoms between the sexes. Attacking the First Amendment because it allows men to read bad books undermines the rights of women to read and write about reproductive health and gender roles. For a young woman to have freedom to control her own body, she must first have the freedom to learn about it.

It is more than a little crazy for women to think that censorship will make them free. Feminists who have so eloquently decried their exclusion from the political process can hardly expect to be the community in control if the time comes to excise pornography from the popular media, public schools, and libraries. (They may learn about free speech the hard way.) The First Amendment protects people on the ideological margins of society; in a misogynist world, it may be one right that always works for women. The effort by feminists to censor pornography was a new turn of the same old screw.

Women are not generically weak, submissive, and silent and incapable of countering the propaganda of pornography with feminist propaganda of their own. Women aren't pure, and they ought not to be passive. They need not choose between repression and selfless acquiescence to abuse.

Conclusion

"I have always wanted to do what I have done," M. Carey Thomas, first dean and formidable president of Bryn Mawr, wrote in 1934, at the end of her remarkable life. It is a brave, unfeminine statement, a claim of control and independent decision making; it implies a life chosen and shaped, not haplessly encountered, as women's lives were once supposed to be. But Thomas had embarked upon rebellion early on. "A girl certainly should do what she chooses as well as a boy," she declared at fourteen, in 1871, when conventional wisdom held that, outside the home, a girl couldn't do anything as well as a boy, least of all choose her life's work. People talked, Thomas exclaimed, "as if the whole end and aim of a woman's life was to get *married* and . . . amuse her husband." As a wife or a presumably frustrated spinster, tending to others, at home or in schoolrooms, she fulfilled not just her role but her nature. "Nature" denied women choice and made them attend the interests of others—husbands, parents, and kids—in place of their own. Instead of pleasure, self-control, and rights of self-interest, nature gave women sad duties of self-abnegation.[1]

Some natural imperatives are changing for women, and Thomas—who managed to satisfy herself, obtain a man's education, and provide one for women at Bryn Mawr—would have been pleased by contemporary feminism's gains. But she might have wondered at the old-fashioned view of femininity that still prevails, along with the notion that it is selfish for women to demand equal rights.

Equal rights feminists are still called narcissistic or simply selfish, as they were 100 years ago, and selfishness still signals sexual ambiguity in a woman: Selfish women make bad mothers; they pursue careers for self-fulfillment, not just because of economic need. Selfish women make bad wives; they don't "amuse" their husbands or grant them what M. Carey Thomas called "the *exquisite* pleasure of knowing more."[2] They expect the sacrifices marriage demands of careers to be mutual. Selfish women make bad citizens; they take jobs away from men. (In 1982 President Reagan blamed unemployment on the "ladies" in the work-force.)[3] They rob unselfishly dependent women and children of male support and undermine the family. Very selfish women destroy the family by declining to be wives or mothers at all. Even unmarried women who do have children, on purpose, are selfish: "It's not fair to the child," people say. More selfish still are women, married or not, who refuse to have children by accident. Abortion, a powerful act of self-assertion, has become a powerful symbol of feminist selfishness. Imagine caring about your own life more than a potential one.

M. Carey Thomas didn't have children, nor did she marry, though she once fell in love with a man. At twenty-one, beginning her graduate studies, she was distracted, unhappily, by love. "I cannot help thinking about him," she wrote. "There is limitless time to think between the turning of the leaves of a Greek dictionary." But he married someone else, and marriage never had been an option for her. In the nineteenth century, social mores and the lack of birth control made marriage even more incompatible with careers for women than motherhood is today. For women, marriage was a retreat from the world and the slim enough hope of autonomous intellectual and professional achievement. "There seems no solution of the question of marriage," Thomas observed, "for it is difficult to conceive a woman who really feels her separate lifework to give it all up."[4] Thomas, like most pioneering professional women of her generation, gave up marriage instead, willingly, if not entirely without regret.

Equal rights feminism does not promise women there'll be no more giving up. Most feminists don't expect women to do everything they want or even to want everything they do. Most feminists, like most reasonable people, realize that you can't always please yourself; or, at least, you can't only please yourself. If love involves caring for someone else as much as you care about yourself, then it will always evoke sacrifices, even from men and feminists too. If good citizenship and a sense of community involve linking your interests to the interests of others, then they have a great deal in common with feminism. The staunchest feminist advocate of every woman's individual rights recognizes that every woman's destiny is linked to the destiny of her sex, which is linked to the destiny of his. A fight for civil rights serves a community, and in a feminist world sacrifices to family and community will be offered freely by women, not exacted selfishly from them.

But underlying much resistance to egalitarian feminism is the inarticulate belief that justice for women is incompatible with justice for family and community. Traditional visions of social justice assume a tradition of service by women, which is rationalized and enforced by proclamations about women's nature. Like a mantra, the "only women get pregnant" refrain reverberates through our culture, throughout our history. It's a way of saying "Only women were born to nurture. Only women were born to serve."

The translation of reproductive differences into gender stereotypes is a social or even a psychological problem as much as a legal and political one. It points out the need for egalitarians to insinuate themselves into the popular culture instead of waiting to be absorbed by it. Popular ideas about sex and gender must change along with law, and resistance to changing the "natural" order is profound. From protectionist feminists to communitarians to right-wing social-issue activists, there is general agreement that egalitarian feminists are too masculine, that they modeled the "new woman" after the old man, that the ERA was unnatural, as if inequality were an inescapable fact of life. To recognize this is to confront the enormity of feminism's task.

Demographic changes may lighten it, facilitating a change in gender roles. Over half of all American women over the age of sixteen are in the labor force, and they're not likely to go home; their employers wouldn't want them to and neither would their husbands. Women are beginning to dominate the labor pool; in the 1990s more than half of new entrants to the labor force will be women.[5] Both unions and employers are therefore paying more attention to "women's issues"—child care and maternity benefits.[6] Employer-sponsored day-care and parental-leave programs are slowly being recognized as sound economic policy. A recent article in the *Wall Street Journal* posits this as the corporate model for the twenty-first century: "Future Corporation runs its own day care center to serve mommies and daddies who struggle to work clutching not just their briefcases but their babies. The Future Corp. School, run jointly with other area companies, gives a high quality, elementary education."[7]

A more optimistic view is that Future Corp. will provide generous leaves that ensure that neither mommies nor daddies will "struggle" to work with their babies. A more optimistic view would posit reproductive freedom for women, so that they're having babies only by choice. A less optimistic but equally feasible view is that Future Corp. will have two separate job tracks, one labeled "mommy."

Although ideas about what women may do are changing, prescriptions about how they should feel and what their priorities should be sometimes seem written in stone. The notion that wage earning naturally takes second place for a woman is based, after all, on a belief in her emotional gifts for childbearing, and in their emotional lives men and women seem "as bound as ever" by stereotypes. Men are said to be more inhibited about expressing nominally feminine emotions, like sadness and distress. Women are said to be more inhibited about expressing anger or sexual desire.[8]

These are differences in style: Women experience anger, but they're taught to internalize it, which makes them more prone to depression than acts of violence.[9] There's no clear line, of course, between style and substance; modes of expression help shape what's being expressed, and people who act less angry may become less angry. Still, the subtleties of this process are lost when masculine and feminine styles are equated with natural differences in male and female nature, from which neither men nor women may escape. The emotional sensibilities that culture breeds in women are linked to a "natural" female drive for emotional intimacy, and the tendency of women to strive for intimacy by default, because they've not been allowed to strive for success, is ignored. Masculine expressions of anger are linked to "natural" male agression, which naturalizes the male quest for success and allows men to abdicate responsibility for maintaining emotional ties.

Hoary notions about the naturally divergent emotional orientations of men and women are presented in relatively sophisticated, scientific or pseudoscientific packages for upscale, educated audiences. A recent article in the *Atlantic*, "Some Differences between Men and Women," confirms that women are naturally preoccupied with love, while men seek professional achievement, by dressing up clichés about gender in familiar psychological theories about the Oedipal dramas of girls and boys: Girls identify with their mothers and hence with a primary caretaking role; boys need to separate from Mom and hence from the notion of caretaking in order to establish their masculine identities. This is a perfectly circular theory; it rests on the initial consignment of mothers to primary caretaking roles, which may not be natural at all. But its authoritative, scientific tone, its Jungian references to male and female archetypes, not stereotypes, makes a series of unsubstantiated generalizations—"women escape into love, whereas men fear being made vulnerable by [it]"—sound like a series of facts.[10]

As it was 100 years ago, science is still a powerful voice for protectionist "facts" about sexual difference, perhaps powerful enough to offset the effect of demographic changes in shaping gender ideals. Since science is presumed to proceed from an objective accounting of facts, since scientists are presumed to be more objective than the rest of us, the gender biases underlying scientific theories sometimes takes years to surface. The notion that men were smarter than women because their brains were heavier was once as credible as sociobiology's more recent explanation of gender roles.

Sociobiology is a relatively new science, based on the notion that all behavior is adaptive, a genetic accommodation to environment. All living organisms are said to have been adapted absolutely by evolution, the process of natural selection and the drive to maximize reproductive advantages. This means that all behavior has a purely biological explanation. When applied to beings like insects and birds, this theory has scientific credibility. When applied to human beings, as it was in popular writings of the 1970s, sociobiology is a politicized simplification of the relations between humans and the worlds they inhabit. The notion that people act on their environments, perhaps as much as they are acted on, and the rich blend of natural and cultural causes of human behavior were lost as sociobiology trickled down into the mainstream. What was gained was a biological justification for the status quo and a powerful argument against social change. Popular sociobiology was incisively attacked and discredited by critics within the scientific community,[11] but it was the perfect pop science for a postfeminist world. It debuted in 1975 with publication of E. O. Wilson's *Sociobiology: The New Synthesis*,[12] when feminism's popularity was beginning to decline, anxiety about new roles for women was rising, and the willingness to believe in natural sexual differences was strong.

Of course, there may be natural cognitive and behavioral differences between men and women, and science may yet uncover them. Theories about the effect of male and female hormones and the different organization and functioning of male and female brains abound.[13] They are, however, highly controversial and speculative, and at most they describe average men and women, without foreclosing the possibility of considerable variation. They describe potential—models of men and women untouched by culture. The complex and puzzling interplay between nature and culture is clear in the controversy over the emotional effects of menstruation. Women's mood swings can be linked to cultural attitudes toward menstruation, as well as hormonal fluctuations. Evidence that women's moods reflect hormonal changes has been countered with evidence that they reflect negative cultural and religious attitudes toward menstruation and female sexuality. It's "no coincidence," one researcher has asserted, that women get the blues "along with an event they consider embarrassing, unclean—a curse."[14]

Why a sign of fertility is considered a curse in cultures that value women primarily for their capacity to reproduce is unclear. It is clear, however, that reproduction and everything connected with it has been turned into a source of anxiety for women—anxiety that fiercely enforces gender roles.

A new preoccupation with infertility has emerged in recent years. Women and men flock to fertility specialists for expensive and highly intrusive treatments. The "pain of infertility" has become a cliché—the subject of polite conversations and popular magazine articles. Anxiety about fertility is even stronger than anxiety about the dangers infertility treatments may pose. The infertility industry is largely unregulated, and serious questions about safety are hardly being asked. Biologist Ruth Hubbard fears that infertility treatments involving synthetic estrogen may be the DES of the 1980s.[15] (DES was a drug given to pregnant women from the late 1940s through the 1960s that caused cancer in DES daughters; its effect on DES sons is not clear.)

The business of infertility is one obvious consequence of reproductive technology and the development of fertility treatments, but it's also a response to anxiety about feminism, the changing labor force, and women's demands for reproductive control. Prochoice advocates are accused of "despising" pregnancy and trying to "de-sex" women.[16] A less hysterical view blames infertility on feminists who encouraged women to work outside the home during their childbearing years. Women are reminded of their "biological clocks" and the slim chances of finding a mate past the age of thirty. It's not at all clear that any of this concern about infertility reflects a decrease in the number of fertile women. Infertility is also, in part, a cultural construct. Do we say a woman is infertile because she fails to conceive after one year, or eighteen months, or two years or three?[17]

What concern about infertility and the way we define it does reflect is the profound connection between a woman's self-confidence and her capacity to reproduce. Part of the pain of infertility, after all, is the sense that you're "not really" a woman.

"Real" women have children (only feminists and women who have been duped by them have abortions). Or we might say that "real" women bear children because talk about infertility focuses on highly sentimentalized images of pregnancy and childbirth, not child rearing. Despite all the talk about adoption by President Bush and other opponents of abortion rights, tax policies as well as popular ideals favor raising your "own" child instead of an adopted one.[18] Babies, newborn babies, have been iconized in response to feminist demands for reproductive freedom and economic equality for women; the focus on infertility tells us more about our views of women than our feelings for children and family life.

So much anxiety about feminism is anxiety about reproduction. What will families look like in a feminist world? What will men look like taking care of babies? What will women look like when they cease to define themselves as people with children and people without them? What are the natural and cultural consequences of motherhood, and what ought to be the legal ones?

So much anxiety about reproduction is anxiety about feminism and changing gender roles. The abortion debate may not, in essence, be about fetal life at all. The notion that fetuses, although forms of human life, are not quite human beings is implicitly established in our culture. We don't mourn miscarriages as much as crib deaths, and people who believe abortions should be available to victims of sexual abuse—young girls impregnated by their fathers—do not believe the children born of incestuous relationships should be killed. If Americans valued fetuses as much as antiabortion rhetoric suggests, we would systematically, routinely, unquestioningly, provide decent prenatal health care to poor people. If Americans valued children as much as antiabortion rhetoric suggests, we would not permit so many of them (one-fifth of all children under eighteen) to live in poverty.

Concern, or professed concern, for fetal life is more of an excuse than a reason for concern about abortion. The antiabortion movement reflects profound resentment and fear of feminism's challenge to femininity and traditional gender roles. Demands to prohibit abortion translate into demands that women go home and stay home, taking care of babies. Opponents of abortion rights are almost invariably opponents of equality who believe that traditional divisions of labor and Ozzie and Harriet families are all that's natural and good. When we reject this narrow, simplistic view of human sexuality, when we confront the complexities of nature and the intriguing variation of what's natural for individual men and women, we'll resolve the debate about abortion. When we allow every woman to shape her own notion of femininity and her own destiny as a human being, we'll allow her to determine her reproductive destiny too. If we believed in equality, we'd believe in reproductive choice.

It shouldn't be so difficult, after all, for Americans to reject the inflexible, gender-based hierarchy and authoritarianism offered by the right and the antiabortion movement. Equality, choice, and the notion of inventing yourself are supposed to be American ideals. The principle that people ought not be disadvantaged legally by the circumstances of their birth—like the fact that they're women—is supposed to be fundamental in America. As the dissent in the *Bakke* case stressed, race, gender, and illegitimacy are "immutable characteristic[s] which its possessors are powerless to escape or set aside."[19] Some might add sexual orientation to the list. This means that we generally treat naturally different people alike. (Affirmative action, at issue in *Bakke*, is an attempt to compensate for our failure to do so in the past; it treats culturally different people differently, in an attempt to correct unnatural differences created by discrimination.) Natural sameness or difference is not generally relevant to the allocation of rights. Ignorant and educated, responsible and irresponsible, well- and ill-intentioned people all have the right to vote, regardless of how they use it or whether they use it at all. In this view, law doesn't presume sameness, but it does presume that immutable differences between people don't matter.

Some feminists disagree. Feminists who believe there are natural differences in male and female nature believe these differences matter a lot. Still others who agree that gender isn't necessarily relevant to character, intelligence, or professional capability and ambition disagree about the relevance of pregnancy, to the formulation of disability benefits or child custody laws—to the formulation of some rights in virtually every sphere.

To point out that only women get pregnant doesn't end a debate; it begins one. What do we make of the fact that women get pregnant? What do we make of the social structures pregnancy engenders? What is the developmental impact of reproductive biology on women? How does the mere possibility of becoming pregnant affect a woman's psyche? What role does it play in shaping personality?

The simplest answer—that biology is destiny—is the one we know best. It justifies, indeed celebrates, sexual inequality. It celebrates conformity. Men and women are not the same, protectionists repeat (as if anyone suggested they were), but their argument about sexuality is a prescription for sameness, not diversity. It presumes that every woman is as much like another as she is unlike every man. It is the reductionist view of human nature that underlies every racist or sexist generalization, every system that treats individuals as mere representative types. Protectionist feminism is not necessarily racist (although it has a historical connection to racism), but it does rest on a process of stereotyping that women and minorities should abhor. As the practice of lynching, based on myths about black male lust and white female purity, made clear, racism and sexism are twin processes of iconization.

Stereotypes about sex and gender, visions of women caring, sharing, and nurturing their families and communities as naturally as they breastfeed will fade slowly. Women will have to struggle for at least another generation with the patterns of work and family life and economic inequity that stereotyping has drawn. They may have to struggle as well with limited reproductive freedom, especially if they're poor. They'll have to gain control of the reproductive process and win the argument about abortion, which shouldn't be a legal argument at all. The question of fetal life that opponents of abortion rights exploit is a metaphysical one that women should be trusted to answer for themselves. Yet politicians from whom most voters wouldn't buy used cars are being empowered to answer it for them.

Feminism requires outrage, compassion, and patience—sensitivity to the problems oppressing women today and a commitment to the arduous process of winning their equality. The equal rights movement hasn't succeeded only because it's not over. Its progress was slowed during the 1980s by political resistance to change. It faces more formidable challenges still. President Reagan's judicial appointments stamped the federal courts with a conservative ideology hostile to women and minority males, a belief in a new federalism in areas of civil rights that isn't terribly different from the old states' rights credo that once justified segregation. The Supreme Court appears to have entered a new era of outright opposition to expanding civil rights and remedying discrimination. Some feminists may relent and rationalize women's secondary status with postfeminist paeans to domesticity. Some will intensify demands for protections of women and the establishment of male and female sets of laws. Others will focus on the drive for reproductive choice.

Perhaps most feminists will coalesce around the issue of choice, as they once coalesced around suffrage. But egalitarians and protectionists disagree about the value of choice (more than they disagreed about votes), since they disagree about the value of individual autonomy for women. Because it embraces disagreements about fundamental principles, feminism has always been a pluralistic movement, without an exclusive party line or rulebook on equality. It is a collection of competing ideals and agendas, focused alternately on protections or rights. Pluralism weakens the drive for equality, but it is also part of feminism's strength. Feminism doesn't depend on any single organization or article of faith. It's scattered and subversive. If NOW, the most visible mainstream feminist organization, were to disappear tomorrow, feminism would not.

In the midst of this anarchic, argumentative movement, beset with complex questions about equality and social justice, how do we choose between protections and rights? For the next several years, some will choose in the interests of reproductive freedom. Some will continue choosing according to their circumstances and needs. Whether they're married or divorced, whether they have children or encounter discrimination on the job will answer as many questions for women as ideologies, and ideologies are shaped by experience, as well as temperament. The politically correct position, what's good or bad for women, is not always clear and not always relevant to people's daily lives. Special maternity benefits help some wage-earning mothers, at least in the short run, as protective labor laws helped some female wage earners eighty years ago. Reasonable feminists will differ as to whether the short-term benefits to some women of workplace protections outweigh their long-term harm to women as a class.

In formulating strategies and agendas for women, feminists will differ in the way they balance circumstance and ideology. If the stream of women's issues winds between one bank marked protections and one bank marked rights, some feminists will weave their way across it.[20] Straight ideological guidelines are easy to devise but often difficult to follow, especially in the context of women's varying short-term needs and a legislative system built on compromise. But when ideology fails, we can always rely on one practical, political guide to decision making; lining up with our friends and teammates, we can choose sides on the basis of bedfellows.

Without getting involved in an argument about sexual violence and the First Amendment, we might oppose censoring pornography because Jerry Falwell favors it. We might reject protectionism because of the company it forces us to keep. Protectionism has always aligned feminists with the enemies of emancipation—pronatalists and other champions of traditional gender roles and hierarchical families headed by men. Any feminist who finds herself allied with Jerry Falwell, Phyllis Schlafly, or the late Senator Sam Ervin on matters of sexual justice has good reason to question her judgment.

The need to choose sides and teammates wisely in a debate about equality will not be obscured or made moot by the battle over abortion. It is more likely to be intensified. Feminists who differ in their views of human nature are likely to differ about the place of reproductive choice on a feminist agenda for the 1990s. Protectionists may consider prona-talist measures—special maternity benefits, maternity leaves, and mommy-track jobs—more pressing priorities than individual rights of choice and the individual autonomy choice promises. Protectionism, after all, is based on a belief that women (and men) are defined by their reproductive roles, that their potential to bear children (whether or not it's fulfilled) shapes women's temperaments, talents, and ideals. It reflects an assumption that support for maternity—special protections for mothers, or what some call special rights—matters more than fundamental rights of choice that acknowledge women's integrity as individuals and what Elizabeth Cady Stanton called "the solitude of self."

Egalitarianism is frightening, as Stanton implied. It burdens women with existential questions and the individualized search for identity that sex-role stereotypes let them elude. It reminds women that despite their familial ties, despite their most ferocious affections for husbands, lovers, and kids, "they must make the voyage of life alone." It confronts women with their fate as "human souls," whose rights, responsibilities, and agonies no one else can shoulder.[21]

The 150-year-old debate between egalitarian and protectionist femi-nists will not be resolved or even temporarily suspended by the campaign for reproductive choice because the debate has always been about choice and two opposing views of women as autonomous individuals or mothers first. Equal rights feminism doesn't place women over the family, but its image of family life is shaped by an image of women as thoughtful, self-reliant individuals imbued with rights. The prochoice movement is a movement to acquire rights, a movement based on a belief in the primacy of rights over familial or community relations. Protectionists, like opponents of abortion rights, have always begun with an image of the family, usually the traditional hierarchical family; the protectionist image of women is shaped by an image of family life, marriage, and motherhood.

There has never been more at stake for women in the conflict over protections and rights. In the wake of recent Supreme Court decisions restricting rights to abortion and equal employment, the dangers of protectionism and its underlying premise that women are ruled by the urge to nurture and reproduce have never been closer or more clear. Women's rights of self-determination and self-control are being subordinated to the requirements of traditional familial roles, their right to equal men in the marketplace is being denied, and their secondary status is being rationalized, once again, as only natural. With the Supreme Court, the President, and many of the states marching resolutely backward to a prefeminist world in which sex was presumed to define character and allowed to determine the allocation of rights, and women were supposed to be barefoot and pregnant, feminists must march with as much resolution and whatever unity they can muster toward equality and an image of women as rational human beings, not breeders.

This is a mandate for women to be like men only if intelligence, wisdom, and the will or desire to take responsibility for yourself are natural only to men. It is an abdication of maternity only if reproductive choice is a natural male right and not a human one. It is bad for children only if being born by mistake into a hostile or indifferent world is good for them. The feminist movement for equality and reproductive rights includes a demand that people consciously decide whether or not to have children, considering parenthood an awesome and irrevocable commitment to another human being. It recognizes that men and women share the capacity to make reasoned moral choices.

To suggest that equality requires sameness—that it would emasculate men or compel women to forfeit their femininity and the values it represents—is to suggest that each sex is only half formed. Feminists, a diverse and contentious lot of women, know how aggressive, competitive, and warlike their own sex can be. Perhaps women who display what are considered masculine characteristics aren't male-identified. Perhaps they're merely human. Perhaps people are capable of inventing themselves in spite of their reproductive roles. Of course the equal rights movement hasn't yet delivered women. How could it have in only twenty years? Equality does require a radical revisioning of human sexuality. No feminist ever said it would be easy.

Notes

Introduction

1. Schlesinger Library, Radcliffe College, AG–218, Helen Hamilton Gardener Papers, Folder 2.

2. "The Human Brain Still Puzzles Scientists," *New York Times*, 9 Oct. 1927, sec. 9, p. 3.

3. Helen Hamilton Gardener, "Sex in Brain," in Helen Hamilton Gardener, *Facts and Fictions of Life* (Boston: Arena Publishing Company, 1893), 122–124.

4. Ibid., 112.

5. See generally Sylvia Ann Hewlett, *A Lesser Life: The Myth of Women's Liberation in America* (New York: W. M. Morrow, 1986), and Mary Ann Mason, *The Equality Trap* (New York: Simon and Schuster, 1988).

6. See Lenore Weitzman, *The Divorce Revolution: The Unexpected Social and Economic Consequences for Women and Children* (New York: Free Press 1985).

7. See Ruth Sidel, *Women and Children Last: The Plight of Poor Women in Affluent America* (New York: Viking, 1986).

Chapter 1

1. *Rostker v. Goldberg*, 453 U.S. 57 (1981).
2. S. Rep No. 96-826, 154–156, U.S. Code and Administrative News, 26 (1980): 43–2650.
3. See, for example, S. L. Bem, and D. J. Bem, "Case Study of a Non-Conscious Ideology: Training the Woman to Know Her Place," in D. J. Bem, *Beliefs, Attitudes, and Human Affairs* (Belmont, Calif.: Brooks/Cole Publishing Co., 1970).
4. Simone de Beauvoir, *The Second Sex* (New York: Random House, 1974).
5. Shulamith Firestone, *The Dialectic of Sex: The Case for Feminist Revolution* (New York: W. M. Morrow, 1970).
6. Sylvia Ann Hewlett, *A Lesser Life: The Myth of Women's Liberation in America* (New York: W. M. Morrow, 1986).
7. See, for example, Phyllis Chesler, *Mothers on Trial: The Battle for Children and Custody* (New York: McGraw Hill, 1986).
8. Carol Gilligan, *In a Different Voice: Psychological Theory and Women's Development* (Cambridge, Mass.: Harvard University Press, 1982).
9. See "On 'In a Different Voice': An Interdisciplinary Forum," in *Signs: Journal of Women in Culture and Society* 11 (Winter 1986).
10. Turn-of-the-century protective labor laws primarily protected white women. They focused on the problems of women in industry and retail sales, virtually all of whom were white; black women worked as domestic servants or laundresses or in agriculture. Blacks and whites were also subject to different standards of criminal justice: Black women, considered naturally "immoral," were less likely to be sent to reformatories for minor sexual and morals offenses, but they were more likely to be imprisoned for serious felony offenses.

Chapter 2

1. Ronald Dworkin, *Taking Rights Seriously* (Cambridge, Mass.: Harvard University Press, 1977), 225–229.
2. Schlesinger Library, Radcliffe College, A–71, Miriam Van Waters Papers, Folder 465.
3. *In re Gault*, 387 U.S. 1 (1967).
4. Schlesinger Library, Radcliffe College, A–71 Miriam Van Waters Papers, Folder 466.
5. Schlesinger Library, Radcliffe College, A–71, Miriam Van Waters Papers, Folder 465.
6. *Harris v. McRae*, 448 U.S. 297 (1980).
7. *Roe v. Wade*, 410 U.S. 113 (1973).
8. *Dandridge v. Williams*, 397 U.S. 471 (1970).
9. *Jefferson v. Hackney*, 406 U.S. 535 (1972).
10. *Lindsey v. Normet*, 405 U.S. 56 (1972).
11. See generally Robert N. Bellah et al., *Habits of the Heart: Individualism and Commitment in American Life* (Berkeley: University of California Press, 1985).
12. Michael Sandel, "Democrats and Community," *New Republic* (22 Feb. 1988): 20, 23.
13. See generally Nancy Rosenblum, *Another Liberalism: Romanticism and the Reconstruction of Liberal Thought* (Cambridge, Mass.: Harvard University Press, 1987).
14. Bellah et al., *Habits of the Heart*, 112.
15. Ibid., 86.

16. Sandel, "Democrats and Community," 22.
17. Bellah et al., *Habits of the Heart*, 111.
18. Ibid., 249.
19. Sandel, "Democrats and Community," 22.

Chapter 3

1. Herma Hill Kay, *Sex-Based Discrimination: Text, Cases and Materials* (St. Paul, Minn.: West, 1981), 12–13.
2. Ibid.
3. *Plessy v. Ferguson*, 163 U.S. 537 (1896).
4. *Brown v. Board of Education*, 347 U.S. 483 (1954).
5. See generally Ann E. Friedman, "Sex, Equality, Difference, and the Supreme Court," *Yale Law Journal* 913 (1983): 92; Herma Hill Kay, "Models of Equality," *University of Illinois Law Review* 39 (1985): 1985; Herma Hill Kay, "Equality and Difference: The Case of Pregnancy," *Berkeley Women's Law Journal* 1 (1985): 1; Sylvia A. Law, "Rethinking Sex and the Constitution," *University of Pennsylvania Law Review* 955 (1984): 132; Phyllis N. Segal, "Sexual Equality, the Equal Protection Clause, and the ERA," *Buffalo Law Review* 85 (1984): 33; Ann C. Scales, "Towards a Feminist Jurisprudence," *Indiana Law Journal* 375 (1981): 56; Wendy W. Williams, "Equality's Riddle: Pregnancy and the Equal Treatment/Special Treatment Debate," *New York University Review of Law and Social Change* 325 (1985): 13; Elizabeth H. Wolgast, *Equality and the Rights of Women* (Ithaca: Cornell University Press, 1980).

My own analysis has been informed, confirmed, or refuted by all these writers. I have been most engaged by the trenchant work of Wendy W. Williams and Sylvia A. Law.

6. *California Federal Savings and Loan Association v. Guerra*, 107 S. Ct. 683 (1987)

For the leading egalitarian analysis of the pregnancy/equality debate, see Wendy W. Williams, "Equality's Riddle: Pregnancy and the Equal Treatment/Special Treatment Debate," New York University Review of Law and Social Change 325 (1985): 13.

7. *Wimberly v. Labor and Industrial Relations Commission of Missouri*, 107 S. Ct. 821 (1987).
8. *Gedulgig v. Aiello*, 417 U.S. 484 (1974).
9. *General Electric Company v. Gilbert*, 429 U.S. 125 (1976).
10. *Strauder v. West Virginia*, 100 U.S. 303 (1880).
11. *Hoyt v. Florida*, 368 U.S. 57 (1961).
12. Appearances were not always controlling: The Court recognized that apparently fair, neutral laws might be applied in a discriminatory manner. In 1886 it found discrimination in the enforcement of a San Francisco law prohibiting laundries from operating without permission of city officials; the law was used primarily against Chinese immigrants. *Yick Wo v. Hopkins*, 118 U.S. 356 (1886).
13. *Reed v. Reed*, 404 U.S. 71 (1971).
14. *Frontiero v. Richardson*, 411 U.S. 677 (1973).
15. *Weinberger v. Weisenfeld*, 420 U.S. 636 (1975).
16. *Califano v. Goldfarb*, 430 U.S. 199 (1977).
17. Cited in *Califano v. Goldfarb*, Ibid.
18. *Stanton v. Stanton*, 421 U.S. 7 (1975).
19. *Stanton v. Stanton*, 30 Utah 2d 315. 517P. 2D1010. (1974).
20. *Stanton v. Stanton*, 421 U.S. 7 (1975).
21. *Orr v. Orr*, 440 U.S. 268 (1979).
22. Ibid.

23. *Kahn v. Shevin*, 416 U.S. 351 (1974).

24. *Schlesinger v. Ballard*, 419 U.S. 498 (1975).

25. *Califano v. Webster*, 430 U.S. 313 (1977).

26. *Martin v. Wilkes*, 57 U.S.L.W. 4616, 13 June 1989.

27. *City of Richmond v. Croson*, 57 U.S.L.W. 4132, 24 Jan. 1989.

28. The only law ever to be upheld under strict scrutiny was a World War II military order excluding Japanese Americans from their homes on the West Coast. See *Korematsu v. United States*, 323 U.S. 214 (1944), decided shortly before the war ended; the dissent in this case called it "the legalization of racism."

29. *Kahn v. Shevin*, 416 U.S. 351 (1974).

30. *Craig v. Boren* 429 U.S. 190 (1976).

31. *Michael M. v. Superior Court*, 420 U.S. 464 (1981).

32. *Parham v. Hughes*, 441 U.S. 347 (1979).

33. Theories of fathers' rights are changing. See discussion, Chapter 11. And contrast *Parham* to *Caban v. Mohammed*, 441 U.S. 380 (1979).

34. *Dothard v. Rawlinson*, 433 U.S. 321 (1977).

35. For an excellent analysis of this conundrum and the Supreme Court's confused approach to equality in cases involving sexuality and reproduction, see Sylvia A. Law, "Rethinking Sex and the Constitution," University of Pennsylvania Law Review 955 (1984): 132.

Chapter 4

1. *Bradwell v. Illinois*, 83 U.S. (16 Wall.) 130 (1873).

2. Mary Wollstonecraft, "A Vindication of the Rights of Women," in Barbara H. Solomon and Paula S. Berggren, eds., *A Mary Wollstonecraft Reader* (NewYork: New American Library, 1983), 276.

3. Ibid., 267, 270.

4. John Stuart Mill, *The Subjection of Women* (Buffalo, N.Y.: Prometheus Books, 1986), 27.

5. Helen Hamilton Gardener, "Sex in Brain," in Helen Hamilton Gardener, *Facts and Fictions of Life* (Boston: 1893) 20.

6. Mill, *The Subjection of Women*, Arena Publishing Company, 7.

7. Elizabeth Cady Stanton, "Address Delivered at Seneca Falls, July 19, 1848," in Ellen Carol DuBois, ed., *Elizabeth Cady Stanton and Susan B. Anthony, Correspondence, Writings, Speeches* (New York: Schocken Books, 1981), 33.

8. "Declaration of Sentiments, Woman's Rights Convention, Seneca Falls, New York, 19 July 1848." In *Women's Rights Conventions, Seneca Falls and Rochester* (New York: Arno Press, 1969).

9. Gerder Lerner, *The Grimke Sisters from South Carolina* (Boston: Houghton Mifflin, 1967), 189.

10. For a discussion of female moral reform movements of the 1830s and female religiosity, see Carroll Smith-Rosenberg, "Beauty, the Beast and the Militant Woman" and "The Cross and the Pedestal," in Carroll Smith-Rosenberg, *Disorderly Conduct: Visions of Gender in Victorian America* (New York: Knopf, 1985).

11. Harriet Martineau, *Society in America*, vol. 3 (New York: AMS Press, 1966), 111–112.

12. Mrs. A. J. Graves, *Women in America: Being an Examination into the Moral and Intellectual Condition of American Female Society*, in Nancy F. Cott, ed., *Root of Bitterness* (New York: Dutton, 1972), 141–147.

13. Harriet Martineau, "On Marriage," in Gayle Graham Yates, ed., *Harriet Martineau on Women* (New Brunswick, N.J.: Rutgers University Press, 1985), 63.

14. Catherine Beecher, "On the Peculiar Responsibilities of American Women," in Cott, *Root of Bitterness*, 171–177.

15. Elizabeth Cady Stanton, "Introduction" and "Commentaries on Genesis," *The Woman's Bible*, Chapters 1–4, in DuBois, *Elizabeth Cady Stanton*, 228–233.

16. Ibid.

17. Susan B. Anthony, "Response to a NAWSA Resolution," in DuBois, *Elizabeth Cady Stanton*, 243.

18. Charles Darwin, *The Descent of Man* (New York: Merrill and Baker, 1890), 587.

19. Stephen Jay Gould, *The Mismeasure of Man* (New York: Norton, 1981), 115.

20. Ibid., 104–105.

21. Ibid.

22. Otto Weininger, *Sex and Character* (London: W. Heinemann, 1906), 64–67. For an incisive summary analysis of Weininger's work and misogynist images of women in nineteenth-century European culture, see Bram Dijkstra, *Idols of Perversity: Fantasies of Feminine Evil in Fin de Siècle Culture* (New York: Oxford University Press), 1986.

23. Weininger, *Sex and Character*, 92, 286.

24. Darwin, *The Descent of Man*, 589.

25. See Dijkstra, *Idols of Perversity*, 170–171.

26. Darwin, *The Descent of Man*, 149–159

27. Dijkstra, *Idols of Perversity*, 258–271.

28. Emile Zola, *Thérèse Raquin* (New York: Penguin Books, 1962), 64.

29. William Thackerey, *Vanity Fair*, Vol. 2 (New York: P. F. Collier and Son, 1917), 344.

30. Emile Zola, *Nana* (New York: Penguin Books, 1982), 12 (Introduction).

31. Darwin, *The Descent of Man*, 580

32. W. Douglas Morrison, "Introduction," in Cesare Lombroso, *The Female Offender* (New York: D. Appleton, 1985), xvii.

33. Lombroso, *The Female Offender*, 74, 94.

34. Gould, *The Mismeasure of Man*, 124.

35. Darwin, *The Descent of Man*, 642.

36. Linda Gordon, *Woman's Body, Woman's Right: A Social History of Birth Control in America* (New York: Penguin Books, 1976), 277.

37. Ibid., 278.

38. See generally Gordon, *Woman's Body, Woman's Right*, 136–158.

39. Ibid., 281.

40. Frances Willard, *How to Win: A Book for Girls* (New York: Funk & Wagnalls, 1887), 55–57.

41. Letter from Elizabeth Cady Stanton to Name Tk, June 20, 1853, in DuBois, *Elizabeth Cady Stanton*, 56.

42. Elizabeth Cady Stanton, *Eighty Years and More (1815–1897): Reminiscenses of Elizabeth Cady Stanton* (New York: European Publishing Company, 1898), 145–148.

43. Mary Wollstonecraft, "A Vindication of the Rights of Women," in Solomon and Berggren, eds., *A Mary Wollstonecraft Reader*, 306.

44. Elizabeth Cady Stanton,"The Solitude of Self," in DuBois, *Elizabeth Cady Stanton*, 246.

45. Letter from Elizabeth Cady Stanton to Susan B. Anthony, March 1, 1853, in DuBois, *Elizabeth Cady Stanton*, 56.

46. Carl Degler, *At Odds: Women and the Family in America from the Revolution to the Present* (New York: Oxford University Press, 1980), 332–333 "Legal Discriminations Against Women," *Equal Rights* 1 (17 Nov. 1923): 31.

47. *Helms v. Franciscus*, 2 Bland Ch (Maryland)544 (1830) Cited in *Ex Parte Devine*, 398 So2d 686 (1981).

48. Viviana Zelizer, *Pricing the Priceless Child: The Changing Social Value of Children* (New York: Basic Books, 1985).

49. See generally Michael Grossman, "Who Gets the Child? Custody, Guardianship, and the Rise of a Judicial Patriarchy in Nineteenth Century America," *Feminist Studies* 9 (1983): 235–261.

50. *Coleman v. Buff*, 93 N.Y. 17 (1883).

51. For a historical analysis of family violence, see Linda Gordon, *Heroes of Their Own Lives: The Politics and History of Family Violence, Boston—1880–1960* (New York: Viking Press, 1988).

52. Nicole Hahn Rafter, *Partial Justice: Women in State Prisons, 1800–1935* (Boston: Northeastern University Press, 1985), 13.

53. Lombroso, *The Female Offender*, 152.

54. For a review of the women's reformatory movement, see Rafter, *Partial Justice*.

55. Ibid.

56. Ibid., 132.

57. Angela Y. Davis, *Women, Race and Class* (New York: Random House, 1981), 91–92.

58. Gerda Lerner, ed., *Black Women in White America: A Documentary History* (New York: Vintage Books, 1973), 193.

59. Davis, *Women, Race and Class*, 188.

60. See Degler, *At Odds*, 258.

61. See Smith-Rosenberg,"Beauty, the Beast, and the Militant Woman," in Smith-Rosenberg, *Disorderly Conduct*.

62. Albert B. Gerber, *Sex, Pornography, and Justice* (New York: Lyle Stuart, 1965), 91.

63. The modern version of the Comstock law declares "obscene, lewd, lascivious, indecent, filthy, or vile" literature, "substances," or "devices" to be nonmailable, as well as "every article or thing" designed or intended for "immoral use." 18 U.S.C. section 1461. It has been upheld repeatedly by the Supreme Court in its application to "obscene" literature. See *Roth v. United States*, 354 U.S. 476 (1957), and cases following. It was not until 1983 that the Supreme Court struck down a related prohibition on the unsolicited mailings of advertisements for contraceptives in *Bolger v. Youngs Drug Company*, 463 U.S. 60 (1983).

64. See generally David J. Pivar, *Purity Crusade: Sexual Morality and Social Control, 1868–1900* (Westport, Conn.: Greenwood Press, 1973).

65. Paul S. Boyer, *Purity in Print: The Vice Society Movement and Book Censorship in America* (New York: Scribners, 1968), 17.

66. Pivar, *Purity Crusade*.

67. See generally Gordon, *Woman's Body, Woman's Right*.

68. See William O'Neill, *Everyone Was Brave: A History of Feminism in America* (Chicago: Quadrangle Books, 1971).

69. Letter from Elizabeth Cady Stanton to Susan B. Anthony, 1 March 1853, in DuBois, *Elizabeth Cady Stanton*, 55.

70. Quoted in DuBois, *Elizabeth Cady Stanton*, 97.

71. Phyllis Schlafly, *The Power of the Positive Woman* (NewRochelle, N.Y.: Arlington House, 1977), 76.

72. Elizabeth Cady Stanton, "Home Life," in DuBois, *Elizabeth Cady Stanton*, 131.

Notes

Chapter 5

1. Yankee mill girls began protesting long working hours, low wages, and deplorable working conditions in the 1820s. Their first strike was in Dover, New Hampshire, in 1828. Cotton mill strikes of the 1830s and 1840s gave rise to the first major militant female labor organization, the Lowell Female Reform Association, formed by mill workers in Lowell, Massachusetts, in 1845. For an account of women's early efforts to organize, see Barbara Wertheimer, *We Were There: The Story of Working Women in America* (New York: Pantheon, 1977), and Rosalyn Baxandall, Linda Gordon, and Susan Reverby, eds., *America's Working Women: A Documentary History—1600 to the Present* (New York: Random House, 1971).

2. Wertheimer, *We Were There*, 71.

3. In 1850, 330,000 women worked as domestic servants and 180,000 worked in manufacturing. See Wertheimer, *We Were There*, 61.

4. See Baxandall, Gordon, and Reverby, *America's Working Women*, 42–66.

5. Wertheimer, *We Were There*, 158.

6. Robert W. Smuts, *Women and Work in America* (New York: Schocken Books, 1971), 19–24.

7. Baxandall, Gordon, and Reverby, 93–96.

8. By 1900, only 3.3 percent of the female labor force was unionized. Carl Degler, *At Odds: Women and the Family in America from the Revolution to the Present* (New York: Oxford University Press, 1980), 400. See also Wertheimer, 151–179.

9. Eleanor Flexner, *A Century of Struggle: The Woman's Rights Movement in the United States* (New York: Atheneum, 1972), 199–200.

10. Wertheimer, *We Were There*, 207.

11. Edward O'Donnell, "Women as Breadwinners: The Error of the Age," in Baxandall, Gordon, and Reverby, *America's Working Women*, 168.

12. *Muller v. Oregon*, 208 U.S. 412 (1908). The Brandeis brief submitted in this case is famous for what was then the innovative use of social science data to determine questions of constitutional law.

13. *Lochner v. New York*, 198 U.S. 45 (1905).

14. *Muller v. Oregon*, 208 U.S. 412 (1908).

15. Sheila M. Rothman, *Woman's Proper Place: A History of Changing Ideals and Practices—1870 to the Present* (New York: Basic Books, 1978), 156.

16. U.S. Department of Labor, "The Development of Minimum Wage Laws in the United States, 1912–1927," *Women's Bureau Bulletin* 61 (1928): 1–12.

17. *Adkins v. Children's Hospital*, 261 U.S. 525 (1923).

18. U.S. Department of Labor, "The Development of Minimum Wage Laws," 5.

19. *West Coast Hotel v. Parrish*, 300 U.S. 379 (1937).

20. *United States v. Darby*, 312 U.S. 100 (1941).

21. Kenneth M. Davidson, Ruth B. Ginsburg, and Herma H. Kay, *Sex-Based Discrimination: Text, Cases and Materials* (St. Paul, Minn.: West, 1974), 651.

22. *Radice v. New York*, 264 U.S. 292 (1924).

23. "Night Work for Women," *Equal Rights* 1 (9 Feb. 1924): 413.

24. "Need for Coordinated Effort," *Equal Rights* 21 (15 June 1935): 2.

25. Rothman, *Woman's Proper Place*, 156.

26. *Goesaert v. Cleary*, 335 U.S. 464 (1948). By 1969, twenty-six states still barred women from a range of jobs and occupations. See Davidson, Ginsburg, and Kay, *Sex-Based Discrimination*, 651.

27. See generally Alice Kessler-Harris, *Out to Work: A History of Wage-Earning Women in the United States* (New York: Oxford University Press, 1982), 180–217.

28. Wertheimer, *We Were There*, 166.

29. Blanche Weisen Cook, ed., *Crystal Eastman on Women and Revolution* (New York: Oxford University Press, 1978), 158.

30. Clara Mortenson Beyer, "What Is Equality?," *The Nation* 116 (31 Jan. 1923): 116.

31. Edith Houghton Hooker, "Utilizing the Maternal Instinct," *Equal Rights* 9 (5 July 1924): 106.

32. Beyer, "What Is Equality?"

33. Florence Kelley, "Shall Women Be Equal before the Law?," *The Nation* 114 (12 April 1922): 421.

34. Alice Hamilton, "What the American Woman Thinks," *Woman Citizen* (8 March 1924): 16.

35. Ibid.

36. Ibid.

37. Beyer, "What Is Equality?," 116.

38. Kelley, "Shall Women Be Equal before the Law?," 421.

39. Harriet Stanton Blatch, "Do Women Want Protection?," *The Nation*, 116, 31 January 1923, 115.

40. It is Important to Open More Trades to Women," *Equal Rights* 1 (12 Jan. 1924): 381.

41. U.S. Department of Labor, "The Effect of Labor Legislation on the Employment Opportunities of Women," *Women's Bureau Bulletin* 65 (1928): 50–54.

42. Rothman, *Woman's Proper Place*, 163–165.

43. Quoted in William O'Neill, *Everyone Was Brave: A History of Feminism in America* (Chicago: Quadrangle Books, 1971), 278.

44. Eleanor Taylor Marsh, "Equal Rights and Mothers' Pensions," *Equal Rights* 1 (19 Jan. 1924), 390; "The Woman's Party—Right or Wrong," *Equal Rights* 1 (20 Oct. 1923): 285.

45. Emma Wold, "Teacher's Council of Woman's Party," *Equal Rights* 1 (10 March 1923): 30.

46. Isabelle Kendig, "Boston Teachers Lose Fight for Equality," *Equal Rights* 1 (19 Jan. 1924): 389.

47. Ethel Klein, *Gender Politics* (Cambridge: Harvard University Press, 1984), 18.

Chapter 6

1. Jane Mansbridge, *Why We Lost the ERA* (Chicago: University of Chicago Press, 1986), 20–22.

2. Ibid.

3. See generally Herbert McCloskey and Alida Brill, *Dimensions of Tolerance: What Americans Believe about Civil Liberties* (New York: Russell Sage Foundation, 1983).

4. Phyllis Schlafly, *The Power of the Positive Woman* (New York: Arlington House, 1977), 71–72.

5. Ibid, 117, 20–21, 17, 96.

6. For an early feminist critique of the sexual revolution, see Anselma Dell'Olio, "The Sexual Revolution Wasn't Our War," *Ms.*, Preview Issue (Spring 1972): 72.

7. See Andrew Hacker, "The Pill and Morality," *New York Times Magazine* (21 Nov. 1965): 72; Gloria Steinem, "The Moral Disarmament of Betty Coed," *Esquire* (September 1962): 97; "The Pill: How it is Affecting U.S. Morals, Family Life," *U.S. News and World Report* (11 July 1966): 62.

8. "The Pill on the Campus," *Newsweek* (11 Oct. 1965): 92.

9. "The Pill: How it is Affecting U.S. Morals, Family Life," 62–65.

10. Vance Packard, *The Sexual Wilderness: The Contemporary Upheaval in Male-Female Relationships* (New York: D. McKay Company, 1968), 163; see generally 135–163.

11. Hacker, "The Pill and Morality," 139.

12. Steinem, "The Moral Disarmament of Betty Coed," 156.

13. Helen Gurley Brown Papers, Sophia Smith Collection, Neilson Library, Smith College, Northampton, Massachusetts.

14. Ibid.

15. Ibid.

16. Ibid.

17. D. Hubert, "The Pill and the Girl Next Door," *Mademoiselle* (March 1967): 162; A. Brien, "Sex: The New Status Symbol," *Mademoiselle* (July 1969): 62; E. M. Brucher,"We Are All Our Mothers' Daughters: What Sex Research Reveals about Unhappy Wives," *Redbook* (November 1969): 71; Robert J. Levin, "The Redbook Report on Premarital and Extra-Marital Sex: The End of the Double Standard," *Redbook* (October 1975): 38.

18. H. Van Slyke, "The Sex Life of a Working Wife," *Harper's Bazaar* (August 1974): 52; J. Curtis, "Are Working Women Sexier?," *Harper's Bazaar* (August 1976): 87; Helen Singer Kaplan, "Can Success Ruin Your Sex Life?," *Harper's Bazaar* (January 1976): 98; Karen Durbin, "An Intelligent Woman's Guide to Sex: Can Sex Ruin Your Work Drive?," *Mademoiselle* (May 1975): 64.

19. "You and Your Job," *Harper's Bazaar* (August 1977): 84–89.

20. Lee Salk, "Can You Work and Be a Good Mother," *Harper's Bazaar* (August 1977): 88; "Child Care Alternatives: Good News," *Harper's Bazaar* (October 1977): 177; "The New Working Mothers," *Harper's Bazaar* (October 1977): 180; "Time Savers for the Working Woman," *Redbook* (March 1978): 57.

21. J. Adams, "Women, Success and Men: The New Sexual Triangle," *Glamour* (October 1979): 60; M. Banashek, "Sex: Is It Finally Time to Shut Up About It?," *Mademoiselle* (January 1979): 88.

22. "High Energy Sex Foods," *Harper's Bazaar* (April 1980): 152; T. A. Warschaw, "How to Get Your Way in Bed," *Mademoiselle* (January 1981): 88; Carol Tavris, "The Latest Sexual Problem: Lack of Desire," *Vogue* (August 1982): 147; Rhoda Koenig, "Love for Sale," *New York* (30 March 1983): 48; Glenn Collins, "Love Makes a Comeback," *The New York Times* (25 Nov. 1984): Sec. 2, 1; "The Revolution is Over," *Time* (3 April 1984): 74.

23. "How Men Are Changing," *Newsweek* (6 Jan. 1978): 52.

24. Betty Friedan, "Their Turn: How Men Are Changing," *Redbook* (May 1980): 23.

25. S. Koslow, "How Men Today See Their Changing Sexuality, How You Fit In," *Glamour* (July 1979): 58.

26. "Battle of the Sexes: Men Fight Back," *U.S. News & World Report* (Dec. 1980): 50.

27. "Over the Brink," *Family in America* 2 (Rockford Institute Center on the Family in America, 1988).

28. Schlafly, *The Power of the Positive Woman*, 87.

29. "Is the Women's Movement Stumbling to a Halt? Or Is It Crashing into a New World of Possibilities?," *Glamour* (Jan. 1978): 46.

Chapter 7

1. Pauli Murray, *Song in a Weary Throat* (New York: Harper and Row, 1987), 352.

2. Ibid., 355–358.

3. Ibid., 359–368. See Also Ethel Klein, *Gender Politics* (Cambridge, Mass.: Harvard University Press, 1984), 22–25.

4. Murray, *Song in a Weary Throat*, 361.

5. Ibid., 367.

6. Klein, *Gender Politics*, 23. *Sex-Based Discrimination: Text, Cases and Materials*, *(St. Paul, West: 1981)*, 572573.

7. *Rosenfeld v. Southern Pacific Company*, 444 F.2d 1219 (9th Cir. 1971).

8. *Weeks v. Southern Telephone and Telegraph*, 408 F.2d 228 (5th Cir. 1969).

9. *Diaz v. Pan American World Airways*, 444 F.2d 385 (5th Cir. 1971).

10. Herma H. Kay, *Sex-Based Discrimination: Text, Cases and Materials*, (St. Paul, West: 1981), 572–573.

11. *City of Los Angeles Department of Water and Power v. Manhart*, 435 U.S. 702 (1978).

12. See Sara E. Rix, ed. *The American Woman, 1987–1988* and *The American Woman, 1988–1989* (Women's Research and Education Institute of the Congressional Caucus for Women's Issues [New York: Norton, 1988 and 1989]).

13. See Sara M. Evans and Barbara J. Nelson, *Wage Justice: Comparable Worth and the Paradox of Technocratic Reform* (Chicago: University of Chicago Press, 1989).

14. Ibid., 34–41, 71–72.

15. Ibid., 63.

16. Ibid., 12–13.

17. *County of Washington v. Gunther*, 452 U.S. 161 (1981).

18. *Spaulding v. University of Washington*, 740 F.2d 686 (9th Cir.), cert. denied, 469 U.S. 1036.

19. *AFSME v. State of Washington*, 770 F.2d 1401 (9th Cir. 1985).

20. *Griggs v. Duke Power Company*, 401 U.S. 424 (1971).

21. See, for example, Anne Zusy, "For Women Who Fight Fires, Acceptance and Frustrations," *New York Times* (12 Oct. 1987): Sec. 1, 1.

22. *Regents of the University of California v. Bakke*, 438 U.S. 265 (1978).

23. For a cogent review of affirmative action and problems of systemic bias, see Marjorie Heins, *Cutting the Mustard: Affirmative Action and the Nature of Excellence* (Boston: Faber and Faber, 1987).

24. *Dothard v. Rawlinson*, 433 U.S. 321 (1977).

25. *Wards Cove Packing Company v. Atonio*, No. 87-1887 (5 June 1989).

26. *Watson v. Fort Worth Bank and Trust*, 56 U.S.L.W. 4922 (29 June 1989).

27. Brief of the ACLU, et al., amicus curiae, in support of Petitioner Clara Watson, No. 86-6139.

28. *Teamsters v. United States*, 431 U.S. 324 (1977).

29. Brief of the ACLU.

30. *Johnson v. Transportation Agency, Santa Clara County*, 480 U.S. 616 (1987); *Sheet Metal Workers v. EEOC*, 478 U.S. 3050 (1986); *Local 93, International Association of Firefighters v. Cleveland*, 478 U.S. 501 (1986); *Fullilove v. Klutznick*, 448 U.S. 448 (1980); *United States Steelworkers of America v. Weber*, 443 U.S. 193 (1979).

31. The EEOC has negotiated multimillion-dollar settlements in sex discrimination cases against Goodyear Tire and Rubber Company, Nabisco, Inc., and LOF Glass (a former division of Libby-Owens-Ford). It negotiated a $42 million settlement with General Motors and a $23 million settlement with Ford Motor Company in cases alleging sexual and racial discrimination. With the exception of the Goodyear Tire and Rubber case, all these cases were initiated during the 1970s.

32. *Faro v. New York University*, 502 F.2d 1229 (2d Cir. 1974).

33. Catherine Stimpson, ed., *Discrimination Against Women: Congressional Hearings on Equal Rights in Education and Employment* (New York: R. R. Bowker, 1973), 425–427, 61.

34. Kay, *Sex-Based Discrimination*, 855. See also Stimpson, *Discrimination against Women*, 61.

35. Rix, *The American Woman, 1987 – 1988*, 240–241.

36. Kay, *Sex-Based Discrimination*, 863–864.

37. Heins, *Cutting the Mustard*, 197.

38. *Sweeney v. Board of Trustees of Keene State College*, 604 F.2d 106 (1st Cir. 1979), cert. denied, 444 U.S. 1045 (1980).

39. *Barnes v. Train*, Civ. No. 1828-73 (D.D.C.) cited in *Barnes v. Costle*, 561 F.2d 983 (1977).

40. Ibid.

41. *Barnes v. Costle*, 561 F.2d 983 (1977).

42. *Meritor Savings Bank, FSB v. Vinson*, 477 U.S. 57 (1986).

43. Joseph Rivera, "Women Allege Sexist Atmosphere in Offices Constitutes Harassment," *Wall Street Journal* (10 Feb. 1988): Sec. 2, 1.

44. Pamela L. Enders, "Sexual Harassment in the Workplace," *Joint Commission on the Status of Women Newsletter* 3 (Harvard Medical School, Harvard School of Public Health, Harvard School of Dental Medicine [16 Nov. 1987]): 1.

45. Claire Safran, "What Men Do to Women on the Job: A Shocking Look at Sexual Harassment," *Redbook* (November 1976).

46. Judith Hovemann, "42% of Female Civil Servants Report Sexual Harassment," *Washington Post* (30 June 1988): Sec. 1, 1.

47. Richard Halloran, "Sexual Harassment Cited in Military in Pacific," *New York Times* (17 Sept. 1987): Sec. 1, 1. See also Richard Halloran, "Study Finds Servicewomen Harassed," *New York Times* (21 Feb. 1989): Sec. 1, 18.

48. Women's Legal Defense Fund Draft Report, "Civil Rights Enforcement Policy: The Issues Unsettling the Law in the Reagan Administration" (16 Feb. 1989): 48.

49. *Price Waterhouse v. Hopkins*, 57 U.S.L.W. 4469 (1 May 1989).

50. Ibid., 4471. See also Brief of Amicus Curiae, NOW Legal Defense and Education Fund, ACLU, Women's Legal Defense Fund, et al., in support of respondent Ann B. Hopkins, No. 87-1167.

51. See Brief for the United States as Amicus Curiae, No. 87-1167.

Chapter 8

1. See generally S. L. Bem and D. J. Bem, "Case Study of a Non-Conscious Ideology: Training the Woman to Know Her Place," in D. J. Bem, *Beliefs, Attitudes, and Human Affairs* (Belmont, Calif.: Brooks/Cole Publishing Co., 1970).

2. The most widely read and influential attack on higher education for women was *Sex in Education*, by Dr. Edward H. Clarke, a retired professor of the Harvard Medical School. See Barbara Miller Solomon, *In the Company of Educated Women* (New Haven: Yale University Press, 1985), 56–57.

3. Solomon, *In the Company of Educated Women*, 119–122.

4. Ibid., 63.

5. Catherine Stimpson, ed., *Discrimination against Women: Congressional Hearings on Equal Rights in Education and Employment* (New York: R. R. Bowker, 1973), 209.

6. Ibid., 163. See also Cynthia Fuchs Epstein, *Women in Law* (New York: Basic Books, 1981), 63.

7. Herma Hill Kay, *Sex-Based Discrimination: Text, Cases and Materials* (St. Paul, Minn.: West, 1981), 787.

8. Ibid.

9. See John Markoff, "Computing in America: A Masculine Mystique," *New York Times* (13 Feb. 1989): Sec. 1, 1.

10. United States Commission on Civil Rights, "To Ensure Equal Educational Opportunity," in *The Federal Civil Rights Enforcement Effort, 1974*, vol. 3 (Washington, D.C.: U.S. Government Printing Office, 1975): 224–225.

11. Sara E. Rix, ed., *The American Woman: A Report in Depth*, 1987–1988 (Women's Research and Education Institute of the Congressional Caucus for Women's Issues [New York: Norton, 1988]), 223, 229.

12. *O'Connor v. Board of Education of School District Number 23*, 449 U.S. 1308(19). This was an interlocutory appeal to vacate the stay of an injunction. The final decision in the case by the Circuit Court of Appeals upheld sex-segregated basketball teams. 645 F.2d 578 (7th Cir. 1981). For a discussion of this case and equality in athletics generally, see Karen L. Tokarz, "Separate But Unequal Educational Sports Programs: The Need for a New Theory of Equality," *Berkeley Women's Law Journal* 1 (Fall 1985): 201.

13. Tokarz, "Separate But Unequal Educational Sports Programs."

14. *Attorney General v. Massachusetts Interscholastic Athletic Association*, 378 Mass. 342, 393 N.E.2d 284 (1979).

15. *Darrin v. Gould*, 85 Wash. 2d 393, 540 P.2d 882 (1975). See Tokarz, "Separate But Unequal Educational Sports Programs."

16. *Force by Force v. Pierce City, R-VI School District*, 670 F. Supp. 1020 (W.D. Mo. 1983).

17. *Clark v. Arizona Interscholastic Association*, 695 F.2d 1126 (9th Cir. 1982), cert. denied, 464 U.S. 818 (1983).

18. *Petrie v. Illinois High School Association*, 75 Ill. App. 3d 980, 349 N.E.2d 855 (1970).

19. Ibid.

20. *Abrams v. United States*, 205 U.S. 616 (1919).

21. Kay, *Sex-Based Discrimination*, 803–806.

22. I was a senior at Smith College when this poll was taken.

23. See Marjorie Houspian Dobkin, ed., *The Making of a Feminist: Early Journals and Letters of M. Carey Thomas* (Kent, Ohio: Kent State University Press, 1979).

24. *Mississippi University for Women v. Hogan*, 458 U.S. 718 (1982).

25. *Vorcheimer v. School District of Philadelphia*, 532 F.2d 880, aff'd, 430 U.S. 703 (1977); affirmed by an equally divided Court.

26. *Plessy v. Ferguson*, 163 U.S. 537 (1896).

Chapter 9

1. For a review of Reagan Administration civil rights policies see Women's Legal Defense Fund Draft Reports, "Civil Rights Enforcement Policy: The Issues Unsettling the Law in the Reagan Administration" (16 Feb. 1989) and "The Agencies and the Laws They Enforce" (4 Feb. 1989).

2. In *Grove City College v. Bell* 465 U.S. 555 (1984), the Supreme Court held that Title IX's prohibition of discrimination in federally assisted educational programs applied only to those programs specifically receiving federal aid and not to their institutions. This meant that a school could use budgeting procedures to shield selected departments or programs from antidiscrimination laws. It opened a loophole

that swallowed the Act, and Title IX practically ceased to matter. *Grove City* also affected three other major civil rights laws prohibiting discrimination in federally assisted programs and activities—Title VI of the 1964 Civil Rights Act, prohibiting racial and ethnic discrimination, Section 504 of the Rehabilitation Act of 1973, prohibiting discrimination against handicapped people, and the Age Discrimination Act of 1975. Congress, however, eventually managed to restore these laws, along with Title IX, when it passed the Civil Rights Restoration Act in 1988 after three years of lobbying by civil rights groups. This act made clear that prohibitions of discrimination in federally assisted programs applied to institutions of which discriminatory programs are part. It was enacted over a veto by President Reagan.

3. Claudia H. Deutsch, "The Ax Falls on Equal Opportunity," *New York Times* (4 Jan. 1987): Sec. 3, 1.

4. Women's Legal Defense Fund, "Civil Rights Enforcement Policy."

5. Staff of the Committee on Education and Labor, U.S. House of Representatives, 99th Congress, Second Session, "A Report on the Investigation of Civil Rights Enforcement by the Equal Employment Opportunity Commission" (May 1986), 4–5.

6. Ibid., 13.

7. Women's Legal Defense Fund, "The Agencies and the Laws They Enforce," 12–14.

8. In 1981 the Commission filed 166 systemic cases; in 1982, 1983, and 1984, it filed 69, 75, and 112, respectively. In 1987 it filed 105 systemic cases, about one-fourth of all cases filed.

In 1988 the agency filed a total of 554 lawsuits, having received 58,853 complaints. The EEOC has always been a troubled agency, hampered by an enormous backlog of cases, but its backlog increased during the 1980s (from 37,675 charges in 1980 to 61,686 in 1987). It also increased processing time for individual cases (from 4.8 months in 1980 to 9.3 months in 1988).

See Women's Legal Defense Fund, "The Agencies and the Laws They Enforce," 20–24.

9. Staff of the Committee on Education and Labor, "A Report on the Investigation of Civil Rights Enforcement by the EEOC," 16.

10. *Regents of University of California v. Bakke*, 438 U.S. 265 (1978).

11. Women's Legal Defense Fund, "The Agencies and the Laws They Enforce," 4.

12. *Contractors Association of Eastern Pennsylvania v. Secretary of Labor*, 442 F.2d 159 (3d Cir.) 1971, cert. denied, 404 U.S. 854.

13. See Robert Pear, "U.S. Plans to Ease Rules for Hiring Women and Blacks," *New York Times*, 3 April 1983, sec. 1, 1.

14. Women's Legal Defense Fund, "The Agencies and the Laws They Enforce," 34–36.

15. Ibid.

16. See Philip Shenon, "Chicago Bank to Pay $14 Million in Resolving Discrimination Case," *New York Times* (11 Jan. 1989): Sec. 1, 1.

17. Women Employed Institute, '*Women Employed vs. Harris Bank*': *A Case Study* (Chicago: Women Employed Institute, 1982), 19–22.

18. Women's Legal Defense Fund, "The Agencies and the Laws They Enforce," 9.

19. Robert Pear, "Aide in Justice Department Holds That Brennan Has Radical Views," *New York Times* (13 Sept. 1986): Sec. 1, 1.

20. *Johnson v. Transportation Agency of Santa Clara County*, 480 U.S. 616 (1987).

21. *United States v. Paradise*, 480 U.S. 149 (1987).

22. Women's Legal Defense Fund, "Civil Rights Enforcement Policy," 7.

23. Ibid.
24. Ibid. 8–10.
25. Ibid. 12–14.
26. *Martin v. Wilkes*, 57 U.S.L.W. 4616 (13 June 1989).
27. *City of Richmond v. Croson*, 57 U.S.L.W. 4132 (24 Jan. 1989). And see Martin Tolchin, "Officials in Cities and States Vow to Continue Minority Contractor Programs," *New York Times* (25 Jan. 1989): Sec. 1, p. 18.
28. *Richmond v. Croson*, 57 U.S.L.W. (24 Jan. 1989) (dissent).
29. Ibid.
30. *Bob Jones University v. United States*, 461 U.S. 574 (1983).

Chapter 10

1. See *Gedulgig v. Aiello*, 417 U.S. 484 (1974); *General Electric v. Gilbert*, 429 U.S. 125 (1976). See also discussion, Chapter 3.
2. Florence Kelley, "Shall Women Be Equal Before the Law?," *The Nation*, 114 (12 April 1922): 421.
3. *Muller v. Oregon*, 208 U.S. 412 (1980).
4. *Oil, Chemical, and Atomic Workers v. American Cyanamid Company*, 741 F.2d 444 (D.C. Cir. 1984).
5. Joan Bertin, "Reproductive Hazards in the Workplace," in Sherrill Cohen and Nadine Taub, eds., *Reproductive Laws for the 1990's* (Clifton, N.J.: Humana Press, 1989).
6. *Hayes v. Shelby Memorial Hospital*, 726 F.2d 1543 (11th Cir. 1984).
7. *Zuniga v. Kleberg County Hospital*, 692 F.2d 986 (5th Cir. 1982).
8. *Wright v. Olin*, 697 F.2d 1172 (4th Cir. 1982).
9. *Auto Workers v. Johnson Controls, Inc.*, CA 7, 58 LW 2193, October 10, 1989.
10. *Wards Cove Packing Company v. Atonio*, No. 87-1887 (29 June 1989). Note that under the rule announced in *Atonio* (shifting the burden of proof of business necessity to employees), *Hayes, Zuniga,* and *Wright* could have been decided differently, against the women plaintiffs.
11. Bertin, "Reproductive Hazards in the Workplace," 285–290.
12. See Barry Meier, "Companies Wrestle with Threats to Workers' Reproductive Health," *Wall Street Journal* (5 Feb. 1987): Sec. 2, p. 1.
13. For a description of risks associated with VDTs, see Nine to Five—National Association of Working Women and Service Employees, "Campaign for VDT Safety" (Cleveland, Ohio, and Washington, D.C., undated).
14. Eric Schmitt, "Suffolk Approves Video Terminal Bill," *New York Times* (11 May 1988): Sec. 2, p. 1.
15. "Impact of the Paperwork Reduction Act," *OMB Review of CDC Research* (October 1986): 2, 4. According to this report, prepared for use of the Subcommittee on Oversight and Investigations of the Committee on Energy and Commerce, U.S. House of Representatives, the Reagan White House OMB was "seven times more likely to reject studies with an environmental or occupational health focus than to reject studies that focused on issues such as infectious diseases or other conventional diseases."
16. *Dothard v. Rawlinson*, 433 U.S. 321 (1977).
17. John Conyers, Jr., "Insensitive to Blacks' Health," *New York Times* (28 Dec. 1983): Sec. 1, Op Ed.
18. *EEOC v. Sears, Roebuck and Company*, 839 F.2d 302 (7th Cir. 1988).

19. *EEOC v. Sears, Roebuck and Company*, No. 79-C-4373, Plaintiff's Pretrial Brief—Commission Sales Issues (1984).

20. *Id.*, Posttrial Brief of Sears, Roebuck and Company.

21. *EEOC v. Sears, Roebuck and Company*, 628 F. Supp. 1264 (N.D. Ill. 1986).

22. *EEOC v. Sears, Roebuck and Company*, No. 79-C-43-73, Plaintiff's Pretrial Brief—Commission Sales Issues.

23. "Offer of Proof Concerning the Testimony of Dr. Rosalind Rosenberg," *Signs: Journal of Women in Culture and Society* 11 (Summer 1986): 757.

24. "Written Testimony of Alice Kessler-Harris," *Signs: Journal of Women in Culture and Society* 11 (Summer 1986).

25. Ibid.

26. Ibid.

27. Sylvia Ann Hewlett, *A Lesser Life: The Myth of Women's Liberation in America* (New York: W. M. Morrow 1986), 185.

28. Mary Ann Mason, *The Equality Trap* (New York: Simon and Schuster, 1988), 131.

29. Phyllis Schlafly, *The Power of the Positive Woman* (New Rochelle, N.Y.: Arlington House, 1977), 159.

30. Robert H. Bremner, *Children and Youth in America*, vol. 3 (Cambridge, Mass.: Harvard University Press, 1974), 716–719.

31. Ibid.

32. "Choice for Families with Children Oppose ABC Child Care Bill," *Family Protection Report* (March 1988): 1; "Day Care: The Thalidomide of the 1980s," *Family in America* 1, a publication of the Rockford Institute Center for the Family in America (Nov. 1987): 1 "Family Leave: Will Congress Leave Sense Behind?," *Family Protection Report* 9 (April 1987): 1; "Working Moms, Failing Children," *Family in America* 2 (May 1988): 3.

33. Bremner, *Children in America*, vol. 3, 677.

34. Ibid. 681.

35. Cynthia Harrison, *On Account of Sex: The Politics of Women's Issues, 1945–1988* (Berkeley: University of California Press, 1988), 5.

36. Barbara Bergmann, *The Economic Emergence of Women* (New York: 1986), 25.

37. "Working Mothers Is Now Norm, Study Shows," *New York Times* (16 June 1988): Sec. 1, 19; "Employers Offer Aid on Child Care," *New York Times* (17 Jan. 1988): Sec. 1, 25.

38. Claudia Wallis, "The Child-Care Dilemma," *Time* (22 June 1987): 54.

39. Lawrence Ingrassia, "Day Care Business Lures Entrepreneurs," *Wall Street Journal* (3 June 1988): Sec. 2, p. 1.

40. "Employers Offer Aid on Child Care," *New York Times* (17 Jan. 1988): Sec. 1, 25. See also Cathy Trost, "School Child Care Programs Stir Debate," *Wall Street Journal* (8 April 1988): Sec. 2, p. 1.

41. Claudia Wallis, "The Child-Care Dilemma," *Time* (22 June 1987).

42. "Labor Letter," *Wall Street Journal* (29 March 1988): Sec. 1, 1.

43. Wallis, "The Child-Care Dilemma."

44. Glenn Collins, "Wooing Workers in the '90s: New Roles for Family Benefits," *New York Times* (20 July 1988): Sec. 1, 1; Marilyn Gardner, "Family Friendly Corporations," *Christian Science Monitor* (30 June 1988): 32; Kirsten O. Lundberg, "What's New in Day Care?" *New York Times* (26 Feb. 1989): Sec. 3, 13; Cathy Trost, "Men, Too, Wrestle with Career Family Stress," *Wall Street Journal* (11 Nov. 1988): Sec. 2, 1.

Chapter 11

1. Elizabeth Cady Stanton, "Home Life," in Ellen Carol DuBois, ed., *Elizabeth Cady Stanton and Susan B. Anthony, Correspondence, Writings, Speeches*, (New York: Schocken Books, 1981), 134–135.

2. For a summary of state laws, see Doris Jonas Freed and Timothy B. Walker, "Family Law in the Fifty States: An Overview," *Family Law Quarterly* 21 (Winter 1988).

3. "New York State Task Force Report on Women in the Courts," *Fordham Urban Law Journal* 15 (1986–1987): 65–111.

4. Lenore J. Weitzman, *The Divorce Revolution: The Unexpected Social and Economic Consequences for Women and Children in America* (New York: Free Press 1985).

5. Ibid., 33.

6. Ibid., 183.

7. Ibid., 193–194.

8. Ibid., 143–145.

9. See Tamar Lewin, "New Law Compels Sweeping Changes in Child Support," *New York Times* (25 Nov. 1988): Sec. 1, 1.

10. Wendy Kaminer, "The Divorce Industry: What Lawyers Talk about When They Talk about Divorce," *7 Days* (22 Feb. 1989): 24.

11. See Nancy D. Polikoff, "Child Custody Decisions: Exploding the Myth That Mothers Always Win," *Women's Rights Law Reporter* (Spring 1982): 235. Polikoff asserts that when fathers demand custody, "their chances of winning are substantial." Courts tend to discriminate against women, especially if they're employed, and they tend to favor the spouse with more money (who tends to be the husband). Polikoff advocates a gender-neutral, primary-caretaker custody standard to replace the best-interests-of-the-child standard that now prevails.

12. For a popular, protectionist feminist critique of custody trends, see Phyllis Chesler, *Mothers on Trial: The Battle for Children and Custody* (New York: McGraw-Hill, 1986).

13. Interview with Raoul Felder, December 1988.

14. See generally Amy Dockster, "More Unwed Fathers Push for Equal Say in Adoptions," *Wall Street Journal* (23 Feb. 1989): Sec. 2, 1.

15. Georgia Dullea, "Unwed Father Given Custody Despite Adoption," *New York Times* (9 Dec. 1988): Sec. 2, 13.

16. *Caban v. Mohammed*, 441 U.S. 380 (1979).

17. *Stanley v. Illinois*, 405 U.S. 645 (1972).

18. *Levy v. Louisiana*, 391 U.S. 68 (1968).

19. Harry D. Krause, *Family Law: Cases, Comments, and Questions* (St. Paul, Minn.: West, 1983), 818–825.

20. *Labine v. Vincent*, 401 U.S. 532 (1971).

21. *Weber v. Aetna Casualty and Surety Company*, 406 U.S. 164 (1972).

22. *Trimble v. Gordon*, 430 U.S. 762 (1977).

23. See generally Krause, *Family Law*, 818–821.

24. *Matter of Baby M*, 109 N.J. 396 (1988).

25. Ibid.

26. Mary Beth Whitehead, with Loretta Schwartz-Nobel, *A Mother's Story* (New York: St. Martins Press, 1989), 26.

27. Ibid., 170.

28. Ibid., 139.

29. Ibid., 25–26, 68.

30. *Matter of Baby M*, 109 N.J. 396 (1988).

31. Whitehead, *A Mother's Story*, 158–159.
32. Ibid., 166.
33. *Matter of Baby M*, 109 N.J. 396 (1988).
34. Whitehead, *A Mother's Story*, 136.

Chapter 12

1. *Muller v. Oregon*, 208 U.S. 412 (1908).
2. Gisela Bock, "Racism and Sexism in Nazi Germany: Motherhood, Compulsory Sterilization and the State," in Renate Bridenthal, Atina Grossman, and Marion Kaplan, eds., *When Biology Becomes Destiny* (New York: Monthly Review Press, 1984).
3. Linda Gordon, *Woman's Body, Woman's Right* (New York: Penguin Books, 1977) 311.
4. In 1927 the Supreme Court upheld a mandatory sterilization law applying to inmates of state institutions. *Buck v. Bell*, 247 U.S. 200 (1927). In 1942, however, it invalidated a sterilization law applying to convicted felons, recognizing procreation as a basic civil right. *Skinner v. Oklahoma*, 316 U.S. 535 (1942).
5. Gordon, *Woman's Body, Woman's Right*.
6. Angela Y. Davis, *Women, Race, and Class* (New York: Random House 1983), 214.
7. *Skinner v. Oklahoma*, 316 U.S. 535 (1942).
8. *Relf v. Weinberger*, 372 F. Supp. 1196 (D.D.C. 1974).
9. Davis, *Women, Race, and Class*, 216.
10. Ibid., 218.
11. Gordon, *Women's Body, Women's Right*, 399–400.
12. Davis, *Women, Race, and Class*, 218–219.
13. *Walker v. Pierce*, 560 F.2d 609 (4th Cir. 1977).
14. See, for example, R. J. Herrnstein, "IQ and Falling Birth Rates," *Atlantic* (May 1989).
15. Nancy Gertner, "Interference with Reproductive Choice," in Sherril Cohen and Nadine Taub, eds., *Reproductive Laws for the 1990s* (Clifton, N.J.: Humana Press, 1988), 310.
16. Ibid., 309.
17. Sabra Chartrand, "Experts Assess a Decade of In Vitro Fertilization," *New York Times* (11 April 1989): Sec. 3, 5.
18. For a review of technology and reproductive-choice–related issues and proposals for public policy, see Cohen and Taub, *Reproductive Laws for the 1990s*.
19. *Skinner v. Oklahoma*, 316 U.S. 535 (1942); *Roe v. Wade*, 410 U.S. 113 (1973).
20. See *Bowers v. Hardwicke*, 478 U.S. 186 (1986), upholding a law criminalizing homosexual activity between consenting adults, in the privacy of the home.
21. *Webster v. Reproductive Health Services*, 157 U.S.L.W. 5023 (July 3, 1989).
22. *Harris v. McRae*, 448 U.S. 297 (1980).
23. In her concurring opinion in *Webster*, Justice O'Connor declines to assume the Missouri prohibition on public funding might be broadly applied to private hospitals with tenuous connections to the state; she leaves open the question of whether an action against a private hospital on public land, for example, would be constitutional.
24. *Planned Parenthood of Central Missouri v. Danforth*, 428 U.S. 52 (1976); *Colautti v. Franklin*, 439 U.S. 379 (1979).
25. See *Akron v. Akron Center for Reproductive Health, Inc.*, 426 U.S. 416 (1983) (dissent).

26. Justice O'Connor (and Chief Justice Rehnquist, joined by Justices White and Kennedy) read into the viability testing provision an acknowledgment that physicians may not be required to conduct tests they consider imprudent, so that testing is not quite as mandatory as the language of the statute suggests. Justice O'Connor also qualified the public funding provision.

27. The Court is scheduled to decide two abortion cases in 1990, both involving parental notification laws applying to minors seeking abortions. (*Ohio v. Akron Center for Reproductive Health*, No. 88-805, 57 U.S.L.W. 3851, June 27, 1989; *Hodgson v. Minnesota*, No. 88-1125, 57 U.S.L.W. 3852, June 27, 1989.) The Court has already upheld parental consent laws; upholding the notification requirements in these cases would not significantly change current abortion law, but it would surely make life harder for some minors. (The Bush Administration has asked the Court to use these cases to overturn *Roe v. Wade*, but the Court does not appear likely to do so.)

The most important abortion case of the 1990 term was settled only weeks before the Court was scheduled to hear it. (*Turnock v. Ragsdale*, No. 88-790, 57 U.S.L.W. 3851, June 27, 1989.) *Turnock* involved an Illinois law that subjected private abortion clinics to stringent regulations that could have effectively closed some of them down. Since this law severely restricted access to private, first trimester abortions, it posed a very serious challenge to *Roe v. Wade*. The Illinois Attorney General essentially backed away from this challenge by settling the case at the last minute, in response to renewed support for abortion rights that followed the Supreme Court's decision in *Webster v. Reproductive Health Services*.

28. *Akron v. Akron Center for Reproductive Health, Inc.*, 426 U.S. 416 (1983) (dissent).

29. E. J. Dionne, Jr., "Poll on Abortion Finds the Nation is Sharply Divided," *New York Times* (26 April 1989): Sec. 1, 1.

30. According to a *New York Times* poll conducted in July 1989, 46 percent of people surveyed agreed and 48 percent disagreed with the statement "Abortion should be available for those who really want it, but should not be easy to get." E. J. Dionne Jr., "Poll Finds Ambivalence on Abortion Persists in U.S.," *New York Times* (3 Aug. 1989): Sec. 1, 18.

31. Pennsylvania recently passed a law prohibiting sex-selection abortions at any time during pregnancy, in clear violation of *Roe v. Wade*. See Michael deCourcy Hinds, "Stringent Curbs on Abortion Pass in Pennsylvania" *New York Times* (25 Oct. 1989): Sec. 1, 1.

32. R. W. Apple, "An Altered Political Climate Suddenly Surrounds Abortion," *New York Times* (13 Oct. 1989): Sec. 1, 1.

33. *Harris v. McRae*, 448 U.S. 297 (1980).

34. Hinds, "Stringent Curbs on Abortion Pass in Pennsylvania," Sec. 1, 1.

Anti-abortion provisions similar to those just adopted in Pennsylvania were struck down by the Supreme Court in cases following *Roe v. Wade*. See *Thornburgh v. American College of Obstetricians*, 476 U.S. 747 (1986); *Akron v. Akron Center for Reproductive Health, Inc.*, 439 U.S. 379 (1983); *Planned Parenthood of Central Missouri v. Danforth*, 428 U.S. 52 (1976). Prochoice advocates have promised a judicial challenge to the new Pennsylvania law, and under *Roe*'s rules, they should prevail. But the rules appear to be changing.

35. Michael deCourcy Hinds, "Poll Finds U.S. and Pennsylvania Share Divisions About Abortion," *New York Times*: (4 Oct. 1989): Sec. 2, 22.

36. Dionne, Jr., "Poll Finds Ambivalence on Abortion Persists in U.S.," Sec. 1, 18.

37. See Eileen McNamara, "Fetal Endangerment Cases on the Rise," *Boston Globe* (3 Oct. 1989): Sec. 1. 1. Tamar Lewin, "When Courts Take Charge of the Unborn," *New York Times* (9 Jan. 1989): Sec. 1, 1; "Mother Charged in Baby's Death from

Cocaine, *New York Times* (10 May 1989): Sec. 1, 18; "Mother Who Gives Birth to Drug Addict Faces Felony Charge," *New York Times* (1 Dec. 1988): Sec. 1, 9.

38. Nancy Gertner, "Interference with Reproductive Choice," in Cohen and Taub, *Reproductive Laws for the 1990s.*

39. *Skinner v. Oklahoma,* 316 U.S. 535 (1942).

40. *Griswold v. Connecticut,* 381 U.S. 479 (1965).

41. *Eisenstadt vs. Baird,* 405 U.S. 438.

42. See, for example, *Griswold v. Connecticut,* 381 U.S. 479 (1965); *Poe v. Ullman,* 367 U.S. 497 (1961); and *United States v. Vuitch,* 402 U.S. 62 (1970). Note too that a doctor appeared as a plaintiff in *Roe v. Wade,* though he was denied standing, and an amicus brief in support of abortion rights was submitted by the American College of Obstetricians and Gynecologists and the American Psychiatric Association. The medical community was not entirely united on the abortion question: A brief in support of prohibition was submitted by dissenting members of the American College of Obstetricians and Gynecologists.

43. See Brief for Appellants, *Roe v. Wade,* No. 70-18, 108–109.

44. Mary Ann Glendon, *Abortion and Divorce in Western Law: American Failures, European Challenges* (Cambridge, Mass.: Harvard University Press, 1987).

45. *Zablocki v. Redhail,* 434 U.S. 374 (1978).

46. *Wisconsin v. Yoder,* 406 U.S. 205 (1972); *Pierce v. Society of Sisters,* 268 U.S. 510 (1925); *Meyer v. Nebraska,* 262 U.S. 390 (1923).

47. *Bellotti v. Baird,* 443 U.S. 622 (1979).

48. See, for example, Catherine MacKinnon, " 'Roe v. Wade': A Study in Male Ideology," in Jay L. Garfield and Patricia Hennessey, eds, *Abortion: Moral and Legal Perspectives* (Amherst, Mass.: University of Massachusetts Press, 1984).

49. *Bowers v. Hardwicke,* 478 U.S. 186 (1986).

50. *Stanley v. Georgia,* 394 U.S. 557 (1969).

51. *Bolger v. Youngs Drug Company,* 463 U.S. 60 (1983), striking down a prohibition on unsolicited mailings of contraceptive advertisements. And see Felicity Barringer, "U.S. Appeals Panel Backs Clinics on Right to Counsel on Abortion," *New York Times* (10 May 1989): Sec. 1, 24. (Federal Courts have split on the right to abortion counselling, and the issue may eventually reach the Supreme Court.)

52. *Harris v. McRae,* 448 U.S. 297 (1980).

53. Ibid., dissent.

54. See, for example, Sylvia A. Law, "Rethinking Sex and the Constitution," 132 *University of Pennsylvania Law Review* 955 (1984). The equality argument was also advanced early on in an amicus brief submitted in *Roe v. Wade* by Nancy Stearns for the Center for Consitutional Rights.

55. *Gedulgig v. Aiello,* 417 U.S. 484 (1974); *General Electric Company v. Gilbert,* 429 U.S. 125 (1976).

Chapter 13

1. Herma Hill Kay, *Sex-Based Discrimination: Text, Cases and Materials* (St. Paul, Minn: West, 1981), 906.

2. *Coker v. Georgia,* 433 U.S. 584 (1977).

3. See David Ranii, "States' New Rape Laws Taking Hold: They Help Victims But Are They Fair?" *National Law Journal* (15 Dec. 1983): 1. And see Patricia Searles and Ronald J. Berger, "The Current Status of Rape Reform Legislation: An Examination of State Statutes," *Women's Rights Law Reporter* (Spring 1987): 25.

4. Ranii, "State's New Rape Laws Taking Hold."

A Fearful Freedom

5. *People v. Liberta*, 64 N.Y. 2d 152 (1984).

6. *Michael M. v. Superior Court*, 450 U.S. 464 (1981).

7. *Country v. Parrett*, 684 F.2d 588 (8th Cir. 1982).

8. See *People v. Superior Court (Hartway)*, 19 Cal. 3d 388 (1977) (dissent).

9. *Commonwealth v. Dodge*, 287 Pa. Super. 148 (1981).

10. *Commonwealth v. King*, 375 Mass. 5 (1977).

11. *People v. Superior Court (Hartway)* 19 Cal. 3d 338 (1977).

12. *United States ex rel. Robinson v. York*, 281 F. Supp. 8 (D. Conn. 1968).

13. *Commonwealth v. Daniels*, 430 Pa. 642 (1968); *State v. Chambers*, 307 A.2d 78 (1973).

14. *Wark v. State*, 266 A.2d 62, (1970), cert. denied, 400 U.S. 952.

15. Kenneth M. Davidson, Ruth B. Ginsburg, and Herma H. Kay, *Sex-Based Discrimination: Text, Cases and Materials* (St. Paul, Minn.: West 1974), 893.

16. Schlesinger Library, Radcliffe College, A-71, Miriam Van Waters Papers, Folder 483.

17. Meda Chesney-Lind, "From Benign Neglect to Malign Attention: A Critical Review of Recent Research on Female Delinquincy," in Sue Davidson, ed., *Justice for Young Women: Close-up on Critical Issues* (Tucson, Ariz.: New Directions for Young Women, 1982).

18. Ibid.

19. See Nicole Hahn Rafer, *Partial Justice: Women in State Prisons 1800–1935* (Boston: Northeastern University Press, 1985), 183–186.

20. See Elizabeth Anne Stanko, "Would You Believe This Woman? Prosecutorial Screening for 'Credible' Witnesses and a Problem of Justice," in Nicole Hahn Rafter and Elizabeth A. Stanko, *Judge Lawyer Victim Thief: Women, Gender Roles, and Criminal Justice* (Boston: Northeastern University Press, 1982).

21. *State v. Wanrow*, 88 Wash. 2d 221 (1977).

22. Cited in *State v. Wanrow*, Ibid.

23. See William Saletan and Nancy Watzman, "Marcus Welby, J.D.," *New Republic* (17 April 1989): 19.

24. Excerpted from pretrial motion papers filed by Chambers's defense attorney, Jack Litman.

25. For an account of the *Herrin* case, see Willard Gaylin, *The Killing of Bonnie Garland* (New York: Simon and Schuster, 1982).

26. This discussion is based on my telephone interview with Monsignor Leonard several months after Levin's killing.

27. See generally Wendy Kaminer, "Pornography and the First Amendment," in Laura Lederer, ed., *Take Back the Night: Women on Pornography* (New York: W. M. Morrow, 1980).

28. Jerry Falwell, Fundraising Letter, 1 Nov. 1980.

29. Phyllis Schlafly, "What's Wrong with Sex Education?" and "A Sex Education Checklist for Your School," *Phyllis Schlafly Report* (February 1981).

30. Remarks by President Reagan on signing the Child Protection Act of 1984, 21 May 1984.

31. Phyllis Schlafly, "New Weapons in the Battle against Pornography," *Phyllis Schafly Report* (June 1984).

32. Catherine MacKinnon, "Not a Moral Issue," *Yale Law and Policy Review* 2 (Spring 1984): 321.

33. Andrea Dworkin, "For Men, Freedom of Speech; For Women, Silence Please," in Lederer, *Take Back the Night: Women on Pornography*.

34. *American Booksellers Association v. Hudnut*, 771 F.2d 323 (7th Cir. 1985).

Conclusion

1. Majorie Houspian Dobkin, ed., *The Making of a Feminist: Early Journals and Letters of M. Carey Thomas* (Kent, Ohio: Kent State University Press, 1979), 48–50, 314.

2. Ibid., 50.

3. See Irvin Molotsky, "Jobless Rate Tied to Bigger Workforce," *New York Times* (18 April 1982): Sec. 1, 37.

4. Dobkin, *The Making of a Feminist*, 132, 140.

5. "Women's Growing Role in the Workforce," *Wall Street Journal* (5 March 1989): Sec. 2, 1.

6. Cathy Trost, "More Family Issues Surface at Bargaining Tables as Women Show Increasing Interest in Unions," *Wall Street Journal* (2 Dec. 1986): Sec. 2, 70.

7. Amanda Bennett, "The Company School: As Pool of Skilled Help Tightens, Firms Move to Broaden Their Role," *Wall Street Journal* (8 May 1989): Sec. 1, 1.

8. Daniel Goleman, "Sex Roles Reign as Powerful as Ever in the Emotions," *New York Times* (23 Aug. 1988): Sec. 3, 1.

9. Ibid.

10. Ethel S. Person, "Some Differences between Men and Women," *Atlantic Monthly* (March 1988): 71.

11. See R. C. Lewontin, Steven Rose, and Leo J. Kamin, *Not in Our Genes: Biology, Ideology, and Human Nature* (New York: Pantheon Books, 1984).

12. E. O. Wilson, *Sociobiology: The New Synthesis* (Cambridge, Mass.: Harvard University Press, 1975).

13. See Daniel Goleman, "Special Abilities of the Sexes: Do They Begin in the Brain?," *Psychology Today* (November 1978): 48; Melvin Konner, "The Aggressors," *New York Times Magazine* (14 Aug. 1988): 33.

14. Karen E. Paige, "Women Learn to Sing the Menstrual Blues," *Psychology Today* (September 1973): 41.

15. Remarks by Dr. Ruth Hubbard, professor of biology, Harvard University, at a seminar on "Reproduction, Technology, and Public Policy," Kennedy School of Government, Harvard University, 4–5 May 1989.

16. Maggie Gallagher, "The New Pro-Life Rebels," *National Review* (27 Feb. 1987): 37.

17. Remarks by Elizabeth Bartholet, professor of law, Harvard University Law School, at a colloquium and seminar on "Reproduction, Technology, and Public Policy," Kennedy School of Government, Harvard University, 4–5 May 1989.

18. Ibid.

19. *Regents of the University of California v. Bakke*, 438 U.S. 265 (1978) (dissent).

20. I owe this image to my editor, Jane Isay.

21. Elizabeth Cady Stanton, "The Solitude of Self," in Ellen Carol DuBoise, ed., *Elizabeth Cady Stanton and Susan B. Anthony, Correspondence, Writings, Speeches* (New York: Schocken Books, 1981), 246.

Index

Abortion, 13, 22, 169–81, 211–15. *See also* Pregnancy; Reproductive choice
  access to, limited by poverty, 16, 169–70
  fetal rights and, 175–76, 211
  Hyde amendment and Medicaid funds cut-off for, 179
  privacy rights and, 172–73, 176, 177
  prochoice movement for, 174–75
  public opinion on, 173–75
  racist population control, sterilization and, 166–67
  Uniform Abortion Act, 177
Academia
  opportunities for women in higher education, 113–14
  sex segregation in, 118–22

workplace equality issues in, 99, 105–7
Adkins v. Children's Hospital, 69
Adoption laws, 153–54, 211
Affirmative action, 12–13, 30–32
  education and, 101–2, 212
  federal government's failure to enforce, 123–32
  as protectionism vs. compensation, 32
AFSME v. State of Washington, 99–100
Age-of-consent laws, 28
Aid for Families of Dependent Children (AFDC), 76, 142
  court cases involving, 16
Alimony, 28, 148–50
American Bar Association, 177, 187
American Civil Liberties Union (ACLU), 23–24, 72, 135

American Cyanamid Company, 134–35, 164, 180–81
American Federationist, 66
American Federation of Labor, 66, 71
American Woman Suffrage Association, 47, 58
Anthony, Susan B., 41, 47, 48, 64
Anti-vice movement, 19th century, 55–57
Art and literature, women in 19th century, 44

Baby M case, 157–61
Barnes, Paulette, 108
Barnes v. Costle, 108
Barry, Leona, 66
Battered wife syndrome, 195
Beecher, Catherine, 40, 113
Beecher, Henry, 47
Bertin, Joan, 135
Biological determinism, 21, 22, 212–13. *See also* Nature and gender; Sexual differences, ideology of
contemporary sociobiology and, 209–10
19th century, 45–47
protectionist labor laws and, 73–74
Birth control. *See also* Abortion; Reproductive choice
eugenics and, 164–65
19th century, 46–47, 57
sexual revolution of the 1960s and, 82–83
Birth Control Federation of America, 165
Blackwell, Elizabeth, 56
Blatch, Harriet Stanton, 74
Bona fide occupational qualification (BFOQ), 94–97
Boston University, 106
Brandeis, Louis, 67
Broca, Paul, 42
Brown, Christine, 107
Brown, Helen Gurley, 84–85
Brown v. Board of Education, 22–23

Bush, George, 171, 174

Caban v. Mohammed, 154–55
Califano v. Goldfarb, 27, 28
Califano v. Webster, 30
California Federal Savings and Loan Association v. Guerra, 23–24
Carnegie Commission, 115
Censorship, 55–57
Central Park jogger rape case, 198–99
Chambers, Robert, "preppie murder" case, 195–99
Childbearing, surrogate, 157–61
Child care, xv, 140–43, 207–8
Child custody, 88, 152–61
fathers' rights and, 153–57
19th century, 50–52
surrogate parenting and, 157–61
Children, nonmarital, 156–57
Child support, 150
City of Los Angeles Department of Water and Power v. Manhart, 97
City of Richmond v. Croson, 31, 130–31
Civil rights. *See also* Equality; Legal equality
American public support for, 79–80
establishment of modern women's, 91–93, 123–24
federal government resistence to expanding/enforcing, 124–32
Civil Rights Act of 1964, 13, 93, 115. *See also* Title VII of the 1964 Civil Rights Act; Title IX of the 1964 Civil Rights Act
Civil Rights Commission, 115
Clements, William, 174
Coker v. Georgia, 184–85
Collins, Eliza, 109
Combat, prospect of women in, 2–3
Commission on Pornography, 201
Communitarianism
critique of equal rights feminism, 18–19
view of justice, 11–12
Community, feminism and concept of, 7, 18–19

Comparable worth, 98–100
Competitiveness in males vs.
    females, 6–7
Comprehensive Community Child
    Care Development Act, 141, 142
Comstock, Anthony, 56
Comstock law, 178
Constitutional law, 21–34. *See also*
    Legal equality; Supreme Court
    decisions
    amendments
        First Amendment, 179, 200, 202,
            203
        Fifth Amendment, 92
        Fourteenth Amendment, 24, 27,
            32, 80, 92, 102, 116, 123, 180
    equality issues and women, 92–93
        affirmative action, 30–32, 129–31
        pregnancy disability, 23–26,
            96–97
        sex discrimination, 26–30, 33
    pornography and, 178–79
    protectionism and, 21–22, 25–26,
        32, 33
    race and, 22–23, 26–27, 32
    social vs. political equality and,
        22–23
    theories of, and social in/equality
        issues, 16–18
Conyers, John, 137
Cooperation in males vs. females, 7
Cornell University, 114
Cosmopolitan magazine, 84
Country v. Parrett, 186
County of Washington v. Gunther, 99
Craniology, 42, 44
Criminal behavior, 19th century
    views of women's, 44–45, 52–53
Criminal justice system, 187–98. *See
    also* Prisons
    double standard in, 188–91
    female equality linked to female
        criminality, 190–91
    prostitution laws, 187–89
    women in 19th century, 44–45,
        53–54, 188

Custody. *See* Child custody

Dandridge v. Williams, 16, 17
Darwin, Charles, 41, 42–44, 46, 56
Day care. *See* Child care
De Beauvoir, Simone, 4
Depo–Provera, 165
Descent of Man, The (Darwin), 41
DES drug, 210
Diaz v. Pan American World Airways,
    96
Disparate impact rule, 100–105
    criminal justice and, 192
    enforcement under Reagan
        administration, 125–26
    fetal protection policies and, 135–36
Divorce, 145–53. *See also* Marriage
    child custody and, 50–52, 152–53
    child support and, 150
    distribution of marital property on,
        147–48, 150
    19th century, 50–52, 58
    no–fault, 146–52
    reforms, 146–53
    social inequality vs. legal equality
        in, 12, 13
    spousal support and, 148, 149–50
Doctors as guardians of reproductive
    rights, 167–68, 176–77
Domestic violence, 191, 195
Dothard v. Rawlinson, 33–34, 137
Draft, prospect of female military,
    2–3
Dworkin, Andrea, 202
Dworkin, Ronald, 12

Eastman, Crystal, 72
Education, xiii, 22–23, 113–22
    affirmative action and, 101–2, 212
    athletics, women's, 116–18
    ideal of educated motherhood, 40,
        49, 113
    male/female student ratios in 1960
        and 1970, 114
    marriage and levels of, 114

Education (*cont.*)
protectionist ideas in, 113–14, 115, 116
separate-but-equal model in, 115, 121
sex discrimination in, 114–15
single-sex environments in, 118–22
Title IX, 115–16, 120–21
women in higher, 113–14
Egalitarian feminism, 19th century
challenges to sexual stereotypes by, 36–37
legal/social equality, efforts to create, 37–41, 48, 57–59
vs. protectionism, 47–49
racism and, 47, 54
Eisenhower, Dwight D., 127
Employment opportunities. *See* Workplace equality
Equal Education Opportunity Act, 120
Equal Employment Opportunity Commission (EEOC), 93–94
failure to enforce Title VII, 124–26
Equality, xii. *See also* Civil rights
in divorce and parenting (*see* Divorce; Marriage; Child custody)
equated with selfishness in women, 205–7
feminist vision of, 1–2, 4, 9
legal (*see* Constitutional law; Legal equality)
vs. protectionism, xiv–xv, 8–10, 23, 213–16
in labor laws, 61–63, 71–77
sexual differences and, 9–10
social problems as obstacles to, xv, 5, 10, 12–18
in the workplace (*see* Workplace equality)
Equal Pay Act, 99, 105, 106
Equal Rights Amendment (ERA), 2, 22
opposition to, as a threat to protectionism, 71–73, 75, 76–77, 80–81, 145–46

ratification failure, 79–80
Equal treatment vs. treatment as an equal, 12–13
Ervin, Sam, 22, 215
Eugenics
advanced reproductive technology and, 167–68
19th century, 46–47
sterilization and, 164–65
Executive Order 11246, 126–28

Fair Labor Standards Act, 70
Falwell, Jerry, 215
Family issues, 140–43. *See also* Child custody; Divorce; Marriage
child care, xv, 140–43, 207–8
privacy rights, 177–78
surrogacy in childbearing, 157–61
violence, 52, 191, 195
women's conflicts between work and, 86
Family Protection Act of 1981, 200–201
Faro v. New York University, 105
Fathers, 153–57
Federal Bureau of Investigation (FBI), 128
Federal Economy Act of 1932, 77
Federal government, failure to effectively enforce civil rights acts by, 124–32
Feminist movement
antipornography movement in, 201–3
biological determinist ideology and, 21–22
competing views of justice in, 11–12
contemporary disdain and hostility toward, 3–4, 5
critique of privacy rights by, 178–80
equality envisioned by, 1–2, 4, 9
equality vs. protectionist views in, xiv–xv, 8–10, 11–12, 213–16
in labor laws, 61–63, 71–77
identification of the sexual revolution with, 81–82, 85

19th century (*see* Egalitarian
  feminism, 19th century)
revivial of protectionism in, 5–7,
  14, 21–22
Fetal protection policies in the
  workplace, 134–37, 164
Fetal rights and abortion, 175–76, 211
Force, Nichole, 117
Friedan, Betty, 87
Frontiero v. Richardson, 27, 28

Gardener, Helen Hamilton, xiii–xv,
  37
Garland, Bonnie, 196–97
Gedulgig v. Aiello, 25
Gender. *See* Nature and gender
General Electric Company v. Gilbert, 25
Gilligan, Carol, 6, 15, 81
Glamour magazine, 86, 87
Goesaert v. Cleary, 71
Gompers, Samuel, 66, 71
Griffiths, Martha, 94
Griggs v. Duke Power Company, 100,
  102
Grimke, Angelina, 38
Grimke, Sarah, 38
Griswold v. Connecticut, 176

Habits of the Heart, 18–19
Hacker, Andrew, 83
Hamilton, Alice, 73
Hammond, William, xiv
Harpers Bazaar magazine, 86
Harris, Alice Kessler, 139–40
Harris Trust and Savings, Chicago,
  127–28
Harris v. McRae, 16, 179
Harvard University, 114
Hayes v. Shelby Memorial Hospital, 135
Herrin, Richard, 196–97
Holmes, Oliver Wendell, 118
Homemakers, potential effects of the
  Equal Rights Amendment on,
  80–81
Hooker, Edith Houghton, 72–73
Hopkins, Anne, 110
Howe, Julia Ward, 47, 56–57

Hubbard, Ruth, 210

In a Different Voice (Gilligan), 6
Individual rights. *See* Civil rights;
  Legal equality
Inequality, social, and legal equality
  issues, 12–18
Infertility, 210–11
Intelligence, women's, 19th century
  views of, xiii–xiv, 36–37, 42

Jefferson vs. Hackney, 16
Job tests, standardized, 100–102
*Johnson v. Transportation Agency of
  Santa Clara County*, 129
Justice, xiv. *See also* Legal equality
  competing views of, 11–12
  relationship to gender nature,
    9–10, 21
  service-based approach to, in
    juvenile courts, 14–15
Justice Department, stance against
  affirmative action programs by,
  124, 128–32
Juvenile court system, socialization
  of, 14–15

Kahn v. Shevin, 29, 33
Kelley, Florence, 73, 74
Kennedy, John F., 92, 127
King, Martin Luther, Jr., 128
Krug, Judith, 200

Labor Department, slackened
  enforcement of affirmative action
  by, 124, 127
Labor laws, protective, 61–77. *See also*
  Worker's rights
  creation of dual labor market by,
    65–66
  effects of, on male workers, 71
  effects of, on workplace
    opportunities, 70–71
  equality vs. protectionism and,
    61–63, 71–77
  Equal Rights Amendment and,
    71–73, 75, 76–77

fetal protection laws, 134–37, 164
Labor Laws (*cont.*)
  improved working conditions,
    63–66
  maximum-hour laws, 67–68
  minimum-wage laws, 69–70
  women singled out for, 67–69
Labor market
  dual (sexually segregated), 66–67,
    97–98, 100, 137
  white collar, 104–5
Labor unions, 65, 66
Ladies Home Journal, 84–85
Laughlin, Gail, 76
Le Bon, Gustave, 42
Legal equality, 11–19, 213–16. *See also*
  Civil rights; Constitutional law
  communitarianist criticism of
    feminism and 18–19
  competing views of justice and,
    11–12
  in divorce (*see* Divorce)
  in employment (*see* Workplace
    equality)
  19th century feminists' efforts to
    create, 8, 37–39
  opposition to women's, 2, 206–7
  reproductive choice and, 169–81
  social in/equality issues and, 12–18
Legislation
  judicial deference to, 32
  rational relation test of, 32
  strict standard of review of, 32–35
Leonard, Thomas, 196–98
Levin, Jennifer, "preppie murder"
  case, 195–99
Levy v. Louisiana, 156
Lindsey v. Normet, 16–17
Lochner v. New York, 67
Lombroso, Cesare, 44–45, 53, 191
Lynchings, 54–55

MacKinnon, Catherine, 200
Mademoiselle magazine, 85, 86
Maintenance awards, 148
Marriage. *See also* Divorce
  educational levels and, 114

19th century, 49–52, 57–59
  sexual violence/rape in, 52, 178,
    185
  E. C. Stanton's views on, 58–59,
    145, 146
Married Women's Property Act, New
  York State, 52
Martineau, Harriet, 39, 40
Martinez, Bob, 174
Martin v. Wilkes, 31, 130
Maximum working hours, 67–69
Meese, Ed, 201
Men
  changing role of, in the
    postfeminist era, 87–88
  effect of double standard in
    criminal justice system on,
    188–91
  effect of protective labor laws on,
    71
  effect of protective
    marriage/divorce/custody laws
    on, 153–57
  effect of sexual segregation in
    sports on, 116–18
  failure to provide sufficient
    workplace safety for, 135, 136
  fears of, exploited by Reagan
    administration, 126
  pornography and social ideas of
    male sexuality, 200–201
  sexual revolution of the 1960's and,
    81, 83–84
Meritor Savings Bank, FSB v. Vinson,
  108–9
Michael M v. Superior Court, 33, 186
Military, U.S.
  benefits, 27
  promotion and discharge in, 30
  prospect of women in combat, 2–3
  sexual harassment in, 109
Mill, John Stuart, 4, 8, 36, 37
Minimum wage laws, 69–70
Mississippi University for Women v.
  Hogan, 120–21
Morality in women, 6, 8

19th century views on, 44–45,
52–53, 55, 56–57
sexual revolution of the 1960's and,
82–85
Mothers
appeal for education of, 40, 49, 113
child custody challenges to, 152–53
dual labor market and, 137
Nazi view of, 164
pensions for, 75–76
problems of working, 86, 140–43
social attitudes toward
motherhood, 163–64
unwed, 153–56
Muller v. Oregon, 67–69, 164

National American Women's Suffrage
Association, 41
National Consumer's League, 72, 73
National Federation of Business and
Professional Women, 75
National Institute for Occupational
Safety and Health, 136
National Organization for Women
(NOW), 23–24, 93
National Women's Party, 71, 72,
76–77
National Woman Suffrage
Association, 47
Nature and gender. *See also* Biological
determinism; Sexual differences
cultural presumptions about, 2,
6–8, 208–9, 212–13
protectionism and, 8–9
protectionist feminism's view of,
5–7, 21–22
relationship of justice to, 9–10,
21–22
sexual violence and, 183–84, 196,
197–99
women's sexuality and, 42–44, 55
workplace issues and assumptions
about, 96, 97, 110–12, 137–40
Nazi Germany eugenic policies, 164
New England mills, working
conditions in, 63–64

Newsweek magazine, 87
New York Female Moral Reform
Society, 55
Nixon, Richard, 141, 142
No-fault divorce, 146–52

Obscenity laws, 56
Occupational hazards, 133–37
Occupational Safety and Health Act
(OSHA), 135
Office of Federal Contract
Compliance (OFCCP), 127
Office of Management and Budget
(OMB), 136
Orr v. Orr, 29

Packard, Vance, 83
Parental leave, 143
Parenting and child custody cases,
152–57
Parham v. Hughes, 33
Pay equity, 98–100
Pennsylvania, abortion in, 174–75
Pensions, 76, 97
Pill, contraceptive, 82–83
Plessy v. Ferguson, 22, 23, 122
Pornography, 5
movement against, 81, 201–3, 214
19th century movement against,
55–56
privacy rights and, 178–79
sexual violence and, 199–203
Postfeminism, 3, 5, 87–89, 92, 149
Poverty
access to abortion limited by, 16,
169–70
feminization of, 5
legal rights and, 16–18
Pregnancy, 5, 9, 212–13. *See also*
Abortion; Reproductive choice
disability coverage, 23–26, 63,
96–97, 133
fetal rights and mother's behavior
during, 176
infertility and, 210–11
medicalization of, 167–68

Pregnancy (*cont.*)
  reproductive role and (*see*
    Reproductive role, women's)
  teenage, 186
  workers' rights and, 13
  workplace hazards and, 133–36
Pregnancy Discrimination Act, 24,
  135, 180
Presidential Commission on the
  Status of Women, 92
Price Waterhouse v. Hopkins, 110–12
Prisons
  pay equity in, 99
  sexual violence in, 34, 136–37
  women in 19th century, 53–54
Privacy rights
  family issues and, 177–78
  feminist critique of, 178–80
  pornography and, 178–79
  reproductive choice and, 172–73,
    176, 177, 179
Property, distribution of marital,
  147–48, 150
Property tax exemption, widow's, 33
Prostitution, 187–89
Protectionism
  affirmative action as compensation
    or, 32
  in childcare and family issues,
    140–43
  constitutional law and, 21–22,
    25–26, 32, 33
  vs. equality, xiv–xv, 8–10, 23,
    213–16
  vs. equality in labor laws, 61–63,
    71–77, 133–37
  feminist retreat into, 5–7, 14,
    213–16
  ideal of femininity and, 8–10, 21–22
  idea of justice and, 11–12
  ideology of sexual differences in
    the 19th century and, 36,
    47–60
  in the law (*see* Constitutional law;
    Labor laws, protective)

  for labor (*see* Labor laws,
    protective; Workers' rights
  marriage/divorce issues and,
    145–47, 152
  sexual revolution of the 1960's and
    revival of, 81–82
  sexual violence and ideas of,
    183–85
  surrogate childbearing and, 161
  women's education and ideas of,
    113–14, 115, 116

Race
  abolition movement of the 19th
    century, 39
  affirmative action and, 12–13,
    31–32, 101–2
  constitutional law, social/political
    equality, and, 22–23
  educational segregation and, 121,
    122
  federal government's slackened
    enforcement of
    anti-discrimination laws on,
    124–32
  19th century views on, 42, 46–47,
    53–55
    black women, 53–54
    lynchings, 54–55
  reproductive choice and racism,
    164–67
  sex discrimination cases vs. cases
    about, 26–27
  working conditions and, 65
  workplace equality issues and, 94,
    137
Radcliffe College, 114
Radice v. New York, 70
Rape. *See* Sexual violence
Reagan, Ronald, administration of,
  92, 111, 201
  record on civil rights policies
    toward women, 124–32
  reduction of day–care subsidies
    under, 143
Redbook magazine, 85, 86, 87, 109

Reed v. Reed, 27, 32
Reform movements of the 19th
    century, 8, 55–57. *See*
    also Egalitarian feminism, 19th
    century; Protectionism
*Regents of University of California v.
    Bakke*, 101, 126, 212
Relf v. Weinberger, 165
Religion and 19th century women,
    39, 40–41, 203
Reproductive choice, 13, 163–81,
    210–13. *See also* Abortion
    eugenic sterilization, 164–65
    infertility, 210–11
    legal equality and, 169–73
    medicalization of birth and, 167–69
    privacy rights and, 172–73, 176
    racism and, 165, 166–67
    sterilization of welfare recipients,
        165–66
    workplace protective laws and,
        134, 164
Reproductive role, women's
    constitutional law and, 33–34
    19th century views of, 41–44, 46–47
    protectionist views of the effect of
        higher education on, 113–14
    sexual violence and, 186–87
Retirement benefits, 30
"Reverse discrimination" cases, 31,
    129
Reynolds, William Bradford, 128
Rockford Institute Center on the
    Family in America, 141
Roe v. Wade, 16, 169–78
Roosevelt, Franklin Delano, Jr.,
    93–94, 127
Rosenberg, Rosalind, 139
Rosenfeld v. Southern Pacific Company,
    95

Salk, Lee, 86, 160
Sandel, Michael, 19
Sandler, Bernice, 106–7
Sanger, Margaret, 46, 179
Savvy magazine, 86

Schlafly, Phyllis, 58, 80, 88, 141, 200,
    201, 215
Schlesinger v. Ballard, 30
Science and 19th century view of
    women, xiv, 41–47
Sears, Roebuck Company sex
    discrimination case, 137–40
Self-defense, rights to, 192–95
Seneca Falls Declaration, 37
Separatist feminists, 11
Seven Sister Colleges, 113, 119
Sex and Character (Weininger), 42
Sex-based classification schemes, 30,
    32, 33. *See also* Affirmative action
Sex discrimination, 26–30, 33
    in education, 114–15
    in employment, 93–112, 137–40
    federal government's slackened
        enforcement of acts against,
        124–32
    presumed sexual differences and,
        xiii–xiv, 2–3, 4, 8 (*see also*
        Sexual differences, ideology of)
    prostitution laws and, 187–88
    race and, 26–27
Sex education, 200–201
Sex/gender stereotypes. *See* Sexual
    differences, ideology of
Sex segregation
    in education, 118–22
    in labor, 66–67, 97–98, 100, 137
    in sports, 115–18
Sexual differences, 208–10. *See also*
    Nature and gender
    antiEqual Rights Amendment
        arguments based on, 80–81
    athletic abilities and, 115, 116
    competitiveness vs. cooperation
        and, 6–7
    discrimination and, xv–xvi, 2–3, 4,
        8 (*see also* Sex discrimination)
    equality and, 9–10
    morality and, 6, 8 (*see also* Morality
        in women)
Sexual differences, ideology of, 4,
    21–22

Sexual differences (*cont.*)
female chauvinism, 5–7
19th century, 35–60
criminal behavior, 44–45, 52–53
cult of True Womanhood, 39–41, 51, 54
egalitarian feminism, 36, 37–41, 47–49
legal/social restrictions on women, 35, 38–39, 50–52
marriage and custody rights, 49–52
protectionism and, 36, 47–60
translated into gender stereotypes, 207–9
Sexual harassment, 107–10
Sexuality of women
19th century views of, 42–44
protectionist views of morality and, 55
sexual revolution of the 1960s and, 81–85
Sexual revolution
birth control and, 82–83
costs of, 86–87
death of, 86–87
identification of feminism with, 81–82, 85
revival of protectionism during, 81–82
women's sexuality and, 81–85
Sexual roles
American views of civil rights and, 79–80, 91–92
changing men's, in the postfeminist era, 87–88
changing women's, beginning in the 1960's, 83–89
reproductive (*see* Reproductive role, women's)
Sexual violence, 5, 34, 57, 183–87, 192–203
against black women, 54
Central Park jogger rape case, 198–99

Chambers "preppie murder" case, 195–99
expanded definition of, 185–86
in marriage, 52, 178, 185
pornography and, 199–203
rape as political control, 183–84
rape penalties, 184–85
rape reform laws, 192
self-defense rights against, 192–95
Skinner v. Oklahoma, 176
Smeal, Ellie, 141
Smith College, 119
Social feminists, 11, 47, 54, 56
opposition to the Equal Rights Amendment, 72–73
Social problems of women, equality vs. protectionism and, xv, 5, 10, 12–18
Sociobiology, 209–10
Sociobiology: The New Synthesis (Wilson), 209
Sodomy law, 178
Spaulding v. University of Washington, 99
Sports
gender-neutral rules in, 117–18
impact of Title IX on women in educational, 115–18
Stanley v. Illinois, 155
Stanton, Elizabeth Cady, 37, 40–41, 47, 48, 49, 58, 215
on marriage and divorce, 58–59, 145, 146
State v. Wanrow, 193–95
Steinem, Gloria, 83–84
Sterilization
eugenics and, 164–65
forced, for welfare recipients, 165–67
Stern, William and Elizabeth, 157–61
Stone, Lucy, 47, 58
Strasser, Adolph, 71
Suffrage, women's, 8, 37, 47–48
Supreme Court decisions
affirmative action cases, 30–32, 129–31

educational opportunity cases,
120–22
effects of 1960's reformism on,
92–93
ideology of sexual differences and
19th century, 35
on legal rights and social
in/equality issues, 16–18
nonmarital children cases, 156–57
pregnancy disability cases, 23–26,
96–97
protective labor law cases, 67–71
on race and social/political equality,
22–23
in Reagan administration, 124, 213
on reproductive choice, 16, 169–80
review of legislation in rights
questions, 32–33
sex discrimination cases, 26–30, 33
sexual equality in parental rights,
154–56
sexual violence cases, 184–86
workplace equality cases, 95, 96,
97, 99–105, 108–12, 135–36
Supreme Judicial Court of
Massachusetts, 116
Surrogate childbearing, 157–61
Sweeney, Christine, 107

Taub, Nadine, 168
Thackery, William, 44
Thomas, Clarence, 124–26
Thomas, M. Carey, 205–6
Time magazine, 86, 143
Title VII of the 1964 Civil Rights Act,
25, 70, 93–112
disparate impact rule, 100–105,
125–26, 135–36, 192
federal government's slackened
enforcement of, 124–26
fetal protection policies and, 134,
135
market forces and, 100
sex as a bona fide job qualification,
94–97

sex discrimination amendment,
93–94
Title IX of the 1964 Civil Rights Act,
106, 115–16, 120–21
effect on sports, 116–18
federal government's failure to
enforce, 124
sex segregation in education and,
120–21
Treatment as an equal vs. equal
treatment, 12–13
True Womanhood, 19th century cult
of, 39–41, 51
racism and, 54
Truman, David, 119
Truman, Harry, 127

Uniform Abortion Act, 177
United States ex rel. Robinson v. York,
189
United States v. Darby, 70
United States v. Paradise, 129
Universities. See Academia
University of North Carolina, 114
U.S. News & World Report magazine,
88

Van Waters, Miriam, 15, 16, 190
Video display terminals, hazards of,
136–37
Violence. See Sexual violence
Vorcheimer v. School District of
Philadelphia, 121
Voting Rights Act, 131

Wages, equity in, 98–100
Walker v. Pierce, 166
Wall Street Journal Report, 109
Wanrow, Yvonne, 193–95
Wards Cove Packing Company v.
Atonio, 102–3, 104
Watson v. Fort Worth Bank and Trust,
103–5
Webster v. Reproductive Health Services
169–71

*Weeks v. Southern Telephone and
    Telegraph*, 95
Weinberger v. Weisenfeld, 27, 28
Weininger, Otto, 42
Weitzman, Lenore, 149
Welfare recipients, coerced
    sterilization of, 165–66
Welfare rights, 16
Wells, Ida B., 54
West Coast Hotel v. Parrish, 69
Whitehead, Mary Beth, 157–61
Willard, Frances, 47, 54, 56, 57, 113
Wilson, E. O., 209
*Wimberly v. Labor and Industrial
    Relations Commission of Missouri*,
    24
Wollstonecraft, Mary, 8, 36, 48–49, 57
Woman's Bible, The (Stanton), 41
Woman's Peace Party, 72
Women's Bureau study of the effect
    of labor laws on women, 75
Women's Christian Temperance
    Union (WCTU), 47, 57
Women's Equity Action League
    (WEAL), 106
Women's Legal Defense Fund, 128
Women's Trade Union League, 72
Workers' rights, 13. *See also* Labor
    laws, protective; Workplace
    equality
    disability cases, 23–26, 63, 96–97
    fatigue, 73
    maximum hours, 67–69
    minimum wage, 69–70
    night work, 70–71
    pay equity, 98–100
    retirement case, 30
    working conditions, 63–66
Workplace, women in. *See also* Labor
    laws, protective; Worker's rights;
    Workplace equality
    changes effecting, in the 1960's and
        1970's, 85–86
    creation of dual labor market in the
        19th century, 64–66

modern dual labor market, 123,
    137–40
safety issues, 133–37
Workplace equality, 91–112. *See also*
    Affirmative action
academic discrimination, 105–7
employment opportunities and, xv
    educational levels and, 114–15
    19th century, 35, 40
    in prisons, 33–34, 136–37
    protective labor laws and, 70–71
    in the 1960s, 85, 93–94
federal government's failure to
    enforce policies on, 124–32
feminist reforms of the 1960s,
    91–93
fetal protection policies and,
    134–37, 164
job standards, 100–102
pay equity, 98–100
pregnancy disability and, 133–36
sex discrimination and stereotypes
    of femininity, 110–12, 137–40
sexual harassment and, 107–10
sexually segregated job market,
    97–98
Title VII of the 1964 Civil Rights
    Act
    decreased enforcement of,
        124–26
    disparate impact rule, 101–105
    market forces and, 100
    sex as a bona fide job
        qualification, 94–97
    sex discrimination amendment,
        93–94
Wright v. Olin, 135

"Yale murder" case, 196–97

Zelizer, Vivian, 51
Zola, Emile, 44
Zuniga v. Kleberg County Hospital, 135